Japanese Monograph No.118

OPERATIONAL HISTORY
OF NAVAL COMMUNICATIONS

December 1941 - August 1945

PREPARED BY
MILITARY HISTORY SECTION
HEADQUARTERS, ARMY FORCES FAR EAST

DISTRIBUTED BY
OFFICE OF THE CHIEF OF MILITARY HISTORY
DEPARTMENT OF THE ARMY

DEPARTMENT OF THE ARMY
OFFICE OF THE CHIEF OF MILITARY HISTORY
Washington 25, D. C.

CMH

SUBJECT: Distribution of Manuscript

TO   : Addressee

The inclosed manuscript is forwarded for your use and retention.

FOR THE CHIEF OF MILITARY HISTORY:

1 Incl
 Ms

D. C. SWEGER
Colonel, Artillery
Executive

Published by Books Express Publishing
Copyright © Books Express, 2012
ISBN 978-1-78039-840-2

Books Express publications are available from all good retail and online booksellers. For publishing proposals and direct ordering please contact us at: info@books-express.com

FOREWORD

Due to the technical nature of the subject matter contained in this monograph, editing was limited to grammatical changes.

The translation of this text was performed by individuals not versed in the field of communications, and therefore technical terms used herein are not purported to be absolutely correct but are the closest interpretations of the Japanese characters.

26 May 1953

Preface

Through Instructions No. 126 to the Japanese Government, 12 October 1945, subject: Institution for War Records Investigation, steps were initiated to exploit military historical records and official reports of the Japanese War Ministry and Japanese General Staff. Upon dissolution of the War Ministry and the Japanese General Staff, and the transfer of their former functions to the Demobilization Bureau, research and compilation continued and developed into a series of historical monographs.

The paucity of original orders, plans and unit journals, which are normally essential in the preparation of this type of record, most of which were lost or destroyed during field operations or bombing raids rendered the task of compilation most difficult; particularly distressing has been the complete lack of official strength reports, normal in AG or G3 records. However, while many of the important orders, plans and estimates have been reconstructed from memory and therefore are not textually identical with the originals, they are believed to be generally accurate and reliable.

Under the supervision of the Demobilization Bureau, the basic material contained in this monograph was compiled and written in Japanese by former officers, on duty in command and staff units within major units during the period of operations. Translation was effected through the facilities of Military Intelligence Service Group, G2, Headquarters, AFFE.

This Japanese Operational Monograph was prepared in English by the Japanese Research Division, Military History Section, Headquarters, Army Forces Far East and is based on the translation of the Japanese original.

TABLE OF CONTENTS

Chapter		Page
I.	ORGANIZATION AND DEVELOPMENT	1
	Central Agency	1
	Development of Communications Facilities	4
	Policy for Control of Civil Communications Facilities	31
	International Communications	33
	Japanese-German Communications Agreement	34
	Combined Fleet Communications Regulations	36
	General	37
	Operational Communications	37
	Routine Communications	42
	Communications Inspection	42
	1941 Naval Wartime Communications Plan	42
	Revisions of the Communications Plan	46
II.	RESEARCH IN WAVE PROPAGATION	51
	Results of Research, 1939-1940	55
	Results of Research, 1941	56
	Results of Research, 1942-1943	57
	Results of Research, 1945	58
III.	COMMUNICATIONS SECURITY	63
	Cryptographic Functions	63
	Code Printing Techniques	64
	Encoding of Call Signs	66
	Communications Defense Countermeasure Committee	68
	Countermeasures for Equipment	70

Chapter		Page
	Essential Points of the Revised Communications Procedure	71
	Unification of the Code Regulations	75
	Revision of Code Books	76
	Distribution System of Cryptographic Publications	77
	Enforcement of the Code Area System	81
	The Exchange of Code Books with the Army	84
	Security "Accidents" and Countermeasures	85
	List of Code Books	91
	Disposal of Code Books After the End of the War	94
IV.	COMMUNICATIONS PREPARATIONS FOR WAR	96
	Wire Communications Facilities	102
	Communications of Carrier Task Force	103
	Selection of Fleet Flagship	104
	Communications Equipment for Ships	105
	Development of Radar	109
	Radar Research	109
	Radar Production	112
V.	NAVAL AIR FORCE COMMUNICATIONS	131
	Radio Equipment for Aircraft	131
	Base Air Force Communications	138
	Base Communications Equipment	144
	Communications of Air Squadrons	146
	General Situation	146
	Frequency System	172
	Radio Equipment	177

Chapter		Page
	Communications Procedure	190
	Communications Plan for Homeland Air Defense Operation	194
	Policy	194
	Plan	195
	Intelligence and Air Defense Command Centers	195
	Lookout Communications Net	195
	Transmission of Air Defense Intelligence	196
	Ground Control of Interceptor Fighters	199
	Summary of Installation Work	200
	Communications Between the Army and Navy	201
	Radio Navigation	202
	Utilization of the Radio Direction Finder	203
	Radio Beacon	206
VI.	COMMUNICATIONS IN ESCORT OPERATIONS	207
	General Situation	207
	The Communications Plan of the General Escort Command	208
	Communications of the General Escort Command	217
	Ship Communications	218
	Aircraft Communications	221
	Radio Intelligence	222
	Office of the Resident Naval Officer and Communications	224
VII.	OPERATIONAL COMMUNICATIONS OF SUBMARINES	226
	Summary of Communications Plan	226

Chapter		Page
	Summary of Submarine Communications Operations	229
	Radio Direction Finder	230
	Submarine Communications Bases	231
	Development of Principal Equipment for Submarines	231
	Transmitter	231
	Very-low Frequency Wave Receiving Set	232
	Very-low Frequency Wave Transmitter	232
	Radio Direction Finder	232
	Very-low Frequency Wave Receiving Antenna	233
VIII.	COMMUNICATIONS IN FIRST PHASE OPERATIONS	234
	Operational Plan	234
	Policy	234
	Communications Procedure	234
	Communications Security	243
	Radio Intelligence	244
	Army-Navy Communications Agreement for Southern Operations	244
	Special Measures Adopted for Southern Operations	249
	Communications in Hawaiian Operation	250
	Communications in the Indian Ocean Operation	254
IX.	COMMUNICATIONS IN SECOND PHASE OPERATION	255
	Communications Plan for Midway Operation	255
	Communications Plan for 1st Task Force	256
	Communications in the Midway Operation	258
	Operations of the 1st Combined Communications Unit	261

Chapter	Page
Northern Force Communications Plan	262
Communications Plan for 2d Task Force	264
Communications in the Aleutians Operation	268
Communications in the Solomons Area Operation	272
Communications Plan of the South Seas Force for Port Moresby Operation	274
Port Moresby Occupation Force Communications Plan	275
Communications Plan of the Port Moresby Task Force and Air Force (29 April 1942)	277
Communications of the Tulagi Occupation Force	282
Communications of the Port Moresby Occupation Operation (Battle of the Coral Sea)	283
Communications Plan of the Eighth Fleet	287
Communications Plan	287
Communications in the Battle of Savo Island	291
Communications in the Battle of Eastern Solomons	292
Outline of Communications Plan	292
Base Communications	294
The Problem of Wave Propagation	295
Air Combat Communications	296
Communications Unit on Guadalcanal Island	298
Communications in the Battle of Santa Cruz	299
Policy	299
Communications Plan of the Support Force	300
Summary of Operations	300
Aircraft Communications	302

Chapter		Page
	Radio Intelligence	304
	Communications in the Battle of Guadalcanal	304
	Advance Force Communications Plan	304
	Raiding Force Communications Plan	305
	Operations of the Raiding Force	307
	Operations of the Advance Force	309
X.	COMMUNICATIONS IN THIRD PHASE OPERATIONS	311
	General Situation	311
	First Mobile Fleet Communications Plan	313
	Summary of First Mobile Fleet Operational Communications	317
	Operational Communications Regulations of the 1st Mobile Base Air Force	326
XI.	COMMUNICATIONS PLAN FOR KETSU-GO OPERATION	342
	Establishment of Communications Centers and Nets	345
	Establishment of Lookout Posts	348
	Establishment of Weather Communications Nets	349
	Communications Among the Principal Operational Command Centers	349
	Air Fleet Headquarters Broadcast Communications Nets	355
	Air Base Telecommunications	355
	Communications Plan for Surface and Underwater Special Attack Units	358
	A-Type Communications Net	360
	B-Type Communications Net	361
	C-Type Communications Net	361

Chapter	Page
Lookout Communications Net	361
Broadcast Communications Nets	361
Special Attack Craft Communications	362
External Communications	362
Weather Communications	364
Frequency System	364
Communications Equipment for Secret Bases of Special Attack Planes	368
Radio Equipment for the Surface Special Attack Unit Bases	369
Problem of Communications Personnel	370
Communications Preparations Relative to the Moving of Imperial General Headquarters	375
Operational (Communications) Preparations of the Navy General Command	376
Communications Plan	376
Maintenance of Command Posts	381
The Technical Advisory Staff	381
Training and Guidance	382
General Communications Training Maneuver	384
Training of Apprentice Radiomen	384
Survey of Reserve Equipment	385
Communications Preparations of Fifth Air Fleet	385
Communications Preparations of Third Air Fleet	389
Communications Plan	390
Situation of the Various Air Fields	395
Personnel Problems	397
Communications Preparations of Tenth Air Fleet	398

Chapter	Page
Communications Plan	401
Situation of the Bases at the End of War	403
Wire Communications	405
Installation and Increase of Radars	405
Transfer of the Command Post to the Yokosuka Naval District	406
Aircraft Communications Equipment	406
Visual Communication Facilities of Bases	407
Reinforcement of Personnel	407

CHARTS

No.		Page
1.	Communications Units Utilized for Interception	7
2.	Radio Direction Finding Stations' Table of Equipment (As of 1 Dec 44)	8
3.	T/E of Naval Communication Units	19
4.	Operational Communications Assignment	38
5.	Air Communications Assignments (Incomplete)	40
6.	Radio Communication Nets and Stations	44
7.	Code Area System	82
8.	Prewar Preparations Plan for Communications Unit	97
9.	Expansion of the Tokyo Communications Unit 1942 - 1944	98
10.	Standard Table of Equipment for Communications Units, 1943	99
11.	Mobile Communications Equipment Production Plan	101
12.	Plan for Increasing Radio Equipment on Naval Vessels	108
13.	Installation Standard of Radar for Ships, 1942	113
14.	Installation Standard of Radar for Ships, 1944	114
15.	Radar Production Schedule	115
16.	Types of Lookout Posts	116
17.	Search Radar Assignment	117
18.	Aircraft Communications Equipment Production	132
19.	Standard Radio Communications Equipment in Aircraft	135
20.	Authorized Strength of Base Air Force Communications Department	140
21.	Standard Communications Equipment for Mobile Land-Based Air Force	145
22.	Base Communications Equipment	146
23.	Major Air Base Communications Equipment Maintained in 1937	147

No.		Page
24.	Major Air Base Communications Equipment Maintained from 1938 to 1940	149
25.	Major Air Base Communications Equipment Maintained from 1941 to 1943	155
26.	Major Air Base Communications Equipment Maintained in Japan at Termination of War	162
27.	Frequency Classification	173
28.	Frequency Assignment Standard	174
29.	Organization of Communications Net	175
30.	Standard Radio Equipment for Various Types of Aircraft (Excluding Radar)	178
31.	Communications Equipment in Actual Use at Start of War	179
32.	Experimental Communications Equipment at Start of War	181
33.	Summary of the 1943 - Experimental Equipment (Excluding Radar)	184
34.	Radio Communications Equipment in Actual Use (Jan 43 - Oct 44)	186
35.	Experimental Radio Equipment	188
36.	Lookout Communications Nets	197
37.	Communications Nets	198
38.	Organization of Command Communications Nets	199
39.	Communications Net	200
40.	Escort Unit Communications Net	209
41.	Monitoring by Surface Escort Unit or Ship	211
42.	Air Base Net and Frequency for Escort Plan	213
43.	Monitoring by Aircraft	214
44.	Submarine Communications Bases	231
45.	Ship, Aircraft and Submarine Communications	235

No.		Page
46.	Communications Unit (Base) Communications	236
47.	Communications Operations Time Chart	239
48.	Communications Relay	240
49.	Broadcast Specifications	241
50.	Place Indication System	245
51.	Radio Intelligence	247
52.	Ship and Aircraft Communications Nets	251
53.	Communications Net for Midway Operation	257
54.	Communications Assignment	263
55.	Communications Nets	265
56.	Aircraft Communications	267
57.	Communications Nets	276
58.	Aircraft Communications	279
59.	Homing Procedure	280
60.	Receiving of Communications	281
61.	Communications Assignments	288
62.	Communications Plan	289
63.	Classification of the Use of Low Frequencies	289
64.	Land-Based Communications Unit	290
65.	Communications Net	293
66.	Communications Assignment	294
67.	Aircraft Communications	305
68.	Communications Assignment	306
69.	Aircraft Communications	306

No.		Page
70.	Radio Communications Net	313
71.	Communications Assignment	314
72.	Target and Content Indication Signs	315
73.	Singapore Area Fixed Communications Net	320
74.	Radio Transmission and Receiving Standard for Each Unit (or Base) of the 1st Mobile Base Air Force	334
75.	A-Type Base Radio Communications System and Assignments	336
76.	B-Type Base Radio Communications System and Assignments	337
77.	Warning Nets	339
78.	Aircraft Communications Plan and A-Type Aircraft Radio Communications Frequency System of the 1st Mobile Base Air Force	340
79.	Communications Control	330
80.	Control Procedure	332
81.	Communications Centers and Nets	346
82.	Frequencies of Flight-Weather Communication Net	350
83.	Operational Command Centers	356
84.	Emergency Central Communications Net	359
85.	Communications Centers	360
86.	Special Attack Craft Communications	363
87.	Special Attack Squadron Frequency System (Incomplete)	366
88.	A Comparative Table of Authorized, Required and Available Communications Personnel (As of 1 March 1945)	371
89.	Advance Graduation of Officers and Enlisted Trainees and Discontinuance of Enrollment	373
90.	Base Telephone Communications	378
91.	Special Attack Squadron Base Communications	379
92.	Yamato Communications Net (HQ 3d Air Fleet)	394
93.	Tenth Air Fleet Headquarters Telephone System	404

CHAPTER I

Organization and Development

Central Agency*

In the Navy General Staff of Imperial General Headquarters, the Communications Department, or what was also designated as the 4th Bureau, was the responsible organ for the preparation of plans and policies pertinent to all communications matters of the Navy. These plans and policies were implemented by the 4th Bureau after approval by the Navy General Staff. The Navy General Staff, in turn, submitted requests to the Navy Ministry for any necessary funds, materials and manpower to support the operational plans and policies as set forth by the 4th Bureau.

Within the 4th Bureau there were three sections (9th, 10th, and 11th). Details pertaining to communications plans, operational control, international communications, communications training, equipment and installations, control and censorship of communications and communications security were handled by the 9th Section. The 10th Section was responsible for code plans, code training, compilation, maintenance and revision of code books and crytographic tables, encoding and decoding and forwarding of radio messages

---

*The term "Central Agency" actually does not refer to an established office as such but is merely the closest interpretation of what the Japanese Navy officials referred to as the highest authorities concerned with communications in the Navy General Staff and the Navy Ministry.

to and from the Navy General Staff and overall control of communications within the Navy. The 11th Section was responsible for research, plans, training and execution of matters regarding radio intelligence. This section also supervised communications censorship, control and security.

With reference to the function of radio intelligence under the 11th Section, its importance was greatly elevated from the time of the outbreak of the China Incident (1937) which had international repercussions. With the subsequent focus of foreign powers on the Orient, radio intelligence became an indispensable function, as increasing demands for information poured into the 11th Section.

It was not until the end of 1940 that the function of radio intelligence became a separate entity under the Communications Department, despite opposition voiced by the senior officers of the 4th Bureau. Radio intelligence or the Special Duty Group, as it was called, was established with the policy that it would chiefly be an enforcement agency with a status equivalent to the other bureaus of the Navy General Staff. A member of the 3d Bureau (Intelligence) and a member of the 4th Bureau (Communications) were assigned to this new group to assist in formulating plans by presenting the ideas of their respective bureaus in regard to intelligence and communications operations. The Special Duty Group was also responsible for the preparation of plans pertaining to the distribution of radio intelligence reports and preparation of an annual radio intelligence program.

In the Navy Ministry, two bureaus and two departments were directly concerned with communications planning and policy, i.e., the Military Affairs Bureau, the Military Preparations Bureau, the Navy Ship and Ordnance Department and the Navy Aeronautical Department. Within each of these bureaus and departments there were sections primarily concerned with the technical aspects of communications among other general functions such as plans, budgets, policies and personnel requirements. The 1st Section of the Military Affairs Bureau and the 1st Section of the Military Preparations Bureau were concerned with communications plans, budgets, policies and personnel requirements.

The Navy Ship and Ordnance Department was concerned with the administration of planning, research, construction, testing, maintenance and supply of equipment (excluding aircraft); design, examination, construction, repair, research, testing and control of wire communications equipment; design and examination of installations of Navy construction and repair depots (excluding air installations). Furthermore, it controlled through the Navy ordnance inspectors, technical depots, Navy yards and the Navy Construction and Repair Department. Thus, in regard to the execution of war preparations, it was the direct supervisory agency.

The Navy Aeronautical Department generally handled design, maintenance and supply of air equipment design and examination of ground installations pertaining to aviation and equipment for ships mobilization of plants and munitions essential to construction and repair of equipment and the training in aviation technique. The 2d Naval Technical Depot and all Navy air depots came under its authority regarding aviation technical matters.

Development of Communications Facilities

As a result of Japanese operations in China, efforts were made toward improving the Navy communications by modernizing communications equipment, increasing communications installations and intensive training of personnel. Moreover, stringent radio control became necessary because of the change in operational policy necessitated by the rapid development of aircraft and the progress of radio technique, particularly in the field of radio direction finders and radio intelligence techniques. Close cooperation with land-based air units deployed over vast areas had to be maintained and the improvement of communications installations to cover a wider range was essential. It was realized then that such accomplishments would necessitate the establishment of a single system of naval communications centered around land communications units. However, at that time Japan's efforts were concentrated on improving and expanding naval sea units, and little progress was realized in the improvment of land-based communications units.

The entire Navy communications system was centered at the Tokyo

Communications Unit. In 1937, additional construction was started and the project was completed in autumn of 1941. The work consisted of the installation of a Type-0 No 03 transmitter, a Type 97 No 01 high frequency transmitter, a Type-98 No 02 high frequency transmitter and a Type-99 No 2 high frequency transmitter. Furthermore, the umbrella-type antenna was discarded and an inverted L-type antenna was installed as well as a very-high frequency radio control mechanism.

The so-called Owada Receiving Station, which specialized in broadcast interception, was established as a detachment of the Tokyo Communications Unit. Interception was used with successful results during the China Incident, utilizing 23 large receivers, 200 small receivers and a total of 13 low, medium and high frequency radio direction finders. Subsequently, increasing demands for this service necessitated the expansion of the Owada facility and steps were taken to increase personnel and equipment to the extent where it could function as the coordinating unit covering radio intelligence for the Navy General Staff.

In obtaining intelligence data, it was most effective to set up intercept organizations as near to the target of interception as possible. In particular, since radio waves from the European areas pass the polar region, locations in northern Japan proved more satisfactory than Tokyo, insofar as reception was concerned. In those areas where specialized interception stations could not be established, owing to the lack of appropriations, regular communications units were utilized in interception work by assignment of additional personnel and equipment. (Chart 1)

Initially the Navy had little idea of the value and use of a radio direction finding organization and the use of a radio direction finder to obtain strategic information was not considered. However, with the development of aircraft and radio intelligence technique, the acquisition of strategic information was demanded. The technical progress of radio direction finders made the acquisition of such information possible and facilities and personnel were expanded for that purpose. (Chart 2)

With the development of aircraft, the strategic value of the South Sea Islands increased. As a result of research and frequent maneuvers, the establishment of communications installation in this area was deemed necessary from the standpoint of strategy and security. Communications facilities at advanced bases such as Palau, Truk and Kwajalein and the relay base on Saipan were to be improved. Also, radio direction finding organizations and stations in these areas were to be improved and increased in number.

The Fourth Naval Armament Replenishment Plan of 1939 provided for the improvement of radio navigation installations at the air bases on Palau, Truk and Ponape, and the improvement of radio communications facilities on Palau and Truk. The plan also provided for the installation of radio direction finding stations at Ponape,

Chart 1

Communications Units Utilized for Interception

Interception Organization	Targets of Interception	Equipment	
Takao Comm Unit (Shinjo Det)	United States Britain Indian Ocean Area China Area	High freq large receiver Low freq receiver High freq receiver Special receiver Mark 2 Telephone Low freq RDF High freq RDF Model 2, medium freq RDF High freq trans 0.5 KW	6 2 2 20 1 1 2 1 1
Maizuru Comm Unit (Nakahojo Det)	Soviet Union	Special receiver High freq RDF Medium freq RDF Low freq RDF High freq trans 1 KW High freq trans 0.5 KW	9 2 2 1 1 1
Maizuru Comm Unit (Shibata Det)	Soviet Union	Special receiver High freq RDF Medium freq RDF Low freq RDF High freq trans 1 KW High freq trans 0.5 KW	7 2 2 1 1 1
Shumushu Comm Unit	United States Aleutian-Alaska Area	Special receiver Mark 2 Telephone	26 1
Kaibun Comm Unit	Soviet Union	Special receiver Low freq RDF Medium freq RDF High freq RDF High freq trans 1 KW High freq trans 0.5 KW	17 2 2 3 1 1
6th Comm Unit (Kwajalein)	United States Hawaii Area	Special receiver Low freq RDF Medium freq RDF High freq RDF High freq trans 1 KW High freq trans 0.5 KW	12 3 3 4 1 1

Note: RDF -- Radio Direction Finder

Chart 2-a

Radio Direction Finding Stations' Table of Equipment
(As of 1 Dec 44)

Equipment			Communication Unit	1	Yokosuka			Owada
			Detachment	2	Hatsuse	Shirakata	Hachijo-jima	
Radio Direction Finder	Low Freq	Type 87		3	3			
		Type 93 No 1		4		1	1	3
	Medium Freq	Type 89		5	3			1
		Portable		6		1	1	
		Type 21		7	1			2
	High Freq	Type 93		8				1
			Improved	9	3	1	1	6
		Type 3		10				2
TM-type	High Freq Portable		Improved 1	11				2
			Improved 2	12			1	
	Light		Improved 1	13	1		1	
			Improved 2	14		1		
Receiver	No 2 Telephone			15	1			1
	Low Freq	Type 92		16				1
	High Freq	Type 97		17				4.19
		Type 92		18				2
	Special	Type 92	Improved 3	19	7			
			Improved 4	20	20	4	4	12
		Type 3		21				8
Transmitter	Low Freq	Type 92	No 3	22				
			No 4	23				
	High Freq	Type 95 No 3		24				
		Type 95 No 4		25	1			
		Type 95 No 5		26		1	1	1
	Special	Type 91 No 4		27				1
		Type 97 No 5		28				
Monitor	High Frequency, (Improved)			29	2.1	1	1	6
	Low Frequency, (Improved)			30	1	1	1	3
Generator				31	40KVAx1	15KVAx1	15KVAx2	60KVAx1 25KVAx1
Direct Current				32	50KWx2 15KWxa 7KWx1			5Kx2 7Kx2 20KWx2
Others				33	Model 5x10 Model 6x40			Model 1x12 Model 4x200

T/E of Radio Direction Finding Chart 2-b
Stations, as of 1 Dec 44 (cont'd)

1	Chichijima		Ominato				Shimushu
2	Ogiura	Iwojima	Sekine	Nemuro	Rosaku	Nosappu	
3			2				
4	3	1	1	1	1	1	
5	3	1		1	1	1	
6							
7	1		1	1			2
8	1		1	1		1	
9	3	1	4	2	1	2	3
10							
11							
12		1			1		
13							
14			1	1	1		
15		1	1			1	
16							
17							
18			1				
19			2			2	
20	2	4	7	10	4	11	15
21						2	
22							
23				1			
24							
25		1		1			
26							
27							
28							
29	2	1	2	3	1		3
30	1	1	1	2	1	1	1
31	6KVAx2	15KVAx2	3KWx1	6KVAx1 6KWx1	15KVAx1	15KVAx1	
32			5KVx1	10KWx1			
33							

T/E of Radio Direction Finding
Stations, as of 1 Dec 44 (cont'd)

Chart 2-c

	Shimushu		Osaka	Maizuru		Kure	Sasebo
2	Musashi	Matsuwa	Shiono-misaki	Shibata	Nakahojo	Miyazaki	Namba
3							1
4	1	2	1	1	1	1	
5	1	2		1	1		
6			1			1	1
7			1	1	1	1	1
8	1						
9	1	2	1	2	2	2.1	3
10							
11						2	
12			1				
13			1				
14				1	1	1	1
15	1						1
16							1
17							2
18							1
19				7	7		9
20	6	6	4		2	7	3
21							
22							
23							
24		1					
25							
26				1	1		
27		1		1	1		
28							
29	1	2	2	3	3	2	4
30	1	2	1	2	2	1	3
31		60KVAx2	6KVAx2	25KVAx1	25KVAx1	6KVAx1	40KVAx1
32		5KWx2 20KWx2					15KWx2 5KWx2
33							

T/E of Radio Direction Finding Stations, as of 1 Dec 44 (cont'd)

Chart 2-d

		Sasebo			Rashin		Chinhae	
2	Hakata	Ee	Tanega-shima	Kaibun	Eiko	Ushijima	Rakuto
3							
4	1	1	1	2	1	1	2
5			1	2	1	1	2
6	1	1					
7							
8				1			
9	1	1	1	2	1	1	2
10							
11				1		1	1
12	1	1	1				
13						1	
14	1	1		1			
15							
16							
17							
18							
19				12			
20	4	4	4	5	4	4	6
21							
22							
23							
24				1			
25				1			
26							1
27							1
28					1	1	
29	1	1	1	2	1	1	2
30	1	1	1	1	1	1	1
31	15KVAx1	15KVAx1	15KVAx2	25KVAx1	15KVAx1	15KVAx2	25KVAx2
32				16KWx2			
33							

T/E of Radio Direction Finding Stations, as of 1 Dec 44 (cont'd) Chart 2-e

	Chinhae	Takao	2d	4th Truk	6th Kwajalein	8th Rabaul	10th Singapore
2	Heikai	Shinjo	Main Force	2d Nichiyoto	1st Jaluit	2d Gasmata	2d Singapore
3							
4	1	1		3	3	1	
5	1			3	3		1
6							
7				2		2	2
8		1			1		
9	1	4	2	5	3	3	2
10							
11							
12	1	1			1		
13	1						
14				1	1	1	1
15		1		1	2	2	
16							
17		6					
18							
19		1			5		
20	4	19	10	7	7	20	15
21							
22							
23					1		
24					1		
25					1		
26						1	
27							
28	1					1	
29	1	3	1	3	2	3	2
30	1	3	1	1	2	1	
31	15KVAx2	40KVAx1	15KVAx1	15KVAx2	6KVAx2 15KVAx1 150KVAx2	15KVAx2	
32		15KWx2 5KWx2		5KWx2	25KWx2 80KWx2		
33					Model 2x120		

T/E of Radio Direction Finding Station, as of 1 Dec 44 (cont'd) Chart 2-f

	10th Singapore	12th Rangoon		21st Soerabaya		24th Amboina	
2	3d Saipan	2d Rangoon	3d Andaman	2d Soerabaya	4th	2d Amboina	3d Kupang
3							
4			1	1	1	1	1
5							
6							
7	2	2	2	2		2	2
8					2	2	2
9	2	2	2	3			
10							
11							
12	1						
13		1					
14	1			1		1	1
15				1		1	2
16							
17							
18							
19							
20	5	18	14	5	7	6	11
21							
22			1				1
23							
24			2				
25			3				1
26	1			1		1	1
27							
28			1				
29	3	2	5	3	1	3	5
30	1		3	1	1	1	3
31	15KVAx2		6KVAx2 60KVAx2	25KVAx2		15KVAx2	15KVAx3 60KVAx1
32			7KWx2 30KWx2				
33							

T/E of Radio Direction Finding
Stations, as of 1 Dec 44 (cont'd)

Chart 2-g

1	25th	31st Manila	32d Davao	Base Force	
				Okinawa	Port Arthur
2	Main Force	2d Manila	2d Davao	Koroku	Dojoshi
3				1	
4		1	1		1
5				1	1
6					
7	1			1	
8		3			
9	2		3	1	1
10					
11					
12			1		
13					
14		1	1		
15		1			
16					
17					
18					
19				2	4
20	10	15	25	18	
21					
22					
23					
24					
25					
26		1			
27					
28					
29	2	1.1	1	2	1
30	1	1.1	1	1	1
31	3KVAx1 25KVAx1	15KVAx1	6KVAx1 6KWx2	25KVAx1	3KWx1
32					3KWx1
33					

T/E of Radio Direction Finding
Stations, as of 1 Dec 44 (cont'd)   Chart 2-h

1	Bako	Hainan	Base Force 10th	11th Indochina	22d Balikpapan
2	Tetsusembi	Tokyo	Miri Base	2d Saigon	
3	3				
4		2		1	
5	3			1	
6					
7					
8					
9	3	3	2	2	2
10					
11					
12				1	
13					
14				1	
15				1	1
16					
17					
18					
19					
20	2	6	5	7	12
21					
22					
23					
24		2			
25		2			
26			1		
27			1		
28					
29	1	2	1 (Type 99)	1	1
30	1	2	1 (Type 99)	1	1
31	3KWx3	60KVAx2	6KVAx1	6KVAx2	15KVAx1
32		5KWx2 30KWx2			
33		Model 4x120 Model 6x125			

T/E of Radio Direction Finding Chart 2-i
Stations, as of 1 Dec 44 (cont'd)

	Base Force	Garrison Units	
	23d Makassar	Marcus Is.	Wake Is.
1			
2	1st Makassar		
3			
4		2	
5		2	
6			
7		1	1
8		1	
9	2	2	2
10			
11		1	
12		2	
13			
14	1	1	
15	1	2	
16			
17			
18			
19			
20	5	22	12
21			
22			
23			
24		2	2
25		4	
26			
27			
28	1 (Type 2)		
29	1	6	3
30	1	5	2
31	15KVAx1	15KVAx2 60KVAx2	40KVAx2
32		7KWx2 30KWx2	
33		Model 4x120	

Woleai and Ulithi. The 1940 Naval Armament Replenishment Plan provided for additional improvement of radio navigation installations for the air bases on Palau and Truk, the improvement of radio communications facilities at Jaluit and the improvement of the Truk Radio Direction Finding Station. In addition, the 1941 Emergency Supplementary Naval Armament Replenishment Plan provided for the overall improvement of communications installations at important bases in the South Sea Islands. By the end of 1941, just before the outbreak of war, important temporary communications installations were improved considerably. However, there were very few bombproof installations and their improvement had to be carried out after the outbreak of the war (See Chart 3 for T/E of naval communications units).

To centralize control over the communications facilities, the 1st Combined Communications Unit was activated in May 1941. This new organization was comprised of the Tokyo and the Owada Communications Units and was placed under the command of Captain Kakimoto, Gonichiro.

To expedite the operations of the newly established Combined Communications Unit, the authority of the chief of the Naval General Staff to instruct and the authority of the C in C, Combined Fleet to direct were specified in Administrative Secret Order No 515, May 1941, which read:

The commanders of the Combined Communications Unit, the Naval Communications Unit and other specially established communications units will be given instructions by the chief of the Navy General Staff in regards to communications necessary for tactics and operations.

The commandants of the Naval Districts and Guard Districts will place the commanders of their subordinate communications units, insofar as it does not interfere with their other duties, under the C in C, Combined Fleet, with regard to communications, utilization of radio intelligence and radio direction findings of the Combined Fleet.

The communications units which had been newly organized in the Southwest Occupied Area after the completion of the First Phase Operations did not cooperate satisfactorily with the Combined Fleet, especially in the control of radio direction finding. Therefore, there was a strong desire for a central unit to direct and control effectively communications units in that area. In August 1943, the 3d Combined Communications Unit was activated and assigned to the Southwest Area Fleet and communications in this area became considerably improved.

When Saipan fell to the enemy in June 1944, the headquarters of the 1st Combined Communications Unit stationed there was annihilated. This unit had been engaged in radio intelligence, deviating somewhat from the original purpose for which it was established -- the supervision and coordination of naval operational communications in that area. It was realized that if the unit were to be reestablished and perform the duties for which it was originally intended, it would be necessary to find an energetic commander and staff to

T/E of Naval Communication Units   Chart 3-a

Location of Communications Unit	Equipment / Type		Key to Unit Name	Transmitter				
				High Frequency				
				50 KW	15 KW	5 KW	2 KW	1 KW
Tokyo Comm Unit	Tokyo Main Body	A C	1					
	Funabashi Detachment	B	2	2	4	4	11	1
	Totsuka Det	B	3		12		8	3
	Kanigaya Det	C	4					
Yokosuka Comm Unit	Yokosuka Main Body	A C E	5					
	Mutsuai Det	B	6				2	6
	Hatsuse Det	C D E	7					1
	Kinugasa		8					2
	Hemmi		9					
Kure Comm Unit	Kure Main Body	A C	10					
	Yakeyama Det	B	11				2	4
	Miyazaki Det	D	12					
	Nakakurose Det	C E	13					
Sasebo Comm Unit	Sasebo Main Body	A C	14					1
	Hario Det	B	15			1	4	6
	Mamba Det	C D E	16					
	Hakata Det	D	17					
	Ei Det	D	18					
	Tanegashima Det	D	19					
Maizuru Comm Unit	Maizuru Main Body	A C E	20					
	Shiraku Det	C E	21					
	Uesugi Det	B	22				2	3
	Shibata Det	D	23					
	Nakahojo Det	D	24					

T/E of Naval Communication Units (cont'd)　　　Chart 3-b

Key to Unit Name	Transmitter									
	High Frequency			Medium Frequency			Low Frequency			
	500 Watt	250 Watt	200 Watt	250 Watt	7 Watt	Telephone 50 Watt	30 KW	5 KW	2 KW	1 KW	500 Watt
1											
2				1		1	1	4	1		
3				2		1					
4					2	1					
5	4			1	1	3					2
6	6		1	1						3	2
7	2	3	1			1					
8	2	1		1		2				2	2
9	5	2		2							1
10	1		2	1		1					1
11	3			1		1			3		2
12			2								
13											
14			3	1		1					1
15	3	1		1		1		2	2		2
16	1					1					
17			1								
18			1								
19			1								
20	1		2	1		1					1
21											
22	2	2		1		1			3	3	1
23	1	1									
24	1	1									

T/E of Naval Communication Units (cont'd) Chart 3-c

Receiver					Others			
High Frequency			Low Frequency		Radio Direction Finder			Audio Frequency Amplifier
Key to Unit Name	Large	Small		Large	Small	High Freq	Med Freq	Low Freq	High Freq
		High Freq	All Wave						
1			51						
2			5						
3			6						
4	12								
5		3	52						
6			3						
7	1		37			3	1	3	
8			3						2
9									2
10		2	21		2				
11			2						
12			7			3	2	1	
13			16						
14		2	22		2				
15			2						
16	3		22	1		3	2	1	
17			4			1	1	1	
18			4			1	1	1	
19			4			1	1	1	
20			17		2				
21			13						
22			2						
23			7			2	2	1	
24			9			2	2	1	

T/E of Naval Communications Units (cont'd)   Chart 3-d

Location of Communications Unit	Type	Equipment	Key to Unit Name	Transmitter High Frequency			
				15 KW	.5 KW	2 KW	1 KW
Ominato Comm Unit	Ominato Main Body	A C E	1				
	Chikagawa Detachment		2	2	1	5	7
	Nosamu Det		3				
	Makubetsu Det		4				
	Sekine Det	D	5				
	Nemuro Det	D F	6				
	Wakkanai Det	A B C D	7				
	Henashi Det	D	8				
Chinkai Comm Unit	Chinkai Main Body	A C	9				
	Jonan Det	B	10			1	2
	Rakuto Det	D	11				
	Gyuto Det	D	12				
	Heikai Det	D	13				
Takao Comm Unit	Takao Main Body	A C	14				
	Hozan Det	B	15	1	1	2	9
	Shokozan Det	B	16			4	4
	Shinjo Det	D	17				
Osaka Comm Unit	Osaka Main Body	A C	18				
	Moriguchi Det	B	19				
	Shionomisaki Det	D	20				
Owada Comm Unit	Owada Main Body	A C D E	21		3		
	Ohira Det	C	22				
1st Communications Unit	Determined by C in C Combined Fleet	A B C D	23				
2d Communications Unit		A B C D	24				

T/E of Naval Communications Units (cont'd) Chart 3-e

Key to Unit Name	Transmitter								
	High Frequency			Medium Frequency		Low Frequency			
	500 Watt	250 Watt	200 Watt	250 Watt	Telephone 50 Watt	5 KW	2 KW	1 KW	500 Watt
1	1		2	1	1				
2	3			1	1	1	1	2	1
3					1				
4	1	1			1				
5					1				
6			1						
7	1				1				
8									
9	1				1				
10	4	1			1		2	2	1
11									
12									
13									
14		1							
15	5				1				
16									
17	1				1				
18					1				
19									2
20					2				
21			2		2				
22									
23									
24	1	1							1

T/E of Naval Communications Units (cont'd)　　　　　　　　　　　　　　　Chart 3-f

Key to Unit Name	Receiver					Others		
	High Frequency			Low Frequency		Radio Direction Finder		
	Large	Small		Large	Small	High Freq	Med Freq	Low Freq
		High Freq	All Wave					
1		1	62		2			
2			2					
3			13					
4		1	2					
5		1	9			5	1	3
6			10			1	2	3
7			21		2			
8			4			1	1	1
9			26					
10			2					
11								
12								
13								
14			29					
15		1	2		1			
16								
17	6	2	20		2	2	1	1
18			25					
19			2					
20			4			1	4	1
21	23	1	62	1		8	2	3
22								
23								
24			10			2		

T/E of Naval Communications Units (cont'd) Chart 3-g

Location of Communications Units	Equipment Type	Key to Unit Name	Transmitter High Frequency			
			15 KW	5 KW	2 KW	1 KW
3d Comm Unit	Koror, Palau Main Body	A B C	1				
	Peleliu 1st Det	D	2				
	Ailai 2d Det	B	3		2	2	5
4th Comm Unit	Dublon, Truk Main Body	A C	4				
	Chare*, Dublon 1st Det	B	5			1	7
	Sunday 2d Det	D	6				
	Ponape 3d Det	A B C	7				
	Uman 4th Det	B	8			2	4
	Moen 5th Det	B	9	4			
5th Comm Unit		A B C D	10				
8th Comm Unit	Rabaul Main Body	A C E	11				
	Rabaul 1st Det	B	12		1	2	6
	Vunakanau, Rabaul 2d Det	D	13				
Shumushu Comm Unit	Shumushu Main Body (Kataoka Transmitting Sta)	A B C	14			2	3
	Paramushiro Det	D E	15				
	Matsuwa Det	D	16				1
Chichijima Comm Unit	Chichijima Main Body	A C E	17				1
	Yoakeyama 1st Det	B	18				2
	Ogiura 2d Det	D	19				
10th Comm Unit	Singapore Main Body	A C E	20				
	Singapore 1st Det	B	21	7	1	3	8
	Singapore 2d Det	D	22				
	Sabang 3d Det	D	23				
	Penang 4th Det	D	24				

T/E of Naval Communications Units (cont'd)　　　　Chart 3-h

Key to Unit Name	Transmitter							
	High Frequency		Medium Frequency				Low Frequency		
	500 Watt	250 Watt	250 Watt	7 Watt	Telephone		5 KW	2 KW	1 KW
					150-Watt All Wave	50 Watt			
1						1			
2									
3	2	1				1	1	1	2
4						1			
5	4	5				1		1	1
6									
7									
8	1	2			2	1			1
9						1	1	1	
10									
11						1			
12	4	2			1	1			
13		1				1			
14	1	2	2			2			1
15						1			
16	1								
17						1			
18	4	2				1	1	1	
19									
20	1			2		2			
21	6				2		1	1	3
22									
23									
24									

T/E of Naval Communications Units (cont'd)　　　Chart 3-i

Key to Unit Name	Transmitter Low Frequency		Receiver				Others Radio Direction Finder		
	500 Watt	250 Watt	High Frequency Large	Small High Freq	Small All Wave	Low Freq Small	High Freq	Med Freq	Low Freq
1			3	7	36	4			
2									
3	1				1				
4			2		36				
5									
6									
7									
8					2				
9					2				
10									
11					42				
12	1				2				
13					20		3	2	
14	1				31			2	3
15					6		1	1	2
16					6		2	2	2
17					39	1			
18	1	2			2				
19					2		3	3	4
20			2		44				
21	1								
22					15		2	2	
23									
24									

T/E of Naval Communications Units (cont'd)

Chart 3-j

Location of Communications Unit	Equipment Type	Key to Unit Name	Transmitter High Frequency			
			25 KW	15 KW	5 KW	2 KW
25th Communications Unit		A B C D	1				
32d Comm Unit	Davao Main Body	A C E	2				
	Davao 1st Det	C	3				
	Davao 2d Det	B	4				
	Davao 3d Det	B	5				
	Davao 4th Det	D	6				
12th Comm Unit	Main Body	A C	7				
	1st Det	B	8			2	
	2d Det		9				
21st Comm Unit	Soerabaja Main Body	A C E	10				
	Soerabaja 1st Det	B	11		1	1	6
	Soerabaja 2d Det	D	12				
	Malabar 3d Det	B	13				
	4th Det	D	14				
24th Comm Unit	Ambon Main Body	A C E	15				
	1st Det	B	16				
	2d Det	D	17				
31st Comm Unit	Manila Main Body	A C E	18				
	Manila 1st Det	B	19	1		1	2
	Manila 2d Det	D	20				
Rashin Comm Unit	Rashin Main Body	A C E	21				
	Rashin Meikodo Det	B	22				
	Kaibun Kaibun Det	D	23				
	Eiko Eiko Det	D	24				

T/E of Naval Communications Units (cont'd) — Chart 3-k

Key to Unit Name	Transmitter									
	High Frequency			Medium Frequency				Low Frequency		
	1 KW	500 Watt	250 Watt	250 Watt	7 Watt	Telephone			2 KW	500 Watt
						150-Watt All Wave	50 Watt	KW		
1										
2										
3	3					2				
4	1	2				1	1			1
5										
6										
7										
8	6	2			2	1				
9										
10			1				1			
11	6		5	3	2	1			1	1
12			1				1			
13								400 100		
14										
15										
16	2	3	4			1	1			
17			1	1			1			
18		1					1			
19	5	3				3	1	300	1	1
20		1					1			
21							1			
22	1	3				1	1		1	1
23										
24										

T/E of Naval Communications Units (cont'd)

Key to Unit Name	Receiver		Others			Key to Type Column:
	High Frequency		Radio Direction Finder			
	Large	Small All Wave	High Freq	Med Freq	Low Freq	
1						A. Taking command of communications and handling radio transmission and reception as telephone control.
2		36				B. Provided mainly with transmitting equipment.
3		28	3		1	C. Provided mainly with receiving equipment.
4		2				D. Provided mainly with radio direction finders.
5						E. Radio direction finder control.
6						
7		15				
8						
9		15	2	2		
10	2	34				
11		2				
12		18	3	2	1	
13						
14						
15		23				
16		2				
17		6	2	2	1	
18		49				
19		2				
20			3	1	1	
21		20				
22		2				
23						
24						

lead it. At that time, there was a scarcity of suitable personnel and even the post of chief of 4th Bureau remained unfilled.

As communications in the area supervised by the 3d Combined Communications Unit had become, on the whole, satisfactory, the existence of this unit was not always necessary and it was felt that as long as some of the staff officers concerned were assigned to Headquarters, Southwest Area Fleet, the unit could be deactivated. It was decided therefore, to deactivate the 3d Combined Communications Unit and appoint the commander of this unit, Captain Onishi, Keiichi, to the post of chief of 4th Bureau and concurrently commander of the reestablished 1st Combined Communications Unit. To effect command liaison, it was decided to have a member of the 9th Section, 4th Bureau, serve as a staff member of the new unit and orders effecting this change were issued on 20 August 1944.

Policy for Control of Civil Communications Facilities

Although no positive policy had been adopted for guidance of communications facilities outside the naval service, the Navy had contended that there should be a consistent policy to assume control of shipping communications. The majority of private ships were equipped with low frequency transmitters, but only a few of the first-class ships subsidized by the Navy were equipped with high frequency transmitters. Most of the transmitters installed on merchant vessels had such varied frequencies that the Navy anticipated difficulty in escorting merchant vessels in wartime.

With the enactment of the Antiaircraft Defense Law in 1937, ocean-going fishing boats were required to report information pertaining to air defense. With the support and guidance of the Navy, the Communications Ministry (civil government agency) conducted training classes at fishing boat bases, but the fishing boat companies were not very enthused about the unification of communications facilities because of the expense involved. As such, a centralized control facility to control this new communications net did not materialize.

About 1940, the Navy overcame some of the difficulties and made progress in the control of civil ship communications by prescribing the limit of permitted deviation of frequency and making gradual improvements in transmitters. The first-class vessels subsidized by the Navy were directed to install high frequency sets, a means by which to control these vessels, especially ocean-going vessels, during wartime. When control of shipping affairs was transferred to the Navy, it was decided that merchant ships would be equipped, in accordance with its requirements, with radio sets to conduct simultaneous low and high frequency communications.

Because of the necessity to direct communications in escort operations, the need for surface traffic security, reports of submarine warnings and prevention of exposure of anticipated movements of important vessels, it was decided to dispatch Navy officers to principal coastal radio stations to direct communications. In July 1942, Navy officers were dispatched to the coastal radio stations in Choshi, Tsunoshima, Shiomisaki, Nagasaki, Ochiishi and Keelung; and subsequently, officers were also dispatched to the four coastal radio stations at Shanghai, Tsingtao, Mokpo (Korea) and Naha (Okinawa).

In order to provide long-range communications in the event of war, the communications plans prepared annually provided for the wartime requisitioning of powerful transmitters owned by companies outside Navy control. However, concrete measures such as contracts with those companies were not taken.

By 1941, with the domestic and foreign state of affairs indicative of imminent war, it was feared that unless concrete preparations were expedited, it would become impossible for the Navy to requisition necessary equipment once the Army started requisitioning. Such being the case, negotiations were conducted with the Army and the Communications Board and an agreement was concluded regarding transmitters to be requisitioned by the Navy in wartime.

International Communications

Prior to the conclusion of the Japanese-German Military Alliance, the Japanese Navy had limited its activities in the field of international communications to support of the Communications Ministry in regards to technical matters and frequency assignments, and had not adopted an international communications policy. With the conclusion of this alliance, the Navy was required to adopt a policy to provide for direct communications between Tokyo and Berlin in order to establish closer liaison and exchange information between the Japanese and German Navies. Initially, the attitude of the Japanese Navy was that German authorities in Japan in communication with Germany and German vessels should use Japan's communications facilities and that direct communications would not be authorized. After further study, the Navy changed its attitude and a communications agreement was concluded which authorized the Japanese Embassy in Berlin and the German Embassy in Tokyo to communicate directly with their respective countries.

Japanese-German Communications Agreement

1. Direct communications between the Japanese Navy Ministry in Tokyo and the German Navy Ministry in Berlin:

    a. The Japanese Navy will use the Funabashi Transmitting Station of the Tokyo Communications Unit and the German Navy will use the Norddeich Naval Transmitting Station. A transmitter with approximately 20 kilowatts power will be used exclusively.

    b. Continuous liaison will be maintained and agreements will be made on frequencies in accordance with atmospheric and communications conditions.

    c. It will be made possible for the Japanese Embassy in Berlin and the German Embassy in Japan to communicate directly with their respective countries.

2. Transmittal of information to German vessels:

    a. The Japanese Navy will transmit information regarding enemy mines and submarines to German vessels and submarines in Japanese waters.

      b. The Japanese Navy will transmit with the frequency used for Tokyo Broadcast No 2 in the same manner as shipping communications are being conducted.

   3. Communications between German vessels and Japan through the Choshi Coastal Radio Station and the Naval Communications Unit at Singapore will be commenced immediately and communications with the Naval Communications Unit at Jogjakarta will commence when communications facilities there are completed.

   4. Communications between Japanese submarines and German Navy radio stations will be through either the German Norddeich Radio Station or the submarine base radio station. Necessary information will be transmitted in the same way German shipping communications are conducted.

   5. The Japanese naval representative in German-occupied areas and German naval representatives in Tokyo, Singapore, Jogjakarta and Penang may communicate directly with their respective countries and receive shipping communications.

When the agreement was put into effect in 1942, the Japanese Navy communicated with German submarines in accordance with the agreement, and in early 1944 the scope of communications stipulated in the agreement was expanded. The transmitting of radio messages by Japanese and German naval representatives in occupied areas through naval communications facilities was authorized; and as the German submarines began to use the Penang base in early 1944, the German radio station there was equipped with transmitters made at the Japanese Navy depot. German radio operations were authorized to communicate freely with German submarines, and it was agreed that the Japanese Navy retain ownership of the transmitters. Frequencies for communications between Tokyo and Norddeich were carefully studied for it was almost impossible to communicate in the daytime. However, communications were conducted satisfactorily between 1800 and 0700 hours.

Although the Japanese-German communications agreement was secret, the Italian Navy soon learned of it and demanded that it become a party to the agreement. As the motive of Italy was regarded with suspicion, her demand was rejected. Subsequently, however, Italian vessels in Japanese waters were authorized to receive information on enemy mines and submarines. In 1943, call signs and other communications data were completely revised when Italy withdrew from the Axis Powers.

Combined Fleet Communications Regulations

All naval communications were to be conducted in accordance with the communications plan of the Navy General Staff and the Naval Communications Regulations prescribed by the Navy Ministry. Each fleet commander was to prescribe detailed regulations necessary for efficient communications within his fleet. However, the communications regulations formulated by the Combined Fleet were regarded as the best example of communications regulations for operational forces and therefore, communications regulations of the fleets not under the command of the Combined Fleet were, as a rule, patterned after the Combined Fleet Regulations.

In preparing a communications plan, forces temporarily activated normally used the plan of the Combined Fleet and simply modified the details of the plan in accordance with the disposition of its force. Although the communications plans of the various fleets may have differed in some details, essentially all naval communications actually adhered to the Combined Fleet Radio Communications Regulations, which were as follows:

General

Article 1. Radio communications within the Combined Fleet will be conducted in accordance with the Naval Communications Regulations, the Army-Navy Communications Regulations and as specified in the following articles.

Article 2. Each fleet commander will be authorized to prescribe the necessary regulations in regard to communications within his fleet and will immediately report or notify the quarters concerned of his regulations.

Operational Communications

A. Communications within the fleet

Article 3. Communications within the fleet will be ordinarily conducted directly and freely by designated frequencies.

Article 4. The operational communications assignment will be as shown in Chart 4, and the frequency system will be as shown in Chart (omitted in original).

Article 5. Transmission with the simultaneous use of day and night frequencies will be the standard procedure. However, vessels with small communications capacity may choose one frequency which will definitely be received by the addressee.

Article 6. When the enemy is within 60 miles, the tactical communications assignment will be effected in lieu of the strategical communications assignment (specific order for the change will not be issued). Ships leaving the combat area will revert to the strategical communications assignment.

Article 7. When the fleet is cruising or is at anchor in a group, each ship will continue monitoring its designated frequency. However, ships with small communications capacity will be authorized to conduct joint monitoring.

Chart 4

Operational Communications Assignment

Classification & Abbreviation	Communications Net	Fleet FS	High Frequency		Medium Frequency		Low Frequency		Very-high Frequency		Note:
			FS	Gen	FS	Gen	FS	Gen	FS	Gen	
1st Strategy SE-TSU-HA No 1								X			1. Special orders will be issued for the communications assignment. Otherwise radiomen will be assigned in accordance with the 1st Strategy Communications Assignment.
2d Strategy SE-TSU-HA No 2			X	X		X					2. In case of unexpected encounter with the enemy, radiomen will be assigned without orders in accordance with the 1st Daylight Action Assignment.
1st Daylight HI-TSU-HA No 1			X	X		X	X	X		X	3. As a rule the frequency system will be ordered simultaneously with the communications assignment using the abbreviations "YA-TSU-HA No 1" and "TE-SO No 2," etc.
2d Daylight HI-TSU-HA No 2		X	X	X	X	X	X	X	X	X	4. X denotes assigned frequency according to flagship and for general use.
1st Night Action YA-TSU-HA No 1	Night Action Unit		X	X	X	X		X	X	X	Abbreviations:
	Others	X	X			X		X		X	FS ...... Flagship
2d Night Action YA-TSU-HA No 2	1st Night Action Unit	X	X	X		X		X			Gen ...... General
	2d Night Action Unit	X	X			X		X			
	Others					X					
3d Night Action YA-TSU-HA No 3	Night Action Unit	X		X							
	Others					X		X			

Article 8. As the ships of a fleet enter port, the ships having entered the port are authorized to dispense with the low frequency wave after the arrival of the flagship of the division to which it belongs.

Article 9. When a ship dispenses with the low frequency wave of the fleet, it will monitor the medium frequency wave during the last quarter of every hour from 0600 to 2200 hours every day.

Article 10. Replies to calls from ships other than from its own division will be made by the division flagship.

Article 11. The standard speed of transmission will be 85 code digits per minute.

Article 12. A ship within visual communications range is authorized to withdraw its communications watch after notifying its division commander.

Article 13. The air communications assignment will be shown in Chart 5. (Incomplete)

Article 14. As a standard procedure, aircraft communications will be relayed by its carrier. When necessary, direct communications may be conducted by preparing necessary frequency.

Article 15. The submarine communications assignment will be as shown in Chart (not entered in original text).

Article 16. As a standard procedure, submarine communications will be relayed by its flagship. When necessary, direct communications may be conducted by utilizing the necessary frequency.

B. Communications Outside of the fleet

Article 17. Each fleet flagship (or ship representing the fleet) will join the nearest local communications net.

Article 18. When a ship cruises independently, it will be authorized to join the local communications net and conduct communications.

Article 19. Communications outside of the fleet will be conducted through the flagship.

C. Communications security

Chart 5

Air Communications Assignments (Incomplete)

Force	1st Air Comm Assignment	2d Air Comm Assignment	3d Air Comm Assignment	4th Air Comm Assignment
1st Fleet as nucleus strength	A		A	E
2d Fleet as nucleus strength		B	B	F
1st Air Fleet as nucleus strength			C	G
11th Air Fleet as nucleus strength			D	H

Article 20. Plain language communications will be authorized only when there is no alternative.

Article 21. The radio silence standard will be as follows:

(1) Very Strict Radio Silence (TE-SE-KA) will be conducted when utmost control is necessary. All radio transmission will be prohibited except emergency messages absolutely necessary for operations. The local supreme commander will control radio transmission.

(2) Strict Radio Silence (TE-KE-KA) will be conducted when strict control is necessary. All radio transmission will be prohibited except messages absolutely essential for operations. Commanders of all levels will control radio transmission of their unit.

(3) Radio Silence (TE-TSU-KA) will be conducted when ordinary strict control is necessary. All radio transmission will be prohibited except messages important for operations, safety precaution and rescue. Commanders of all levels may entrust control of radio transmission to the communications officers.

D. Radio jamming

Article 22. Commanders of all levels will be authorized to conduct radio jamming when deemed effective.

Article 23. Joint jamming will be conducted in accordance with frequency assignments.

Article 24. When it is detected that the friendly communications are being jammed by the enemy, measures will be taken as follows:

    Method 1. Communications will be continued with the same frequency utilizing the intervals of the enemy jamming. This method will be used in general except in those cases covered by special orders.

    Method 2.)
) (Contents omitted in original)
    Method 8.)

Routine Communications

Article 25. The routine communications of the fleet will be conducted in accordance with the operational communications assignment.

Article 26. The use of radio communications will not be authorized for reporting results of gun and torpedo practice firing.

Article 27. Without requiring specific orders, medium frequency of the fleet will be monitored in the following cases:

(1) When passing through narrow channels

(2) When leaving or entering ports

(3) When conducting fleet maneuvers

(4) When visual communications are impossible due to poor visibility

Article 28. When the main part of the fleet is anchored at places other than a naval port or naval station, a communication liaison with the shore facilities will be established. Special orders will be issued each time in assigning the ship responsible for the establishment of a land communications post.

Communications Inspection

Article 29. The fleet flagship (or delegated ship) will inspect communications and prepare necessary records. Important matters will be reported immediately and other matters will be reported at the beginning of each month.

1941 Naval Wartime Communications Plan

In 1941, instructions were issued converting existing peacetime communications plans to a wartime footing. The main object of this revision to wartime conditions called for converting, without undue change, existing communications facilities and practices into operational communications. The communications capacity of the main advance operational bases were to be increased to the degree necessary for them to become operational communications centers. The Tokyo Communications Unit was to be the communications center for the entire area, while the auxiliary stations at Takao, Ominato, Truk and Sasebo were to be respectively, the communications sub-centers for the southwest, northeast, southeast and Asiatic mainland areas.

As the center of communications, the range and capacity of the Tokyo Communications Unit was to be increased in order to lighten the load on the auxiliary communications. The range of this station was to be the area of the long-range communications zone, while the range of the auxiliary stations was to be the short-range communications zone. Vessels within the range of one of the auxiliary stations were to enter the local short-range communications net and conduct its communications through the local auxiliary stations. Vessels outside the range of any short-range communications net were to conduct communications through the Tokyo Communications Center (Chart 6). The Central Broadcast Net was to be used by the Tokyo Communications Unit to communicate with naval officers abroad and with units in as well as outside the naval service. The Primary Radio Net was to be used for communications between secondary ship and land-based radio stations through the Tokyo Communications Unit. The Secondary Radio Net was to be used for communications between ship and land-based auxiliary radio stations through the secondary

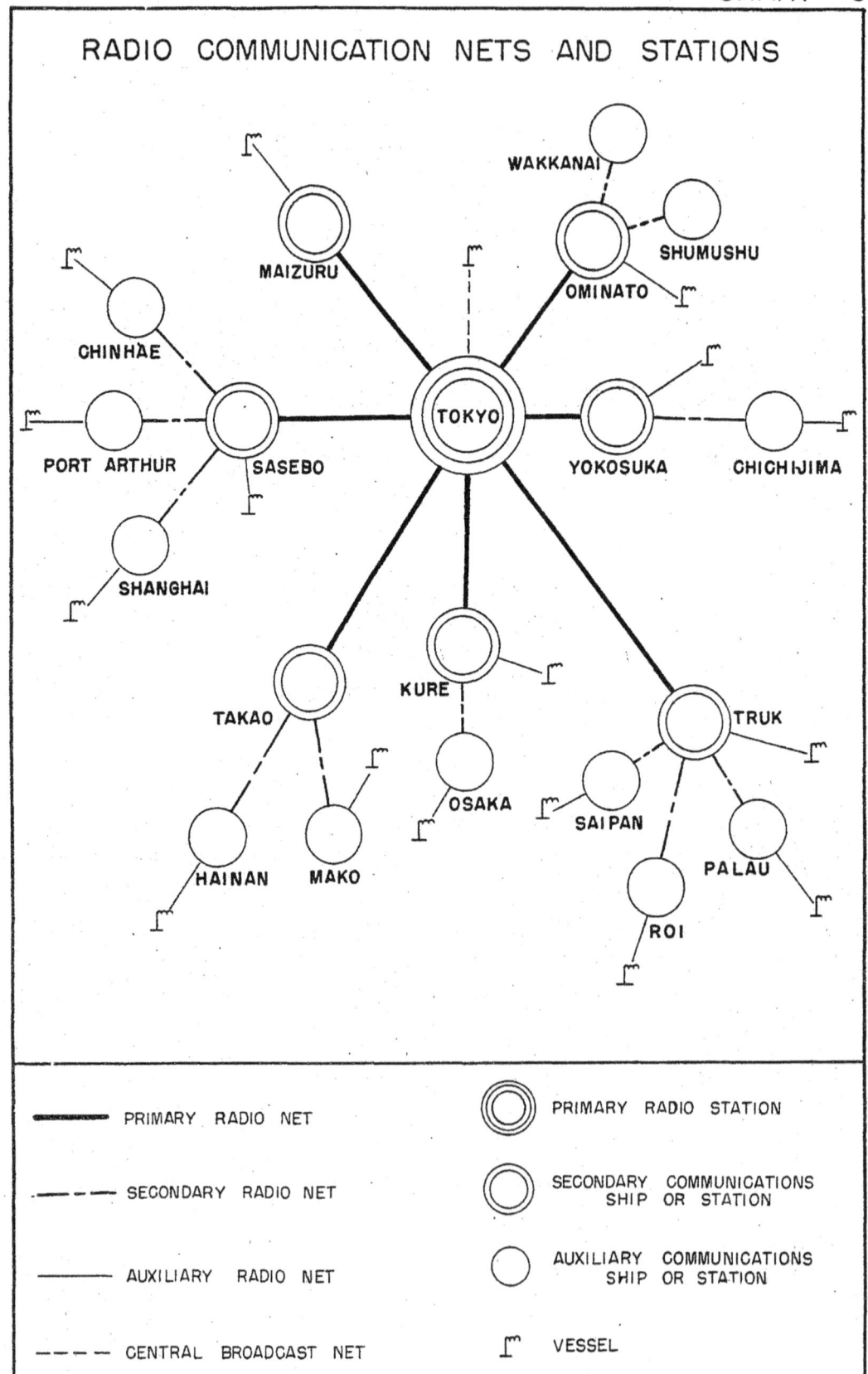

radio stations. The Auxiliary Radio Net was to be used for communications between ship and radio stations through the auxiliary radio station. The Force Radio Net was to be used for communications within the fleets or between ships and land stations or within Naval District and Naval Guard District units.

Each communications unit was the communications center of the area concerned and, as a rule, ships and stations assigned to each communications net (except those specially designated) communicated with proper parties through the central communications unit of the assigned communications net. All ship and land radio stations were attached to the Central Broadcast Net and when necessary, the fleet flagship or other ship or land radio station was to be attached to the Primary Radio Net to communicate directly with the Tokyo Communications Unit. In addition, ship and land radio stations were required to SOS on 500 KC frequency and for urgent dispatch on 215 KC frequency. In the event of an urgent dispatch, a ship or land radio station was authorized to call the desired station on the urgent dispatch frequency but was required, after contact had been made, to transmit on its proper frequency. The use of the urgent dispatch frequency was to be strictly controlled in order to maintain communications security against the enemy. Special attention was to be given to the utilization of wire communications to maintain communications security and to lighten the burden of radio traffic on Primary and Secondary Radio Nets. Transmissions by the communications unit nearest to the fleet anchorage were to be remotely controlled by wire or else conducted by low-powered transmitters from flagships.

Communications with the Army were to be conducted in accordance with the Landing Operations Manual and the Army-Navy Radio Communications Agreement. Details regarding frequency and procedure were to be decided through consultation with all forces engaged in the operations to avoid radio interference.

Radio intelligence instructions designated Great Britain and the United States as the primary targets for radio intelligence while the secondary targets were the Soviet Union and China. The radio intelligence teams gathered information which was forwarded to the Central Radio Intelligence Group for decoding. Based on information received from these teams and through their own facilities, the Central Intelligence Group was responsible for the preparation and dissemination of the estimate of the situation.

The main target for radio direction finding was designated as the enemy forces located in the Pacific operational waters, and the secondary target as those in the Japan Sea, the China Sea and on the Asiatic mainland.

Revisions of the Communications Plan

When the theater of operation expanded considerably with the occupation of territories in the Southern Area and the increase of forces in this area, there developed a great increase in communications traffic which taxed to the limit the capacity of the Tokyo Communications Unit. The situation reached the stage where it was impossible to conduct smooth and prompt communications through the existing method. In June 1943 therefore, revisions were made in the Navy Communications Regulations to strengthen wire communications and to strengthen radio control.

As the existing communications regulations concerned only radio communications and in view of the importance of wire communications, matters concerning wire communications were added to the regulations. Radio and wire communications were more closely coordinated to lighten the load on radio facilities as well as to increase efficiency. Communications between units having both wire and radio facilities were, as a rule, to be conducted by wire.

The existing long-range and short-range communications zones were abolished and transmission communications zones were established. They were classified into the central broadcast communications zone (entire area) and the local broadcast communications zone, and the frequency of all stations was fixed so that the transmission of any one station could cover the entire theater of operation. This called for the strengthening of the central broadcast communications net and the establishment of the local broadcast communications net.

Under the revised regulations, ships and stations assigned to each communications net could communicate with other units only through the central communications unit of their assigned communications net. As a rule, all radio ships and stations were to be attached to the central broadcast net in addition to their local broadcast net. However, radio stations with small receiving capacity were not required to be attached to both communications nets but were assigned to only one communications net. A fixed communications net was established between units. Air communications zones and air communications nets were determined in order to unify the air transportation communications and maintain security of communications. In addition, a wire telegraph communications net and wire telephone communications net were established as well as a system for sending telegrams by telephone. When wire telephony was possible between ship and station, it was used as much as possible for unclassified or low classification messages.

As the war approached closer to the Homeland and air raids became intensified, the main operational strength of the Navy was centered on the land-based air forces. Along with the increase in forces and the acceleration of war preparations, the burden placed on communications increased heavily. Communications could not be conducted smoothly because of additional time required to handle more complicated codes and because of incapable personnel. As inefficient communications greatly affected operations, it became necessary to effect other fundamental changes in the communications plan. Therefore in December 1944, the fundamental policy was revised and the preparation of facilities to cope with the changing war situation was also taken into consideration. Because the war situation was unfavorable, it was decided to gradually put the plan into practice before the completion of all preparations. The essentials of this revised policy were as follows:

1. The communications net will be separated into two nets -- the purely operational communications net and the administrative communications net.

2. The main air operation centers will be communications centers corresponding in size and capacity to the communications units.

3. In order to strengthen and increase the communications capacity of the communications units and main air operation centers, broadcast communications will be further strengthened, and as much of the regular fixed communications system as possible will be converted into the broadcast system.

4. Communications nets will be divided into the land communications net and ship communication net in order to facilitate the use of the ships and to strengthen cooperation of the communications unit with forces afloat.

Also included in the revision was the plan for establishing a weather net. The weather reports had been conducted mainly by wire under control of the Communications Board. However, with the intensification of enemy air raids and the expected decisive battle on the Homeland, it became necessary to convert wire communications into radio communications nets centered around the air bases.

The necessity for the immediate execution of this plan to cope with the war situation was recognized, but its materialization was delayed due to enemy disruption of communications and the delay in the preparation of crystals. The plan, therefore, although gradually put into operation, had not been completed when the war ended.

CHAPTER II

Research in Wave Propagation

From about 1930, Vice Admiral Minohara, Tsutomu and Captain Ito, Yoji, both members of the Naval Technical Research Laboratory at the time, were engaged in research work in wave propagation and ionized layer. Experiments were made by the "interference method" which had originally been conducted by Dr. Appleton. In view of the fact that Dr. Appleton's experiment was conducted in 1926, it is worthy of mention that the research by the Japanese Navy began only four years later.

Although the early experiments were conducted by the "interference method," subsequent experiments were conducted by the "impulse method". This was the basis of radio communications used in the Pacific War. By this method, a transmitting station transmitted radio waves modulated by a very short impulse of about 10^{-4} second so that the approximate height of an ionized layer can be estimated by measuring the time difference between radio waves transmitted along ground surface and those reflected by air ionized layers in the upper atmosphere.

A transmitter of this type was installed at the Meguro Naval Technical Research Laboratory (Tokyo) and receivers were set up at Tachibana Mura Receiving Station and at Hiratsuka Receiving Station established in the compound of the Naval Powder Depot in Kanagawa

Prefecture. The results of experiments were recorded simultaneously at both receiving stations. Experiments were conducted with frequencies ranging from 2,000 to 2,999 kilocycles. Continuous measurements at fixed frequencies were conducted chiefly at 4,000 to 4,999 kilocycles. As a result, it was discovered that the ionized layer existed at heights of 90 to 110 kilometers in the daytime and about 200 kilometers at night. Subsequently, photographic strip records were made of the ionized layer at a fixed frequency (4,000 KC). It has been revealed by Dr. Appleton that the layers existing at heights of 90 to 110 kilometers in the daytime and at 200 kilometers at night were different. He called the former E-layer and the latter F-layer.

The measurement of the height of the ionized layer by the Navy was conducted by continuous observation of the various heights of the layers by fixed frequency. In November 1932, the relation of the layers with meteors was investigated. At the time of the solar eclipse on Losap Island in the South Sea Islands on 14 February 1934, research personnel were sent to investigate and to clarify the conditions of the ionized layer in the southern area. At the Hiratsuka Laboratory of the Naval Technical Research Laboratory, the strength of actual radio waves from every part of the world was measured and studies were made of the variations of wave strength during a day and the four seasons.

The measurement of the ionized layer up to that time had been limited to that of the height of the layers. In some cases, investigation of variations in radio waves was conducted occasionally by changing the frequencies. The measurement of density of the electrons (or penetration frequency) which determines the highest possible frequency, important for communications, was not made at all. On the other hand, in 1932, Mr. Namba, Shogo of the Electricity Research Laboratory of the Communications Ministry determined (similar to method by Eckersley) the alternation coefficient for radio waves passing through the ionized layer. He utilized the high frequency field intensity measurement records which were available as a result of cooperation between Great Britain and the United States and which were made public by Burrows. Mr. Namba estimated the ionosphere and announced the method as to how to calculate the high frequency field intensity for long distance communications.

The measurement of the height of the ionized layer as well as the penetration frequency was started in 1934. It was discovered by this experiment that when frequency is increased, radio waves which are originally reflected by E-layer penetrate this layer and are reflected by F-layer. It was also discovered that as the frequency is increased, the radio waves penetrate F-layer and pass beyond the ionosphere. In 1934, experiments for measuring the penetration frequency and the height of the ionized layer were chiefly conducted by the Naval Technical Research Laboratory. As a result, the highest practicable frequency in communications with Tokyo as a center was determinable for any hour of the day or season of the year.

The lowest practicable frequency according to the output of the transmitter was determined, as experimented by Eckersley, by the degree of attenuation of radio waves when they penetrate or are reflected by the E-layer. However, this question of attenuation presented many difficulties. From a theoretical point of view, there are different opinions even today in that numerous unknown coefficients are found in attenuation. Therefore, radio waves with various frequencies in actual communications should be utilized to measure the field intensity according to various ranges and seasons of the year and that attenuation factor be induced from the field intensity. However, such an experiment requires a large number of field intensity measuring sets and many years of observation and careful arrangement of data.

It was discovered that the highest practicable frequency (basis for making a communications plan) can be determined by measuring the ionized layer, regardless of the output of transmitters, and that the lowest practicable frequency can be calculated by the measurement of field intensity and by close observation of the ionized layer, especially E-layer. It was made clear that the basis for the selection of communications frequency lies in measuring the ionized layer and field intensity.

The ionized layer measuring equipment was gradually improved, largely through the efforts of Technician Shinkawa and Lieutenant (Technical) Yamamoto. For the observation of the solar eclipse in

Hokkaido on 19 June 1936, automatic equipment had been devised to record by photograph the penetration frequency by connecting a transmitter and a receiver to the layer measuring equipment and by changing frequencies. Thus, through research in the ionized layer, the necessary data was available for the communications plan. It was after 1934 that penetration frequency for the ionized layer could be measured. From 1934 to 1937, the following facts were made clear:

1. In the variations during a day and a year, the density of the electrons in E-layer varies with the sun's altitude and is approximately in proportion to $\sqrt{\cos x}$ wherein x represents the altitude of the sun. This coincides with the theory advanced by Chapman.

2. Besides regular reflections, there are irregular reflections called sporadic reflections in E-layer.

3. In the daytime, F-layer is divided into F1-layer and F2-layer. In winter, however, F1-layer does not appear. F2-layer appears only at night. The diurnal and annual variations in F1-layer are more irregular than E-layer, but are subject to variations approximately in proportion to $\sqrt{\cos x}$. However, the day-night variation in F2-layer disagrees considerably with Chapman's theory. In other words, the day-night variation is not symmetrical with noon as the dividing line. Penetration frequency becomes rapidly higher with the sunrise, and after sunset it gradually (especially in summer) becomes lower; it reaches the lowest at daybreak. Moreover, the day-night variation is considerably great, amounting from 10 to 20 per cent. In the seasonal variation, the lowest penetration frequency is observed twice—once in winter between December and January and again in June. The highest penetration frequency occurs in spring and fall. Considerable discrepancies with Chapman's theory exist on this point.

Results of Research, 1939-1940

In September 1939, an observatory was established on Palau

Island to conduct the observation of the ionized layer in the South Sea Islands area. By this observation, valuable data was obtained for communications in the equatorial area. The short and medium range high frequency propagation charts were prepared based on attenuation calculations in accordance with observation and measurement of field intensity and they were published December 1939 in Tokyo. This chart contained frequency, time and correlation of field intensity in every month of the year for ranges of 300, 500, 700, 1,000, 1,500, 2,000 and 2,500 kilometers, and served as a guide to communications in medium latitudes and during the period of maximum sunspots. The short and medium frequency wave propagation chart for the South Sea Islands area, based upon a one-year observation on Palau Island, was published and distributed by the Naval Technical Research Laboratory in September 1940.

Results of Research, 1941

As a result of research, data on penetration frequency (density of the electrons), the height of the ionized layer and field intensity was obtained. Research was made for day-night and seasonal variations and their relation with sunspots. The relationship of the density of the electorns with the sunspots is as follows:

1. Marked correlation between the day-night variation of the electrons and that of the sunspots cannot be observed.

2. There is a marked positive correlation between the mean monthly value of density of the electrons and that of the sunspots, and both make corresponding changes.

Therefore, practical radio frequency varies with the sunspot cycle. In other words, high frequency can be used during the maximum value of sunspots. Because high frequency is subject to less attenuation, it makes communications easier. Too high a frequency cannot be used for communications during the minimum value of sunspots when penetration frequency is low because it will penetrate the ionized layer. It was also discovered that communications become difficult on account of attenuation in this period.

The government organization of the Radio Physics Research Committee, which had been advocated by the Electronics Research Committee of the Scientific Research Council, was promulgated in April 1941. The elevation of the committee to the status of the Radio Physics Research Institute was, at the time, jointly supported by the Army, Navy and the Communications Ministry with the aim of research in wave propagation and the ionized layer.

Results of Research, 1942 - 1943

A wave propagation chart book was distributed in July 1942 by the Naval Technical Research Laboratory. In addition to the wave propagation charts for the equatorial and the medium latitude areas which had been published previously, it contained a wave propagation chart based on the data obtained at Shikuka, and a long-range propagation chart. Since these charts were based upon the data for maximum value of sunspots, many discrepancies were found in the actual communications during the minimum value of sunspots.

High frequency in the equatorial area was reported inadequate because of the minimum value of sunspots, sudden decrease in penetration frequency at daybreak and great attenuation in the equatorial area. Therefore, there arose an urgent need to use medium frequency at night and daybreak and for short distance communications. Such being the case, observations in the southern occupied areas became necessary. The Army planned to establish observatories at Singapore, Bandoeng, Manila and Rangoon; and the Navy at Paramushiro, Kwajalein, Makassar, Sabang and Rabaul. It was decided that the nucleus of these observatory staffs would consist of personnel from the Radio Physics Research Institute.

The Army began to establish its observatories from January 1943 in the order Singapore, Bandoeng, Rangoon and Manila, while the Navy commenced in July on Kwajalein, Paramushiro, Makassar, Rabaul and Penang. The observation party for Rabaul was lost enroute at sea. All members of the Kwajalein party were killed in action while preparing for observations after arrival. They were all costly sacrifices for wave propagation research. The observatories at Paramushiro, Makassar and Penang were established without difficulty and furnished valuable information.

Results of Research, 1945

As the conditions of the ionized layer in each area became clearer through data obtained from the southern area, the Naval Technical Research Laboratory distributed to the Navy a monthly bulletin containing wave propagation information together with the forecast for the following month for use in communications.

With the progress of the war, research in wave propagation for aircraft became an urgent necessity. Only one frequency was used during one flight regardless of day or night. However, it was revealed that since the range of ground waves could be increased more in the case of aircraft owing to its high flying altitude than in the case of ground communications, the ground waves occupied half the radio waves used in transmitting from fighters operating at short range. This information, the result of calculating the ratio between the flying altitude and the range of ground waves on land and sea, was imparted to air units through the Yokosuka Air Group. Moreover, in consideration of the sky and ground waves with ranges up to 500 kilometers, a disc-type aviation wave propagation chart was devised and distributed to each air unit through the Yokosuka Air Group.

A practical high frequency chart was distributed as Wartime Research No 12, with Yokoyama, Eitaro of the Radio Physics Research Institute in charge. With time and range as the axis, and frequency as the parameter, this was a convenient and easy reference chart for beginners. However, there were gross errors pertaining to waves of 2, 3 and 4 megacycles, particularly in the attenuation in the daytime. Since the use of medium frequency on aircraft was stressed for operational radio waves at night and at daybreak, the books were distributed among the units concerned after corrections were made.

The following is summation of research on radio wave transmission directly connected with organization of the radio system:

1. <u>Observatory in Tokyo, 1934. Condition: Sunspots at minimum.</u>

   In Tokyo, the vertical penetration frequency at F2-layer at noon was 6 to 6.8 megacycles in the spring and fall, and 5.5 to 6 megacycles in summer and winter. At midnight, it was 2.3 megacycles in December and January, and 4.8 megacycles in summer. Communications in high frequency became so difficult and the high frequency band so narrow that the following frequencies were adopted according to the distance of communications:

   Day frequency .... 5 to 13 megacycles
   Night frequency .... 2 to 6 megacycles

   The number of sunspots made a sharp increase which indicated that the sun entered the period of intense solar effect. The penetration frequency at F2-layer at noon was 12 to 13.7 megacycles in spring and fall, and 7 to 8.7 megacycles in summer and winter. The frequency band was greatly expanded and communications became easier. Frequencies adopted:

   Day frequency
       Spring and fall .... 9 to 25 megacycles
       Summer and winter .... 7 to 18 megacycles

   Night frequency
       Winter .... 3 to 8 megacycles
       Summer .... 5 to 11 megacycles

   No inconvenience was experienced in communications by the

high frequency band of more than about 4 megacycles. This precluded the need for using medium frequency. The output of more than one kilowatt increased the range of communications considerably. Therefore, in some cases, it was possible to use only one frequency through the day and night when the right frequency was selected.

2. <u>Observatories at Tokyo, Palau and Shikuka</u>

Sunspots gradually entered a period of decrease in number, with 1938 as the period of maximum frequency. Penetration frequency at the ionized layer also became greatly lowered. In Tokyo at noon, it dropped to 8 to 10 megacycles in spring, fall and winter, and 7 megacycles in summer. At midnight, it was 3 megacycles in winter and 6 megacycles in summer. In Palau at noon, it was 9 to 10 megacycles in spring and fall, and 8 to 9 megacycles in summer and winter. At midnight it was 8 to 9 megacycles in spring and fall, and 6 to 7 megacycles in summer and winter; but at daybreak, it showed a sharp decline to 3 megacycles. In Sakhalin at noon, it was 7 to 8.5 megacycles in spring, fall and winter, 5.5 to 7 megacycles in summer, while at midnight it was 3 megacycles in winter and 5.5 megacycles in summer. The conditions of communication became gradually worse with the decrease in the number of sunspots from about 1937. For night frequency, a frequency of about 3 megacycles became necessary for short distance communications. In the southern area, the density of electrons did not show much decrease from daytime until midnight, whereas it showed a sharp decrease at daybreak which made it very difficult to choose an operational frequency at dawn.

Frequencies adopted:

    Medium frequency
       7 to 16 megacycles ..... in medium and low latitudes
       5 to 13 megacycles ..... in high latitudes

3. <u>Observatories at Tokyo, Palau, Toyohara, Paramushiro, Singapore, Rangoon, Bandoeng, Manila, Makassar and Penang.</u>

<u>Period: 1942 to 1945</u>

Since sunspots were at the minimum value in 1943 and 1944, communications were very difficult. It often happened that at daybreak in the southern area, frequency had to be lowered as far as 1.5 megacycles. Therefore the use of medium frequency of 2 to 4 megacycles became necessary at night and daybreak. A close investigation had to be conducted into the time for change of day frequency to night frequency and vice versa. A very high frequency could not be used for day use as there was too much attenuation. The range of communications by one frequency was diminished and the planning for communications nets became extremely difficult.

Frequencies adopted:

    Day frequency .... 5 to 13 megacycles
    Night frequency .... 2 to 6 megacycles

CHAPTER III

Communications Security

Cryptographic Functions

As was briefly described in Chapter I, cryptography was administered by the 9th and 10th Sections of the Communications Department (4th Bureau, Navy General Staff). The 9th Section had one staff officer in charge who decided the general policy to be integrated in any communications plan of the Navy. The details for code planning, training, equipment, compilation, code books, code tables, encoding and decoding and other implementing functions were the responsibilities of the 10th Section.

Until 1943, the post of chief of the 10th Section was concurrently held by the chief of the Radio Communications Section of the Navy Ministry. In September 1943, a full-time section chief was assigned to the 10th Section and the chief of the Radio Communications Section was delegated the concurrent role of commander of the Tokyo Communications Unit. With this change, the function of encoding and decoding was transferred to the Tokyo Communications Unit as were most of the code personnel. The duties which were retained by the Radio Communications Section consisted of receiving and filling outgoing messages to and from the Navy Ministry, the Navy General Staff and other Navy offices in Tokyo, making copies and distributing incoming messages, security of messages and other matters concerning handling of coded matters.

In the naval districts and guard districts, crytographic materials were handled by the local communications unit stationed in that district. In the units, they were handled by the assistant communications officer or by a code officer independently assigned, but as the number of ciphered messages increased, additional commissioned and warrant officers were assigned.

The printing of cryptographic materials was carried out by the Printing Bureau of the Cabinet, but later when the Naval Code Book A and other publications were contemplated, the printing was undertaken by the printing office in the Navy Ministry. With subsequent increases in the various types and copies of cryptographic publications to be made, the printing services of the Naval Torpedo School and the Naval Communications School were called upon to perform the task.

During the Pacific War, most of the printing except military top secret matters was initiated by the Bunjudo Printing Office in Yokohama (Navy-controlled publishing company). In 1944, the 10th Section of the Navy General Staff was moved to that concern and code books of all description were printed there.

Code Printing Techniques

Combat experiences had shown that it was extremely difficult to dispose of code books immediately in emergencies. Thus various methods were sought to print code books which, when sunk, would be obliterated in water such as: (a) Chemicals which dissolve the contents of a book when soaked in sea water, (b) water-soluble ink which fades away when exposed to sea water, and (c) water-soluble paper. Of these three methods, the chemicals mentioned in (a) had long been under study, but by this method alone, it was impossible to chemically treat all those which were being used. Therefore, careful study was made of (b) and (c). The research for water-soluble ink was made at the Technical Research Laboratory (by Senior Technician Kisa as the person in charge) but the study reached a stalemate because of the following problems:

1. If solvent action was too sensitive, there was danger of the writing fading from rain-water, splashes of sea-water or perspiration when the printed matter is being carried or used, and, if the action was too weak, there was danger of the writings failing to become invisible.

2. The chemical for treating printed or written matter had to be absolute so that it would be impossible for the enemy to use scientific means to cause reappearance thereof.

3. There was the difficulty of eliminating traces of type print.

The German water-soluble ink served as the incentive and water-soluble ink reportedly superior to the German counterpart was concocted. With the use of this ink and starch-coated paper, it was planned that the regulations for its use should be printed first of all. After confirming its practicality, other matters such as the additive tables and the code books were to be printed.

The printing method merely entailed cleaning the type with benzine and then applying the water-soluble ink. No special printing machine was used and the matter to be printed was run off in the usual manner. When the printed matter was thoroughly soaked as a book, the permeation of sea-water through all parts took several hours. Whether the traces of the printing types remained depended largely upon the printing technique and there were some cases in which disappearance was not complete.

Encoding of Call Signs

For the utmost security, it was necessary to encode call signs and names of senders and addressees, particularly since it was vital that movements and locations of the naval forces be kept in strict secrecy. However, naval authorities felt hesitant about further complicating the encoding system as they were apprehensive of the costly delays to communications. On the other hand, it was believed that well-trained radiomen would be capable and the authorities started on the compilation of code books for utmost security. Actually, there was little hope of establishing an intricate system of encoding call signs and names of senders and addressees in view of the marked deterioration of radiomen's skill during the war.

A program to encode the call signs and the names of senders and addressees with the improved "ENIGMA" transcription machine* was planned, but got no further since clerical persons equal to the number of radiomen to dictate were required. In the Hawaiian operations, special code phrases were used by the Combined Fleet and no special measures had been taken by the Central Agency. However, in anticipation of commencement of operational action in November 1941 when the First Air Fleet anchored in Saeki, the "New Code Book for Air Communications, Vol II" and the "New Code Book for Tactical Operation (Part B)" were distributed to each ship of the Fleet to be used in the forthcoming operation.

The code was changed periodically but in case of security "accidents" to code books in the interim, top secret communications were handled by the application of the emergency regulations and use of other code books. Revision of code books was made by improvising on the code books currently in use. In case of "accidents" to the master code books, the emergency regulations were to be applied as a temporary expedient and new code books were distributed to replace the old ones. In case of "accident" to other than the master code books, the emergency regulations were telegraphed by means of other code books, depending upon the urgency and the extent

---

*The "ENIGMA" was originally a German code machine which the Japanese improved and adapted to the "KANA" (Japanese alphabet). This machine transcribed, i.e., encoded from dictation.

of distribution. Units not accessible by telegraph were informed of the regulations through liaison by the nearest senior commanding officer, and the code books, after being revised, were distributed later to replace the old ones.

Communications Defense Countermeasure Committee

With the progress of communications technique, communications intelligence also made rapid progress through the expansion and strengthening of its agencies. As a result of the study of enemy communications, respective agencies often submitted recommendations on items requiring revision of security of friendly communications.

At the time of the northern French Indo-China operations in January 1941, the 2d Carrier Division (the Soryu, Hiryu and 23d Destroyer Division) was ordered to advance to southern Formosa. It sailed southward under radio silence but due to an unforeseen incident in the vicinity of Agincourt, Formosa, a considerable number of messages were transmitted. The British Navy at Hongkong learned of the Japanese movement apparently through interception of these messages. This was confirmed through Japanese interception of their communication which read: "The 2d Carrier Division is sailing south and it is certain that an aircraft carrier believed to be the Soryu reached northern Formosa, but nothing is known since then, and the rest of the force proceeded to Takao."

This incident served as a great impetus to security countermeasures for communications. The results of studies showed there were considerable defects in the current call signs and that monitoring revealed the characteristic of each ship from its transmitting frequencies. It was therefore certain that the enemy, through monitoring, radio direction finding and call signs, was making an intensive study of Japanese communications.

Therefore, in order to establish countermeasures, a Communications Defense Countermeasure Committee was formed in December 1942. The members were as follows:

> Chairman: 4th Bureau chief, Navy General Staff
> Committee members:
>> 9th Section chief (concurrently 10th Section chief)
>> Members of the 9th and 10th Sections
>> Naval Communications School instructors
>> Naval Technical Department members
>> Naval Air headquarters members
>> Yokosuka Air Group instructors
>> Members of Naval Affairs Bureau
>> Technical Research Laboratory members

The committee studied broad problems concerning communications, and in September 1943 submitted a report, the gist of which follows:

1. Revision of Communications Procedure:

> With broadcast communications being the predominant means, the transmittal forms will be revised and adhered

to: strengthening of security, speed and reliability of handling, simplification in administration and discipline in communications.

2. The following code countermeasures are planned:

    a. Rationalization of code revision.

    b. Strengthening and increasing handling speed by mechanization.

    c. Prevention of "accidents" during transportation.

    d. Planning measures for localizing damage in case of "accidents."

3. Countermeasures for equipment:

    a. Investigation of transmitters incapable of radio direction finding.

    b. Elimination of the characteristics of radiation waves.

4. Induce more security measures in basic training at communications schools.

5. Establish efficient inspection agencies for communications.

These countermeasures were put into effect at once. Then revision of the communications rules was taken up, with the Communications School and the Yokosuka Air Group taking the initiative. In August 1944, a draft was prepared but further discussions and studies prolonged final decision until 1945 when it was ready for printing. However, there was no opportunity for its enforcement due to the adverse war situation at this time.

Countermeasures for Equipment

1. Development of a transmitter which could avoid detection

by radio direction finders: A device known as "NB" (medium frequency communications method which eludes radio direction finders to a great extent) had been completed at the end of 1944, and was installed on flagships in January 1945.

2. Elimination of the characteristics of radio waves.

   a. Tone-changing device: In order to offset the characteristic of the tone of transmitters, a device was added by which the tone was varied intermittently.

   b. Monitoring to determine correctness of signal was conducted on main warships. In particular, repairs were made on devices which transmitted notably peculiar radio waves.

The monitoring of friendly communications had heretofore been carried out by higher headquarters of each communications unit without resorting to any special research body. The necessity thereof had been keenly felt, but it did not materialize as there was great difficulty in providing suitable installations and personnel.

Essential Points of the Revised Communications Procedure

The Navy Communications Rules had been revised in 1937, and subsequent to that year, many revisions and additions had been entered. There still existed a need for security in tactical communications, particularly aircraft communications. The problem rested on the need for establishing a suitable transmittal form for messages and the need for communications discipline.

Outline of the revised Navy Communications Rules.

1. The name was changed to Navy Communications Regulations.

Radio, wire communications and radiotelephone were included therein.

2. Because of the peculiarities inherent in aircraft communications and the training of personnel, only matters concerning aircraft communications were extracted and compiled in the "Extracts from the Navy Communications Regulations (Aircraft Communications)."

3. The five types of message transmittal forms were as follows: basic, strategical (divided into general and security), tactical aircraft communications (air-basic, air-No 1 and air-No 2) and emergency.

    a. The basic transmittal form

        This was a transmission form used for direct communications or broadcast communications between bases and for short distances (generally 200 miles to avoid long-distance transmittal) in the routine and strategic communications.

    b. Strategic general transmittal form

        This was used mainly for broadcast communications between ships or stations in strategic moments. It was a transmittal form which had greater security for routine and strategic communications and could be used for general communications.

        Calling: Common signs were used mainly.

        Heading: (1) All prefixes were omitted; (2) the handling of all items, with the exception of those referred to in Code Indicator "KO" Manual or those having a broadcast number or those in numerical or letter code, were somewhat simplified.

        Ending: The heading was to be repeated to prevent errors in broadcast call signs.

    c. Strategic security transmittal form

This was applied in case greater security was required than in the strategic general transmittal form.

Heading: (1) Prefixes were the same as in (b); (2) addressee, for distribution list addressees, part or all of the conventional message text were made into code form and inserted at the end of the text (Call signs were the same as code signs).

d. Tactical transmittal form

This transmission form was to be used when voluminous, prompt and smooth handling was required. The main form of communications was broadcasting and direct communications could be effected when necessary.

Heading: (1) Only necessary matters were to be entered; (2) Senders address and distribution list addressees (these were not inserted in the text, unless special mention was required) were usually omitted.

Ending: Same as the basic transmittal form

e. Aircraft communications transmittal form

Because of the characteristics of aircraft communications, the tactical transmittal form was further simplified for sole use in aircraft communications and in facilitating training. The main form of communications was broadcasting, and direct communications could be effected when necessary. In order to strengthen the security of call signs of aircraft, ship and station communications, a different call and ending was used for this transmittal form, classifying them as air-basic transmission, air-1 or air-2 transmission.

f. Emergency transmittal form

This was the most simplified transmittal form used to transmit only the text and the ending (station callsigns were omitted), and was adopted in case of great urgency.

g. In case acknowledgement was required and direct communications were to be effected in various transmittal forms, the acknowledgement request sign was transmitted at the conclusion of the "ending" to indicate the switch-over from broadcasting.

4. In case the indication of frequency in communications was required, abbreviated frequency code was used for security purpose.

5. The two relay methods were the **ordinary relay method** (usual relay method) and emergency relay method (a method of relay broadcast in which messages received were relayed as they were received in order to minimize delay). Relay instructions were prescribed for such instances wherein there was vagueness or doubt in the receiving of messages.

6. When jamming was perceived, transmission was required to be suspended at once.

7. Radiation of radio wave was so arranged that it could not, under any circumstances, be undertaken without the permission of the communications officer. At the same time, for the prompt handling of communications in case radio control was not in force (in strategic and other areas) for the radiation of radio wave, the communicator (radiotelephone operator) would obtain permission only on the following matters prescribed by the communications officer:

    a. Correction of mistakes in transmission;
    b. Reply to radio transmission (voice transmission);
    c. Reply message in testing and transmitting call signs.

8. The service message was divided into the reply to transmission and service message. The reply to transmission was limited to an extremely small number (in case of aircraft transmission, it

was generally the same as that used in the past), the use of which was left to the operators, depending upon the situation. Except for the above, when the communications officer deemed it necessary, the Navy communications code books (the numerical and sign books, the security of which was better than the currently used procedure signals, and which were easy to use) were to be used for general communications. However, in the case of aircraft communications, the abbreviation "RI-YA-OTSU" was prescribed for those of special importance.

9. The operations liaison (liaison absolutely necessary for operations and security), testing (used exclusively for testing radio sets), and call-reply liaison (call and relay) were as newly prescribed and placed under the single heading "liaison".

Unification of the Code Regulations

The code books had their respective regulations concerning their use but the contents of these regulations were much the same. Therefore, the suggestion for unified regulations was made, but as multiformity of code was rather advantageous from the viewpoint of security, the suggestion was not carried out. However, it was decided that a unified code book should be provided for both the numerical code and letter code including the headings and indexes of the code method to be referred to.

The compilation of the code book "RO", which was to replace

the code book "D", was started in the latter part of June 1942 and completed in the latter part of July. This code book together with the code book "OTSU" which was still valid was, immediately distributed to all the units of the Combined Fleet. The distribution within the Combined Fleet by means of destroyers and aircraft was completed by early September. The distribution to and enforcement by the China Area Fleet took an additional month or two. Since then, new code books were prepared successively and everything proceeded smoothly by the end of 1942.

In view of the fact that the distribution of code books had taken one and a half months even with the assistance of the Combined Fleet, there arose the demand for the urgent study of measures regarding further distribution due to the revision of code books.

Revision of Code Books

With the failure of the Midway operation, the main body of the air fleets was completely destroyed as well as some aircraft carriers. As a result of this situation, it was feared that some of the code books lost were seized by the enemy and necessitated changing all the code books (except those used for information). However, the staff of the Combined Fleet was of the opinion that if there were any code books lost, they would not cause an immediate danger. The Central Agency also held the same opinion and the only action taken was to apply the emergency regulations (using the old code books as the master code) as a temporary expedient.

Subsequently, all the code books were revised in the order of their importance. The additive method (numerical code system) was adopted to a greater extent than before and the titles of code books were revised to disguise any suggestion of their contents. The existing code books were named by their contents and catalogued by the "JIKKAN" system (use of the ten Japanese calendar signs). When code books increased in number, Roman letters were added to the titles.

Code books had hitherto been revised every several years, and the regulations for their use as well as the additive tables were revised every 6 to 12 months. However, in view of the increase in communications, more frequent revisions were made according to the following standard:

1. Strategic code book and its regulations for use:
    Every six months or one year.

2. Additive table and its key table:
    Every one to six months according to the frequency of use.

3. Tactical code book:
    Once a month.

4. Call signs:
    The original was changed once a month; the change by a modification table was made every day or once a week.

Distribution System of Cryptographic Publications

The Navy Library and the Naval District Libraries respectively served as the cryptographic publications distributing organs for the Central Agency and for each naval district.

The Navy Library was attached to the Secretariat of the Navy Minister and its chief librarian was charged with the custody and distribution of Navy publications. A chief librarian was assigned to each Naval District Library with the concurrent position of assistant to the staff officer in charge of the custody and preparation of publications.

Since there was no direct connection of command and supervision between the Navy Library and the Naval District Libraries, distribution could not be carried out smoothly, and the increase in the number of copies and frequent renewal of cryptographic publications necessitated a drastic reform of the distribution system.

In March 1942, the Navy Library became the 5th Section of the Naval Ship and Ordnance Department and the chief librarian of the Navy Library was concurrently assigned to the Naval Ship and Ordnance Department to be in a better position to command and control distribution.

Although this reform of the system greatly facilitated the transportation of cryptographic publications, the marked decline in the general appreciation for the maintenance of secrecy and the importance of the code and cipher caused the frequent loss of these publications. In addition, the whereabouts of many cryptographic publications became unknown during transit. Much time was taken for investigation to determine whether there were any cryptographic publications carried by transport ships when they were sunk. In short, the merits and demerits of this system were about the same and only the Naval Ship and Ordnance Department staff who appreciated the importance of the cryptographic publications made positive efforts in making effective use of the new system.

The results were satisfactory in part, but the conspicuous drawbacks of the new system were that the personnel became lax in safeguarding secrets and that cryptographic publications were found to be missing for long periods of time.

Taking into consideration the capacities of the Navy Library and Naval District Libraries, the cryptographic publications were distributed to each department and the code book contents scheduled to be revised were made known to each department half a year before the revision. However, in consideration of the scope of distribution, this system was changed in 1940 and orders were issued by radiotelegraph because the old system involved complicated procedures due to frequent changes in schedules. It was decided to notify en bloc the schedule and change of schedules in monthly reports by the Telegraph Section.

In order to minimize security "accidents" to code books which had been put into use, it was decided after the Midway operation that only the current code book and that for the next phase of operations should be distributed and that the rest be kept in the libraries. Accordingly, in view of the necessity to distribute successively the frequently revised code books in time for use, it was decided to issue detailed instructions concerning the distribution twice a month in addition to scheduled cancellation notices and other remarks in the Navy Official Report Appendix. These instructions were to be given exclusively to the headquarters and local distribution offices, and other departments were to be notified by their respective commanders.

With reference to the monthly report, a distribution division was instituted in the Telegraph Section to make a detailed investigation of the actual distribution of code books in addition to the compilation of the report in an effort to achieve maximum efficiency in handling code books and safeguarding secrecy. The code books, upon completion, were transferred to the Navy Library directly from the printing office under the supervision of the Bureau of Naval Affairs which immediately transferred them to each Naval District Library. Transmission was effected under the escort of librarians. The local distribution offices conducted mass transportation under the escort of their staff members, but as for distribution to minor offices, the recipients were summoned or the code books were forwarded by registered mail.

The return of code books from various units was made in the Homeland as soon as orders for cancellation were issued; from overseas areas, they were returned when ships were available; and code books in custody of ships were returned when the ships docked in

Homeland ports. Later however, due to frequent "accidents" during transportation and the shortage of transports, the officer in charge of code books was to burn them and then notify the Navy Minister in writing to that effect.

Enforcement of the Code Area System

As the war situation turned unfavorable, many forces were isolated at widely remote places. Accordingly, the distribution of cryptographic publications became very difficult and drastic measures were necessary for this distribution. Thus, it was decided to adopt the code area system (Chart 7).

The entire theater of operations was divided into 11 code areas, and of these, nine were grouped into three categories (W, Y and X in Chart 7) when unification was required from the operational viewpoint. The code books were differentiated as -- the code book used exclusively for communications within the area (non-related to other areas), and the code book used for communications between the headquarters of the area and the Central Agency. Japan Proper, the greater part of China and Formosa were excluded from the code areas and the old code system was observed.

The code book for the exclusive use within a code area was called Code System "HA", and Code Book "HA", the Regulations for Code "HA" and Key Table "HA" were used. As Code Book "HA" had not been compiled in time, Code Book "TEN" was used instead. The code

Code Area System — Chart 7

Area	Theater	Control Center	"I"	"RO"	"HA"
K	South China, Hainan Island	Hq 2d China Expeditionary Fleet; Hq Hainan Guard Dist	No 7; No 14	Special (Common to communications centers)	No 7
M	Malaya, Sumatra, North Borneo	Hq 10th Area Fleet (10th Comm Unit); Hq 1st Southern Expeditionary Fleet (10th Comm Unit)	No 1; No 13		No 1
S	French Indo-China, Thailand	Hq 11th Base Force	No 4		No 4
J	Java, S and E coasts of Borneo, Celebes, Lesser Sunda Islands	Hq 2d Southern Expeditionary Fleet (21st Comm Unit)	No 2		No 2
Y	Covering J, M and S areas	Hq 10th Area Fleet (10th Comm Unit)			No 13
X	Covering K, M and S areas	Hq 10th Area Fleet (10th Comm Unit)			No 14
B	Burma	Hq 13th Base Force (12th Comm Unit)	No 11		No 11
F	Philippines	Hq Southwest Area Fleet	No 10		No 10
G	Area north of Australia	Hq 25th Base Force (24th Comm Unit)	No 3		No 3
O	Bonin Islands, Iwojima, Marcus Island, Wake Island, Pagan	Hq Chichijima Base Force (Chichijima Comm Unit); Hq 27th Air Flotilla	No 5; No 15		No 5
N	Southeast area, East Caroline-Marshall area	Hq Southeast Area Fleet (8th Comm Unit); Hq 4th Fleet (4th Comm Unit)	No 12; No 6		No 12
W	Covering N, O and P areas	Hq Southeast Area Fleet (8th Comm Unit)			No 6
P	West Caroline	Hq 30th Base Force (3d Comm Unit)	No 9		No 9
T	Formosa	Hq Takao Guard Dist (Takao Comm Unit)	No 8		No 8

Remarks:

1. "I" codes were for use between the center of a code area and the Central Agency or C in C Combined Fleet.
2. "RO" special codes, were for use between the following important sections: Central Agency; C in C Combined Fleet; commanders of various fleets; commander of 27th Air Flotilla; commanders of important base forces (those at Kurile Islands, Chichijima, Okinawa, Port Arthur, Rashin, Yangtze River, Amoy, Hongkong, Tshingtao and Mako); 9th, 10th, 11th, 12th, 13th, 15th, 21st, 22d, 23d, 25th, 30th, 32d, 33d Base Forces.
3. "HA" codes were for use between various sections within a code area.

book was common to all the code areas but the regulations for code and the key table were different.

The code book for use within the code area was distributed to every communications organ in the area and arrangements were made so that only the Central Agency and the Combined Fleet headquarters could communicate directly with the areas. The code book was distributed also to the naval districts and guard districts in Japan Proper and Korea to be used for interception. The code method was the numerical code by the additive panel.

The code book used for communications between each communications center was called Code System "I", utilizing Code Book "I", Regulations for Code "I", Key Table "I" and Additive Strip "I". The Code Book "I" had not been compiled in time so that Code Book "RO" was used instead.

In the beginning, it was planned that all the code books and tables should be different for each code area. Actually they were made different except the code book, which was used in common, but there was no code for use in the group areas, W, Y and Z. The Central Agency and the Combined Fleet headquarters possessed all the code books, while the naval districts and guard districts in Japan Proper and Korea possessed only the decoding books. The code method was approximately the same as Code "H", but to strengthen security, the additive "strips" which were attached to the additive panel were frequently changed.

When the distribution of code publications to District F became impossible, Area F used the special "RO" code which had been established for that area before the enforcement of the code area system as well as the code regulations and additive table* specially designated for that area.

The code area system was gradually carried out by areas where the revision of the codes "RO" and "TEN" was not feasible in case of security "accident", and in May 1945, the system was in force in almost all the code areas (excluding Area F). In Area F, the use of this system was not possible. Area B was dissolved because the Burma area was lost before the distribution. Area T (Formosa) was established after the enemy landing at Okinawa.

The Exchange of Code Books with the Army

By the end of 1944, it became necessary to unify codes in order to facilitate operations of the Army and the Navy, and as the first step, it was decided to interchange the currently used code books between the Navy and the Army for mutual utilization. The code books of the Army had a different code form, and the varieties of these books were so numerous that the Navy found it difficult to use. Moreover, administration became complicated because the notification

---

*The additive table consisted of an irregular arrangement of a code group composed of five letters with numbers ranging from 0 to 9 each. The use of this code was limited to once for a unit.

on their usages was apt to be delayed; therefore, the Navy could hardly utilize them. On the other hand, the Army utilized naval code books very effectively in intercepting information for Army air intelligence. However, as air transportation to the Southern Area was disrupted and there was only the air communications mainly to the northern Asiatic continent, the code book for air transportation was used in the communications of the Japan Air Transportation Company.

Security "Accidents" and Countermeasures

Major security "accidents" concerning code and cipher and their countermeasures in the Pacific War were as follows:

Submarine I-1 at Guadalcanal Island:

While transporting provisions to Guadalcanal Island, the submarine was stranded on the coast of Kamimbo during combat with an enemy motor torpedo boat. It listed and exposed part of its hull above the water. The responsible persons evacuated some of the military top secret documents from the craft and buried them in the coastal sands of enemy territory where there was every fear of their being dug out plus the fact that water-soluble ink had been used for only a few of these documents. The loss comprised many code books for future use in addition to those in current use, totalling about 200,000 copies. This fact was reported about a month after the "accident" when the crew involved returned to Rabaul. Although the Submarine Squadron Command issued orders to dig them out and destroy them immediately, one or two of the numerous places where the documents were buried could not be located. Moreover, as there were a considerable number of code books left in the submarine, aerial bombardment and torpedoing by submarines was carried out, but complete destruction was not confirmed.

Countermeasures:

1. Emergency measures were taken and new code books were used.

2. The additive table of the wartime code book was immediately revised and the encoding procedure was altered.

3. The original of the strategic code book was not changed.

"Accident" during transport to Tsingtao:

In 1943, when crytographic publications were being transported from Kure Naval Ship and Ordnance Department to Tsingtao Base Force, the box containing them was inadvertently opened. This was charged to the Naval Ship and Ordnance Department's failure to have a responsible officer cognizant of the importance of cryptographic publications.

Countermeasure:

1. Emergency measures were taken.

"Accident" on Biak Island:

When the enemy assaulted Biak Island in May 1944, the

garrison unit, anticipating danger, had the radio crew carry the code books to another communications room. The radio crew encountered enemy soldiers on the way and the code books were lost in the fighting. This "accident" was reported to the Central Agency about three weeks later because the responsible officer of the shore combat unit was negligent in reporting it earlier. Emergency measures were taken immediately. Since the A-GO Operation was just in the planning stage, overall emergency measures were taken. As a result of prompt and thorough investigation, it was found that only one or two codes were actually missing and nothing had happened to the important codes. However, as emergency measures were taken for many codes on the basis of the careless report, communications were slowed down considerably. In addition, as this "accident" happened immediately before the A-GO Operation, progress on this operation, was seriously affected.

Countermeasures:

    1. Overall emergency measures were taken.

    2. The encoding procedure was partially altered.

    3. The original of the strategic code book was changed.

Jettisoning of code books from transport plane of the Fourth Fleet:

A transport plane of the Fourth Fleet flying from Truk to Rabaul in 1943 cast its cargo into the sea during flight because of motor trouble. It became known that the cargo comprised some code books and there was fear that they might be adrift. For fear that the code books, being tightly packed, would remain adrift for a long period and as the place of "accident" was somewhat near the coast, countermeasures were taken immediately.

Countermeasure:

    1. Emergency measures were taken.

"Accident" of code books washed from transport submarine:

    A submarine was attacked from the air during debarkation of cargo destined for a unit stationed at Salamaua, New Guinea. The craft suddenly submerged and the cargo which was on deck was washed away. Among the cargo were some cryptographic publications.

Countermeasure:

    1. Emergency measures were taken to some extent.

Freight-car door "accident":

    When cryptographic publications were transported by freight train from the Yokosuka Naval District Library to the Ominato Naval Ship and Ordnance Department in 1943, it was discovered at the destination that the lock fastened to the freight-car door had been lost in transit. Whether it had fallen off or the door had been purposely opened could not be ascertained. Nothing was amiss with the packing.

Countermeasure:

    1. No measures were taken.

Loss during railway transportation:

    When cryptographic publications were sent under escort from the Chinhae Communications Unit to its detachment in 1944, they were lost due to negligence during transportation and were not recovered despite thorough search.

Countermeasure:

    1. Emergency measures were taken by distributing duplicates of lost code book.

Besides these seven major code "accident" cases during the two years from 1 January 1943 to the end of 1944, there were a number of minor cases. Approximately 2,000,000 copies of cryptographic publications for current and future use were discarded due to these seven "accidents". For the safeguarding of military secrets, measures to minimize losses due to "accidents" were so earnestly desired that the "strip additive panel" device came to be adopted and put into practical use in part, though the war ended before its results were thoroughly studied.

Apart from the measures taken due to the "accidents" mentioned above, the "additive strip" was used together with the additive table as a measure to further increase security of code from the middle of 1944. In enforcing this system, the revision of the strategic code book was effected by advancing the date for the regular revision.

The Japanese Navy could not obtain any actual proof whether the code was broken by the enemy, although it was presumed that some of the lost code books had fallen into enemy hands. Therefore, the conjecture was that, although secret communications might have been intercepted by the enemy, the important code books in current use could not be directly utilized by the enemy. However, the following factors were taken into consideration:

1. Since the Navy revised its important codes (at least the additive table) about every month, it was quite certain that the codes were not broken by the enemy inasmuch as numerous codes were used at not too frequent intervals.

2. It was presumed that if any messages were broken by the enemy, it was because outpost units used the old code book in re-transmitting radio messages when the new code book had not been distributed to them.

3. As the Army revised the letter substitution table for sending telegrams, the enemy could have broken the code by obtaining cross-checking data concerning matters identical both in the Army and the Navy.

4. Complete reliance was not placed in the diplomatic relations code.

At any rate, the Americans reported that the disaster to Admiral Yamamoto at Buin, Bougainville, was due to cryptanalysis.

However, this was impossible as his movement was never dispatched in the Navy code. Furthermore, from the success in the Kiska withdrawal operations and others, it was concluded that the main code book had not been broken.

List of Code Books

1. For strategic and administrative use:

    a. Naval Code Book (KO):

    Exclusively used for communications between important communication organs.

    b. Naval Code Book (SHIN):

    Used for communications concerning logistics but rarely used because the code personnel were accustomed to the use of Naval Code Book (D).

    c. Naval Code Book (D):

    A numeral code book which was widely and proficiently used for most communications.

2. For tactical use.

    a. Naval Code Book (OTSU):

    Used for tactical communications of surface forces; revised once or twice a year.

    b. Naval Code Book (BO):

    Used for local actions.

    c. Naval Code Book (F):

    Used for air communications; revised every two months.

    d. Naval Code Book (C):

    Used for air communications and other miscellaneous purposes.

e. Naval Code Book (H):

   Used for air communications in the China area; a simple letter transcription method code which could be readily revised at any time.

f. Naval Code Book (KI):

   Used for land combat in the China area. Widely used during the China Incident, but sparingly used after the outbreak of World War II. There was a tendency to use the Naval Code Book (OTSU) in place of this code book.

g. Code Book for the Army-Navy joint operation:

   Its use was suspended due to a security "accident" by the Army.

h. The Combined Fleet Special Code (A).

   A collection of code phrases.

3. For communications of intelligence reports.

   a. Overseas Secret Telegraph Code Book:

      Kept in reserve but was to be used for communications between attache's and the Central Agency.

   b. Naval Code Book (J):

      Used for communications between attache's stationed in Europe and America and the Central Agency.

   c. Naval Code Book (HEI):

      Used for intelligence communications in the China area.

   d. "IC":

      Used by intelligence agents.

      "I C-A": This was distributed to officers stationed in Great Britain, France, Italy, Spain, Portugal, Turkey and Soviet Russia.

"I C-B": Distributed to the headquarters of the Second China Expeditionary Fleet, the officers stationed in Canton, and the headquarters of the Canton Base Force; headquarters of Mako Naval Guard District, headquarters of Takao Naval Guard District and headquarters of Hainan Naval Guard District.

"I C-C": Distributed to the officers stationed in North Korea, Khabarovsk, Manchuria and Korea; headquarters of Chinhae Naval Guard District.

"I C-D": Distributed to the officers stationed in America, Canada, Mexico, Brazil, Argentina and Chile.

"I C-E": Distributed to the officers stationed in Burma.

e. "The New Code Book":

Distributed to the officers stationed on the western coast of America.

4. Code books commonly used for communications with service branches outside the naval service.

a. Shipping Secret Communications Regulations:

Used in communications with merchant ships. These regulations provided for encoding call signs and names of the senders and addressees; and for the text the code from "Naval Code Book (S)" was applied.

b. Naval Code Book (S):

This book was distributed to merchant ships of more than 1,000 tons.

c. Code Book for Fishing Boats:

This was distributed to all vessels.

d. Naval Code Book (W):

Used for reporting all ships (foreign) entering and clearing ports. This book was distributed to principal naval headquarters and above, local resident officers, custom houses and Naval Harbor Master's Offices.

 e. Standard Code Book for the Three Ministries:

Used by the Navy, Army and Foreign Ministries. It was distributed to the diplomatic officials stationed in East Asia and principal Navy and Army headquarters.

5. For miscellaneous uses.

 a. Naval Communications Abbreviations:

Abbreviations for ranks and positions, the names of agencies and communications phrases.

 b. Primary Signal Book:

This was also used in visual signals.

 c. Special Abbreviations for the Combined Fleet:

The abbreviations used for tactical communications, for communications with temporarily established radio stations and for communications inspection.

 d. Naval Call Sign Table:

This was distributed to all communications agencies.

 e. Special Call Sign Table for the Combined Fleet:

Used for tactical communications of the Combined Fleet.

Disposal of Code Books After the End of the War

In the latter part of August, an order was issued to destroy by fire all the cryptographic publications except the following:

Code Book "RO" (3) and (4), their regulations for use

and additive tables; Code Book "TEN" No 1, its regulations for use and additive table; Code Book "HA", its regulations for use and its key table; the Code Book "I", its regulations for use and its key table; call signs and abbreviation signals in use.

It was planned to keep various kinds of code books at the offices of the Central Agency for some time but they were all destroyed due to an error by an officer of the Navy General Staff, and this created temporarily confusion in communications. On the last day of August, all documents were destroyed except Code Book "TEN" and related books and tables, and the call signs and abbreviation signals.

CHAPTER IV

Communications Preparations for War

The communications preparations before the outbreak of war were to have been planned according to the annual War Mobilization Program but since no preparations were made for equipment due to budgetary reasons, no full-scale program was undertaken until the fall of 1941 (Chart 8) (See Charts 9 and 10 for expansion of the Tokyo Communications Unit and standard TO/E for other communications units).

The establishment of the central communications installations for fleets, ground forces and air bases necessary in offensive operations and the completion of the wire communications nets of the Homeland were the main objectives in the communications preparations at the outbreak of war. Since the communications facilities of the naval vessels in the forward combat area had generally been completed (though not entirely adequate), there were no special problems to be considered.

After 1942, during offensive operations, the consolidation of the central communications facilities of the air bases and units in the occupied territory was emphasized. However, the production of fixed radio sets did not increase, so the operations were carried out mainly by means of mobile radio equipment (Chart 11).

Throughout World War II, the maintenance of overseas land com-

Chart 8

Prewar Preparations Plan for Communications Unit

Communication Unit	Summary of Preparations	Objective
Tokyo Communications Unit	1. Strengthen communications capacity. 2. Establish reserve sending and receiving stations.	Effect arrangement for the unit to serve as the central communications unit of the entire Navy.
Takao Communications Unit	Strengthen communications capacity	To serve as the central communications unit in the Southern Operations.
Ominato Communications Unit	Strengthen communications capacity	To serve as the central communications unit in the Northern Operations.
5th (Truk) Communications Unit	Strengthen communications capacity	To serve as the central communications unit in the Pacific Operations.
1st Communications Unit	Provided with: 15 mobile high frequency transmitters 15 receivers	To serve as the mobile communications unit during the French Indo-China and Malay Operations.
2d Communications Unit	Provided with: 20 mobile high frequency transmitters	To serve as the mobile communications unit during the Philippines and Dutch East Indies Operations.

Chart 9

Expansion of the Tokyo Communications Unit
1942-1944

	Project	Completed
Receiving Facilities	Installed underground receiving facilities with the compound for antiaircraft defense. Equipped with 40 receivers	Spring of 1943
	Installed reserve receiving stations at the Naval War College. Equipped with 40 receivers	Middle of 1942
	Reinforced receiving stations: Constructed two strongly built receiving station rooms. Equipped with 40 receivers	Middle of 1943
Transmitting Facilities	Installed Totsuka Transmitting Station No 2: Constructed 3 bombproof transmitting station rooms and installed 16 15-kilowatt transmitters.	Spring of 1944
	Reinforced the Transmitting rooms of the Funabashi Transmitting Station: Constructed 2 strongly built transmitting station rooms and installed 4 2 kilowatt transmitters.	Spring of 1944
	Installed control line between the Koyama Transmitting Station and the Tokyo Communications Unit; enabled use of 2 transmitters	Autumn of 1942
	Installed control line between the Usami Transmitting Station and the Tokyo Communications Unit; enabled use of the 100-kilowatt ultralong-wave transmitter	Autumn of 1942

Chart 10 - a

Standard Table of Equipment for Communications Units, 1943

Classi-fication	Applicable Unit	Station	Table of Equipment	
A	Applicable to the Central Communications Unit of the Combined Fleet	Receiving Station	Receivers, large	2
			Receivers, small	40
		Transmitting Station	5-KW high frequency transmitters	2
			2-KW transmitters	2
			1-KW or less transmitters	12
			0.5-KW low frequency transmitters	2
			0.25-KW medium frequency transmitters	3
		Radio Direction Finder Station	Receivers	20
			High frequency radio direction finders	3
			Low frequency radio direction finders	3
			Medium frequency radio direction finders	3
B	Applicable to the Central Communications Unit of the Fleet	Receiving Station	Receivers, large	2
			Receiver, small	
		Transmitting Station	2-KW high frequency transmitters	2
			1-KW or less transmitters	8
			0.5-KW low frequency transmitters	2
			0.25-KW medium frequency transmitters	3
		Radio Direction Finder Station	Receivers	10
			High frequency radio direction finders	2
			Medium frequency radio direction finders	2
			Low frequency radio direction finders	2

Standard T/E For Communications Units, 1943 (Cont'd)

Chart 10 - b

Classification	Applicable Unit	Station	Table of Equipment
C	Applicable to the central radio station of the unit such as base forces, etc.	Receiving Station	Receivers, small 16
		Transmitting Station	1-KW or less high frequency transmitters ..... 6 0.5-KW low frequency transmitters .... 2 0.25-KW medium frequency transmitters 2
		Radio Direction Finder Station	Receivers .... 6 High frequency radio direction finders .... 2 Medium frequency radio direction finder .... 1 Low frequency radio direction finder 1

Note:
1. When transmitters and receivers are lacking, mobile high frequency radio sets (250 watt) are to be provided, depending on the local situation.
2. All communication facilities are to be made bombproof.
3. Necessary power units and antenna array are to be arranged.

Chart 11

Mobile Communications Equipment Production Plan

Communications Equipment	Planned Monthly Production				
	From January 1942	From July 1942	From January 1943	From July 1943	From January 1944
High Frequency Mobile Radio Set	30	50	100	150	200
Air Base Radio Set No. 5	20	50	100	200	300
Portable Radio Set	100	200	300	400	500
Portable Very High Frequency Radio Set	100	150	200	250	300
Telephone Set	100	200	300	400	300

munications facilities was so poor that operations were always carried out with the facilities in an unsatisfactory condition. The main reasons for this being: (1) impossibility of mass production of communications equipment; (2) transportation difficulties due to American submarine attacks; (3) Inefficient as well as lack of maintenance personnel.

Wire Communications Facilities

The establishment of wire communications nets was accelerated in 1941 as a measure in the preparations for war, and the Navy planned to obtain exclusive use of the wire nets controlled by the Communications Ministry. In the beginning of the war, the first consideration was the installation of the telegraph and telephone circuits connecting Tokyo, the naval districts and guard districts in Japan.

In anticipation of greater production of radios after 1943, plans were made to complete the air defense lookout communications and wire communications between air bases in the Homeland and make extensive use of the wire nets owned by the Communications Ministry. Every effort was made to complete the installation of portable telegraphs and telephones, but due to a shortage of materials and other factors, the work was not completed until about 1945.

As for wire facilities in occupied overseas areas, importance was particularly attached to installations at base air groups.

However, due to transportation difficulties and shortage of materials, no progress was made. When installation was completed, it was immediately destroyed by air raids, thus the work remained unfinished when the war came to an end. The base air groups which were specially designated in the installation plan were: Kanoya, Chitose, Bibai, Paramushiro, Takao, Clark (Philippines), Davao, Kendari, Singapore, Guam and Rabaul.

Communications of Carrier Task Force

In any operation, secrecy of fleet movement had been of absolute necessity. Fleets usually maneuvered in groups, but when dispersed for operations, the distance between each group, as a rule, did not exceed 100 miles. Thus, communications within a fleet were chiefly conducted by the visual method. However, radiotelephone communications by short-distance transmitting frequency was the usual means for radio communications. On the other hand, as total reliance could not be placed upon the radiotelephone, a double or a triple telephone system was generally adopted and the radiotelegraph system by low and high frequencies was also used as alternate and reserve communications means.

As task forces also had to maintain secrecy of movement in their operations, over-all coordination of land-based communications units in the operating area was required. A coordinated system between the task forces and land-based communication units was generally established before the outbreak of war. Moreover, the flagship of a fleet (or the ship in charge of communications with outside units) required transmitters which would not be detected by enemy radio direction finders. Although such transmitters were completed in early 1944, they were not put to practical use until spring of 1944 when task forces actually engaged in operations.

Selection of Fleet Flagship

There were both advantages and disadvantages in using an aircraft carrier as the flagship of a task force, but the Japanese Navy used aircraft carriers as task force flagships throughout the war. From the standpoint of communications, it was more advantageous to use a battleship as a flagship because of its strong protective capacity against possible impairment to communications facilities. However, from the standpoint of directing the operation, the use of an aircraft carrier as a flagship was highly advantageous in that it enabled direct control over air squadrons, the main striking strength of the force, and also the commanding officer could directly control the commander of reconnaissance planes and gain firsthand knowledge of the enemy situation. Therefore, when Japan had flying squadrons equal or superior in fighting power and skill to that of the enemy at the start of war, an aircraft carrier had many advantages as a flagship.

With the progress of the war, the fighting power and skill of the Japanese air squadrons decreased steadily. As such, aircraft carriers became vulnerable to damages which frequently caused the failure of command function at critical moments. Nevertheless, the fact remains that the aircraft carrier was used as a flagship to the very end of the war as the expedient means for combat command. Other means could have been easily taken had the radiotelephone within a task force been developed and improved to the same extent as the wiretelephone.

Communications Equipment for Ships

The number of vessels in the Japanese Navy at the time of the outbreak of the China Incident was approximately 330 (1,250,000 tons), the main strength of which consisted of the following: 10 battleships, 10 aircraft carriers, 35 cruisers, 136 destroyers, 80 submarines, 13 gunboats, 10 torpedo boats and 10 special duty ships. Vessels under construction were based upon the First Plan (four-year plan beginning in 1934), the Second Plan (five-year plan beginning in 1937) and the Third Plan (six-year plan beginning in 1939). (See Monographs 145, 149, 160, 169, 172 and 174).

Although there was some delay in the construction of these new ships, due mainly to the slow production of engines, no difficulty was encountered in the installation of radio equipment. However, from about 1940 when military preparedness began to be accelerated, the production of special radio equipment such as high frequency transmitters for submarines and other large-type high frequency transmitters tended to lag behind schedule.

Military preparations had been strongly stepped up from about 1940, and merchant ships and fishing boats were requisitioned one after another and converted into naval auxiliary vessels. Large-type merchant ships were converted to aircraft carriers and cruisers, and small fishing boats to minesweepers, subchasers and picket boats.

The installation of complete radio equipment on these converted vessels presented considerable difficulty as such equipment on these vessels was often inferior to the standards designated by the Navy. Replacements with new radio equipment were necessary beyond initial estimates, and, moreover, when they were installed, great difficulty was experienced in the problem of enlarging a radio room and of the adaptation of the power source which varied according to each ship.

From the beginning of 1941, a large number of converted vessels were rapidly completed, and these were fitted with either additional equipment or the old equipment replaced altogether. The Construction and Repair Depots undertook the task, which was done as rapidly as possible to minimize the docking period. When the war was in full swing, a new naval construction program was planned (Fourth Plan), which took into consideration the experiences gained in battle and emphasized the preparation of small vessels.

Through appropriations from the Munitions Preparation Expenditure, the preparation of transmitters and tubes for the expeditionary forces was completed. However, the types and amount of equipment to be furnished were decided in accordance with the amount of stockpiled equipment and probable future developments.

From the beginning of 1940, TM-type high frequency portable radio sets had been ordered on a long-term basis for the monthly output of approximately 35 sets, the peak production in civilian industry. At the outbreak of the Pacific War, tubes valued at 60,000,000 yen had been purchased.

After commencement of hostilities, research was continued for ways and means to improve communications, a few of the objectives being:

1. To strengthen the radio room under the armored deck to maintain radio communications.

2. To make medium frequency communications possible.

3. To improve very-high frequency communications for greater security.

4. To improve the capacity for intercepting enemy communications.

To attain these objectives, the amount of radio equipment was increased according to a plan (Chart 12).

The situation of communications equipment for submarines from the fall of 1941 was as follows:

1. Only the high frequency transmitter was used and the low frequency radio tumbler mast was discarded.

2. The 17 KC very-low frequency receiving set (for underwater radio reception) was installed.

3. The installing of medium frequency transmitters was planned but ended in the experimental stage since the antenna array was not completed.

Chart 12

Plan for Increasing Radio Equipment on Naval Vessels

Type of Ship	Details
Capital Warship	1. Radio rooms to be provided in four places and the receiving and transmitting rooms under the armored deck to be made the main radio rooms. 2. Receivers for the interception of enemy communications to be increased: six receivers for the fleet flagship and four receivers for the division flagship. 3. Medium frequency transmitters to be increased: three for the fleet flagship, two for the division flagship and one for other vessels. 4. Installation of 25 W very-high frequency telephones: three for the fleet flagship, two for the division flagship and one for other vessels.
Destroyer	To be equipped with an additional medium frequency transmitter.
Defense Ship	To be equipped with an additional medium frequency telephone.

(For further details, see Chapter VII: Operational Communications of Submarines).

In the latter part of 1942, combat operations became very active and reports on damaged vessels began to come in from about the middle of May. Attention was focused on measures to minimize such damages and at the same time, serious consideration was given to a plan for improving communications on ships and simplifying equipment in order to minimize the amount of labor and materials required. As a result of combat experiences, various measures were taken into consideration such as redesigning the antenna to minimize obstruction and damage by gun fire or bombs, the change of location of radio rooms from the main deck and upper deck as a precaution against damage and the dispersion and care of communications equipment. Other measures instigated from the Munitions Preparation Expenditure, the simplification of command and communications facilities, the abolishment or curtailment of secondary radio batteries and the readjustment of other small equipment.

Development of Radar

Radar Research

When information was received that radar was being used in the European theater by both Great Britain and Germany, Japan became cognizant of the necessity of radar from the tactical standpoint. Thereafter every effort was made to advance radar research for military purposes.

In the initial stage of the war, technical research on radar and communications equipment pertaining to aviation was the responsibility of the Naval Air Technical Depot, while radar and communications equipment for ships and ground installations were handled by the Naval Technical Research Laboratory. However, chiefly because of the poor staff of radar research technicians available in the Naval Air Technical Depot, the research on aircraft radar equipment made little progress, despite the fact the Naval Technical Research Laboratory assisted in the research.

In view of the great effect radar had on operations, research on this type of equipment was accelerated by all departments concerned from the outbreak of the war. Various measures to improve production were studied and Navy Minister Admiral Shimada, presuming that the reason for the slow progress in the production and performance of radar equipment lay in the administrative systems of the Navy Ship and Ordnance Department and the Navy Aeronautical Department, decided to establish the Electronics Development Department as the central administrative agency, despite strong opposition.

The Military Affairs Bureau, the Navy General Staff, the Navy Aeronautical Department and the Navy Ship and Ordnance Department strongly opposed the establishment of the agency for the following reasons:

1. The establishment of an administrative agency would only complicate matters and would not expedite the development of radar equipment. The slow progress in radar equipment was attributable primarily to lack of research facilities.

2. Research and experimental manufacture of radar equipment and production would be impossible without the positive aid and the cooperation of the Navy yards and air depots. Furthermore, under the prevailing shortage of materials, it would be actually impossible for the Electronics Development Department, as an independent agency, to obtain the necessary materials.

Despite all the opposition, the Navy Minister ordered the establishment of the Electronics Development Department in March 1944. The new department took over matters concerning research and testing of radar, communications and sonic equipment which hitherto were assigned to the Navy Ship and Ordnance Department and the Navy Aeronautical Department. The department, organized into two bureaus (General Affairs and Technical), was responsible for research and testing of radar, communications and sonic equipment.

Although the creation of this administrative organization centralized the administrative control over the research and testing of radar equipment and facilities, the decentralized research facilities remained the bottleneck. In November 1944, a committee studied the problem and a new system was established whereby one organization would be concerned with research, testing, production and supply of materials for communications equipment. The Navy Electronics Development was dissolved and the 2d Navy Technical Depot was established on 15 February 1945, through the merger of communications facilities attached to the Central Agency concerned, the Naval Air Technical Depot, Naval Technical Research Laboratory and Yokosuka Navy Yard. The 2d Navy Technical Depot then became the responsible agency for the research, testing production and materials for communications equipment.

Radar Production

From the commencement of hostilities until the spring of 1942, the promotion of construction and installation of radio equipment on vessels was the main task. It was in mid-May that radar No 1 Type 2 was installed on the battleship *Ise* for aircraft detection, and radar No 2 Type 2 was installed on the battleship *Hyuga* for surface craft detection. As a result of these first two experimental ventures which were relatively successful, the radar No 2 Type 1 was installed on aircraft carriers, cruisers and battleships. In March 1943, radar No 2 Type 2 was installed on Subchaser No 43 for surface craft detection, and on Submarine I-158 in April of the same year for submarine use (Chart 13). (Installation Standard of Radar for Ships, 1944, see Chart 14.)

Subsequently the demand for radar equipment placed a tremendous burden upon production. The emphasis on the transition to production of radar and the materials and labor facilities which had hitherto been laid upon general radio equipment required a large-scale study to be made. The Navy General Staff studied the potentialities of various industries to manufacture radar equipment and issued a general production schedule (Chart 15).

The production of radar for lookout posts commenced in the middle of 1942 and installation was carried out under the following plan: (Chart 16)

Chart 13

Installation Standard of Radar for Ships, 1942

Type of Vessel	Order of Installation	Type of Radar and Quantity	
		No 2 Type 1	No 2 Type 2
Battleship	3	1	2
Cruiser	2	1	2
Aircraft Carrier	1	2	
Submarine tender	2	1	
Destroyer (TSUKI-class)	2	1	
Destroyer	2		1
Submarine Chaser	1		1
Submarine	1		1

Chart 14

Installation Standard of Radar for Ships, 1944

Type of Warship	Order of Installation	Type of Radar and Quantity			
		No 2 Type 1	No 1 Type 3	No 3 Type 2	Radar Intercepter
Battleship	3	1	2	2	2
Cruiser	2	1	2	2	2
Aircraft Carrier	1	4		2	2
Aircraft (Small)	2	2	1		2
Submarine tender	2	1	1		2
Destroyer (TSUKI-class)	1	1	1		1
Destroyer	2		1	1	1
Submarine Chaser	1			1	1
Flagship submarine	1		1	1	1
Transport submarine	1		1		1
Submarine	1			1	1
Transport	3				1

Chart 15

Radar Production Schedule

Type	Jul-Dec 1942	Jan-Jun 1943	Jul-Dec 1943	Jan-Jun 1944	Jul-Dec 1944	Jan-Jun 1945
Radar for lookout posts	20	40	50	50	50	50
Portable Radar No 1 Type 3			50	100	150	150
Antiaircraft Radar for ship use	20	30	50	50	50	50
Anti-vessel Radar for ship use	20	30	50	100	150	150
Radar (Air No 6) for aircraft	300	500	800	1000	1000	1000
Radar for firing			20	20	20	20
Radar for searchlight directing				40	40	40
Radar intercept device			100	300	300	300

Type of Lookout Post	From July 1942		From July 1943		Remarks
	Monthly Installation Rate	Number of Radars at One Place	Monthly Installation Rate	Number of Radars at One Place	
E Class	10	2	15	2	Antiaircraft lookout station
F Class			10	1	Anti-vessel lookout station

Chart 16

From 1944, a great increase of radar lookout posts was planned due to the intensification of enemy air raids and the shrinking battlefront. The object of the plan was to perfect a warning system by radar nets throughout the Homeland, Formosa, the Philippines, Malaya, Java and the coast of Central and South China (Chart 17).

Chart 17-a

Search Radar Assignment

Location of Installation	Radar						Radio Equipment					Motor Generator				Description
	Anti-aircraft Search				Surface Search		Transmitter			Mobile High Freq Radio Set	Full-Wave Receiver	Diesel	Gasoline			
	No 11	No 11k	No 12	No 13	No 14	No 22	No 32	250-Watt Low Freq	250-Watt Med Freq	250-Watt High Freq			15 KVA	6 KVA	3 KVA	1 KVA	
Key to Equipment	1	2	3	4	5	6	7	8	9	10	11	12	13	14	15	16	17
Imaizaki	2		1								1		1	1			
Kagenoma	2		1								1		1	1			
Ishikawazaki	2										1		1	1			
Kakumabetsu	2										1		1	1			
Suribachi Bay	2			1							1		1	1			
Musashi Bay	2										1		1	1			
Sutegokoen	(2)																
Matsuawajima	2		2								1			2			
Shinshirujima	(2)										(1)		(1)	(1)			

Search Radar Assignment (Cont'd)

Chart 17-b

Key to Equipment	1	2	3	4	5	6	7	8	9	10	11	12	13	14	15	16	17
Kushizaki	(2)			2							1		(1)	(1)		2	
Rubetsu				1							1					2	
Teiitsu				2							1					2	
Tennei	2			2							1		2				
Kitashiretoko				2													
Nayoshi	2								1	1		1	2				
Nakashiretoko				2												2	
Nishinotoro				1			(1)				(1)			(1)			*
Soyamisaki				2			(1)							(1)			*
Mosamimisaki	1			1							1			1			
Motorimisaki	(1)			2							1		(1)	1			
USA Airfield				2													
Oita Airfield				2													
Tomitaka	2			2							1		1				

Chart 17-c

Search Radar Assignment (Cont'd)

Key to Equipment	1	2	3	4	5	6	7	8	9	10	11	12	13	14	15	16	17
Miyazaki Airfield				2													
Toizaki	2	1			1		1				1		2				*
Kasanohara Airfield				2													
Hinosaki		2		1							1			2			
Ueki							(1)										*
Kanoyamachi				2													
Satamisaki				3			(1)							1			*
Kagoshimamachi				2													
Surigahama							(1)										*
Bononisaki	1			2					1		1	1	1		2		
Tsurigakezaki	2			2					1	1	1		1			2	
Izumi				2						1							
Onnajima	1											1	2				
Osezaki	1			2								1	2				*

119

Chart 17-d

Search Radar Assignment (Cont'd)

Key to Equipment	1	2	3	4	5	6	7	8	9	10	11	12	13	14	15	16	17
Ukushima	2			2					1	1		1	2				
Ikutajima							(1)				(1)						*
Tajimadake	1			2													
Mihoro Airfield			2														
Nemuro	1		1	1							1		1	(1)			
Nemuro Airfield				2													
Akeshi	1		1										1	1			
Erimomisaki	1		1								1		1				**
Chitose				2													
Keizanmisaki				2			(1)				1			2			**
Shirakami							(1)				(1)			(1)			*
Kamoinisaki	(2)			2							1		(1)	(1)			
Shiriyazaki	1		1								1		1	1			**
Ominato	1		1										1				

Search Radar Assignment (Cont'd)

Chart 17-e

Key to Equipment	1	2	3	4	5	6	7	8	9	10	11	12	13	14	15	16	17
Ryuhimisaki	1						(1)				(1)			(1)			*
Kodomari	1										1			1	1		
Samekaku	1		1	1					1	1		1	1				
Kinkazan		1	1	1			(1)		1	1		2		1			*
Matsushima Airfield				1													
Koriyama Airfield				2													
Shioyasaki	2		1	1			(1)		1	1		2	1	1			
Tsukuba Airfield				2													
Hyakurigahara Airfield				2													
Omura Airfield				2													
Wakamiya							(1)				(1)			(1)			*
Okinoshima							(1)				(1)			(1)			*
Futaoishima							(1)				(1)			(1)	1		*
Kaijima	1			2					1	1		1	2				

121

Chart 17-f

Search Radar Assignment (Cont'd)

Key to Equipment	1	2	3	4	5	6	7	8	9	10	11	12	13	14	15	16	17
Hinomisaki	1			2					1	1		1	1				*
Togo	1			2					1	1		1	2				
Miho Airfield				2													*
Kyogazaki	2			2			(1)		1	1		1	1				*
Minazuki	1			2					1	1		1	1				*
Enkozaki							(1)				(1)			(1)			*
Kannonzaki						1	(1)				1			1			*
Kijibana						1	(1)										*
Danzaki	1			1													*
Niigata							(1)				(1)		(1)				*
Kamizaki							(1)				(1)		(1)				*
Gōnozaki							(1)				(1)		(1)				*
Kairyuto							(1)				(1)		(1)				*
Nagasu	(2)			(2)			(1)				(1)		(2)				*

Chart 17-g

Search Radar Assignment (Cont'd)

Key to Equipment	1	2	3	4	5	6	7	8	9	10	11	12	13	14	15	16	17
Makishima							(1)				(1)			(1)			*
Yatabe Airfield				2													
Konoike Airfield				2													
Inubosaki	2	1		1			(1)		1	1	1	2	2				*
Katori Airfield				1													
Taito	1	1								1	1	1					
Mohara Airfield				2													
Kisarazu Airfield				2													
Katsuura	2		1	1			(1)		1	1		2	40 KVA ...1				
Tateyama				2													
Fura		1	1	1		1		2	1			2	1				*
Kannonzaki							(1)							(1)			*
Sendazaki							(1)							(1)			*
Enoshima							(1)							(1)			*

Chart 17-B

Search Radar Assignment (Cont'd)

Key to Equipment	1	2	3	4	5	6	7	8	9	10	11	12	13	14	15	16	17
Atsugi				2													
Okusuyama	1			1													
Oshima				2			1				1	1		2	2	3	*
Niijima				2													
Miyakejima	1			2					1	1	1	1	2		2	3	
Mikurajima				2							1				2	2	
Hachijojima	1	2								1	1	1	2	2			
Chinkai				2													
Maifutsu-to							(1)				(1)			(1)			*
Shorijima							(1)				(1)			(1)			*
Kyobunto				2							1			1		2	
Koshu				2													
Eastern Part of Saishuto							(1)				(1)			(1)			*
Western Part of Saishuto							(1)				(1)			(1)			*

124

Chart 17-i

Search Radar Assignment (Cont'd).

Key to Equipment	1	2	3	4	5	6	7	8	9	10	11	12	13	14	15	16	17
Shorizanto				2							1			1		2	
Chozanshi				2							1					2	
Port Arthur				2							1					2	
Tanegashima				2							1				2		
Southern Part of Tanegashima				2							1			1		1	
Kushincerabuto				2							1				1	1	
Kuchinoshima				2							1				1	1	
Takarajima				2							1				1	1	
Amamioshima				2							1				1	1	
Kikaigashima				1							1				1	1	
Kitadaitojima				2							1				1	1	
Minamidaitojima				2							1				1	1	
Okidaitojima				2							1				1	1	
Aogashima				4							1	1			2	2	

Search Radar Assignment (Cont'd)

Chart 17-j

Key to Equipment	1	2	3	4	5	6	7	8	9	10	11	12	13	14	15	16	17
Torishima				4							1	1			1	1	
Ishimurozaki	1			2	1						1	1	2			4	
Fujieda Airfield				2													
Omaezaki	1		1	1						1		2	2				*
Hamana				2							1	1		1		1	
Irako							(1)										*
Daiosaki	1	1	1	1			(1)		1	1		2	1				*
Nagoya Airfield				1													
Yamato Airfield				2	1				1								
Kashinozaki	2		1	1						1		1					
Shionomisaki				2		1					1	1 (High Freq)					*
Esugizaki				2							1						
Ichiezaki				2			1				1						
Hinomisaki											(1)			(1)			*

Chart 17-k

Key to Equipment	1	2	3	4	5	6	7	8	9	10	11	12	13	14	15	16	17
Kata							(1)										*
Yura							(1)				1						*
Naruo Airfield				2													
Himeji Airfield				2													
Tokushima Airfield				2													
Miyokojima		2							1	1			1				
Ishigaki jima		2							1	1			1				
Yonakuni jima				2											1		
Hokasho				2													
Sanshokaku		1		2										1	1	1	
Suo		1		2										1	1		
Karenko		1		2										1	1		
Shinko				2											1	1	
Taito		2		2							1			2			

Search Radar Assignment (Cont'd)

Chart-17-1

Key to Equipment	1	2	3	4	5	6	7	8	9	10	11	12	13	14	15	16	17
Kotosho				2							1				1	1	
Garampi		1		2							1			1	1		
Toko		1		2							1			1	1		
Takao	2	1		2							1			1	1		
Taikozan	1	1		1							1		1	1			
Tainan				2							1						
Mako	1			4							2		1	1			
Kaiko				2							1			1	1	1	
Taichu	1			2							1			1	1		
Shinchiku	1	1		1							1		1	1			
Tansui		1		2							1			1	1		
Murotozaki	2		1	2						1		1					
Susaki							(1)				(1)			(1)			*
Matsuyama Airfield				2													

128

Chart 17-m

Search Radar Assignment (Cont'd)

Key to Equipment	1	2	3	4	5	6	7	8	9	10	11	12	13	14	15	16	17
Ashizurimisaki	2		1	2						1		1	1	1			
Okinoshima				2							1						
Iwakuni Airfield				2													
Fukashima				2			(1)				1				1		*
Tsuiki Airfield				2													
Uraota							1				1				1		*
Chichijima	1			4					1	1							
Hahajima				4													
Radar School	1		1	1								1					
Koizumi Plant				1												2	
Musashi Plant of Nakajima Co.				1												2	
Nagoya Plant of Mitsubishi Co.				1													
Meiji Airfield				2													
Chigasaki	No 6 ...1	No 62 ...1	No 62 ...1	1													

129

Chart 17-n

Search Radar Assignment (Cont'd)

Key to Equipment	1	2	3	4	5	6	7	8	9	10	11	12	13	14	15	16	17
Fuki kaku				2							1				1	1	

Remarks:

(1) "Description" Column:

    * Indicates stations which were planned and set up as anti-surface craft lookout stations. However, some of them also served as antiaircraft lookout posts.

    ** Indicates posts which were destroyed by air raids.

(2) Number of Equipment:

    The figure in parenthesis indicates the quantity of equipment which was not completed.

CHAPTER V

Naval Air Force Communications

Radio Equipment for Aircraft

In the preparations for war, radio equipment as well as other war materiel depended solely on production by the civilian industries. In 1940, the Navy took further measures to increase production by establishing the Numazu Ordnance Depot (specializing in manufacture of communications equipment). By 1941, large-scale equipping of aircraft was planned and the production of necessary radio equipment was set forth according to a production schedule issued by the Navy General Staff (Chart 18).

At the outbreak of war, the installation aspect of aircraft communications equipment was limited to installing equipment in any available space. The installation was carried out without careful consideration of the requirements in battle or the duties of the radio crew during flight. Therefore, efficiency of radio equipment could not be fully manifested.

In the installation of equipment on aircraft, the fitting of the radio was found to be most defective, and the radio crew had to operate it under very adverse conditions. Receiving was difficult or impossible because of the noise from the defective telegraph set or buzzers, and as a result, some of the important telegraph messages failed to be received. Moreover, it was extremely difficult

Aircraft Communications Equipment Production

Type	Planned Monthly Production				
	From Jan 1942	From Jul 1942	From Jan 1943	From Jul 1943	From Jan 1944
Aircraft Radio Set No. 1	400	500	1,000	1,500	2,000
Aircraft Radio Set No. 2	300	500	700	1,000	1,500
Aircraft Radio Set No. 3	200	300	500	600	1,000
Aircraft Radio Set No. 4	100	100	150	150	150
Very High Frequency Radio Telephone for communications within the Unit	100	100	150	150	150
Homing Direction Finder	500	1,000	1,500	2,000	2,500

to operate the telegraph set in a plane at a high altitude because the apparatus was poorly located and adjustment of the sets could not be made.

The installation work by aircraft manufacturing companies was also very unsatisfactory. In particular, careless supervision and poor testing frequently resulted in wrong wiring and defective high-voltage ground contact or bonding.

In many instances of defective wiring, the sets did not function after they were installed in the plane, and considerable time was required for repairs and maintenance. There was also a considerable number of aircraft on which the equipment was absolutely impossible to repair. Another defect was the noise caused by improper insulation and bonding of the ignition system; moreover in the installation there were frequent cases in which the mounting bases were of different size necessitating adjustments to be made.

There were various factors for the consistently defective installation of equipment. One factor which was quite flagrant was that the equipment itself was considered more important than the installation technique. Actually there were no research personnel specializing in the installation of equipment until 1944. Those who engaged in the planning and research in radio did not engage in the actual equipping of aircraft. They only considered the weight, volume and capacity of any equipment and were not familiar with the actual circumstances of those who operated it during flight.

Another factor was that the electrical engineers of aircraft manufacturing companies who engaged in the planning and experimental manufacture of airframes knew very little about radio equipment, much less its operations. They merely did the work of a carpenter fitting something of a certain size into a certain size into a certain space, and had no idea as to how the equipment could be used effectively.

As for the companies themselves, they were forced to rush production of communications equipment and as a result, they deliberately scamped their work. Factory superintendents were so occupied with procuring materials that the testing of completed aircraft, their primary duty, was neglected.

Thus, as mentioned in the foregoing, there were many reasons for unsatisfactory equipment but the must fundamental one was that the installation work was neglected and that the personnel concerned were indifferent as to its effects upon the fighting power.

The standard radio equipment installed in various types of aircraft in December 1941 and August 1945 is shown in Chart 19.

A general classification of radio equipment for the land-based attack planes was as follows:

1. No 3 aircraft radio.
2. Fixed antenna for No 3 aircraft radio.
3. Trailing antenna for No 3 aircraft radio (75 m).
4. Radiotelephone for inter-unit communications.
5. Controller of radiotelephone for inter-unit communications.
6. Antenna of radiotelephone for inter-unit communications.
7. Loop antenna for radio direction finder.

Chart 19-a

Standard Radio Communications Equipment in Aircraft, December 1941

Equipment	Land Medium Bomber	Carrier Torpedo-Plane	Carrier Dive-Bomber	Land (carrier) Recon Plane	Three-Seater Sea Recon Plane	Two-Seater Sea Recon Plane	Sub-borne Recon Plane	Fighter	Flying Boat
Aircraft Radio Set No 4	X								X
Aircraft Radio Set No 3	X	X			X				X
Aircraft Radio Set No 2			X	X		X	X		
Aircraft Radiotelephone Set No 1	X							X	X
Aircraft Radiotelephone No 4 for communications within the unit		X	X						
Aircraft Radiotelephone No 3 for communications within the unit	X								
Radio Direction Finder for large aircraft use		X	X	X	X	X			X
Radio Direction Finder for small aircraft use								X	

Remarks: X denotes the standard equipment which should be installed in the respective aircraft. However, due to shortages, very few aircraft were fully equipped. Experimental radio equipment is not included in this chart.

Chart 19-b

Standard Radio Communications Equipment in Aircraft, August 1945

Equipment	Large Land Bomber	Medium Land Bomber	Light Land Bomber	Land Recon Plane	Carrier Torpedo-Plane	Carrier Dive-Bomber	Fighter	Night Fighter	Three-Seater Sea Rcn Plane	Two-Seater Sea Rcn Plane	Sea-Plane Bomber	Sub Recon Plane	Flying Boat	Patrol Plane
Aircraft Radio Set No 3	X	X	X	X	X	X		X	X	X	X	X	X	X
Aircraft Radiotelephone Set No 1			X				X							
Large aircraft Radiotelephone for communications within the unit	X	X	X										X	X
Small aircraft Radiotelephone for communications within the unit					X	X			Patrol Plane Unit only X		X			
Radio Direction Finder for large aircraft	X	X	X										X	X
Radio Direction Finder for small aircraft				X	X	X		X	X	X	X			X
Radar	X	X		X	X			Special X	X				X	X
Radar Intercept Receiver	X	X											X	X
Magnetic Detector									Patrol Plane Unit only X					X

136

    8.   Auxiliary antenna for radio direction finder.
    9.   Radar.
  10.   Side antenna for radar.
  11.   Front antenna for radar.
  12.   Radar intercept receiver.
  13.   Antenna for radar intercept receiver.

The radio equipment for other types of aircraft was generally the same as the above.

The radiotelephone was necessary for fighter planes to carry out effective aerial combat and interception operations, but because of its limited range, the pilots became disinclined to use it to the fullest extent. This tendency was probably attributable to the pilot's indifference toward radio and partly to imperfection of the equipment itself, but the basic reason for the poor fighter plane communications was that there were very few officers enthusiastic enough to overcome the drawback and make the best use of existing equipment.

With the appearance of Type 3, No 1 aircraft radio set, radio-telephone capacity increased as it was simpler to manipulate, but maintenance thereof was neglected. Moreover, most of the units had poor communications due to the lack of attention to the screening of electromagnetic elements.

There was originally in existence the Type 96, No 4 aircraft radio set which could be operated by remote control and it was installed in large and medium planes. Then the Type 2, No 4 radio set was experimentally manufactured for remote control purpose but its mass production was shelved because it was deemed impracticable.

However, since the Type 96, No 4 aircraft radio set could not be
operated on medium frequency, the Type 2, No 3 aircraft radio set
was installed in land-based attack planes. This necessitated the
radio operator's seat to be placed far behind the pilot, making
intercommunications difficult.

In small planes, too, with the increase in the amount of equipment carried such as radar and other equipment, the space for radio sets became smaller, thereby increasing even more the necessity for remote control. Remote control for the radiotelephone of fighter planes was adapted for the Type 3, No 1 aircraft radiotelephone with good results, and the application of remote control to radiotelegraph was finally revived in the last Type No 3 experimental aircraft radio set, modified in 1944. This however, was not put into practical use by the operational forces.

Base Air Force Communications

At the beginning of the war, the base air force was organized as a unit of the Combined Fleet; consequently, each unit with its own independent communications system was included in the communications system of the Combined Fleet. Later, with the progress of operations, the base air force became the main striking strength of naval operations, and to cope with this situation, communications facilities of the base air force were gradually increased. However, the capacity of the cooperating land-based communications units was far too limited to satisfy the requirements of the air forces from the standpoint of both personnel and equipment (See Chart 20 for authorized strength of the base air force communications department).

The base air force's independent communications system encompassed two communication nets, namely, the air force communications which was considered an operational communications net, and the administrative communications net. At the time, it was felt that uninterrupted communications could have been maintained through maximum utilization of communications units if the following measures had been taken: boost the capacity of communications units, thereby strengthening broadcasting communications of communications units; adopt mechanical control for regular unit-to-unit communications; and increase their capacity in handling communications.

Operational air communications centers which were projected to be strengthened were Kisarazu, Yamato, Kanoya, Shokozan (Takao), Clark Field, Tinian, Truk, Rabaul and Seletar (Singapore). With the progress of the war, those in Formosa and Japan were enlarged and became flexible organizations with auxiliary centers as reserve installations. As enemy air activity grew in intensity, dispersal in depth of groups of bases and the dispersal of installations in each base was required, and at the same time, a new arrangement of radio-telephone networks to connect dispersed installations became necessary. However, there was no equipment available to meet the foregoing requirement, and moreover, at this stage of the war, the war

Chart 20-a

Authorized Strength of Base Air Force Communications Department

Personnel Classification (See Key on Chart 20-d)			A	B	C	D	E	F	G	H	I	J	K	L	M	N	O	P	Q
Communications Officer			1		1									1					
Divisional Officer					0-1										1	1			
Assistant Communications Officer					1									1					
Warrant Officers and Above		Materiel Assistant to the Communications Officer	2	1	1	1	1	1	1	1		1	1	1	1	1	1		
	Radio Dept	Radio Officer	1			1	1	1	1	1				1	1	1	1		
		General Duty Officer	1											1					
	Code Dept	Code Officer	1																
		Officer and Reserve Officer	1												2	1			
		Special Duty Officer and Warrant Officer		1											2	1	1		
		Assistant Code Officer	1	1										1					

140

Authorized Strength of Base Air Force Communications Department (cont'd)

Chart 20-b

Personnel Classification	A	B	C	D	E	F	G	H	I	J	K	L	M	N	O	P	Q
Special Communications Personnel (Inter-plane Communications)	6	3	3	3	3	3	3	3	3	1	1		3	3			
Advanced Radiomen — Communications Personnel	6	6	3	3	3	3	3	3	3	3	3		13	8	6	4	
Advanced Radiomen — General Equipment Personnel													3	3	2	0	
Radio and Code Dept — Ordinary Radiomen	2	2											50	34	19	13	4
Radio and Code Dept — Code Personnel	15	5		3	3	3	3	3	3	2	2		35	15	10	10	2
Wire Telephone Personnel			1										30	18	12	12	3
Administration Personnel (non-specialist)													21	15	6	6	1

Authorized Strength of Base Air Force Communications Department (cont'd)

Chart 20-c

Personnel Classification			A	B	C	D	E	F	G	H	I	J	K	L	M	N	O	P	Q
Radar Equipment Maintenance Dept and Wire Telephone Maintenance Dept	Warrant Officers and Above	Officer in Charge of Maintenance Section			1	1	1*	1*	1*					1					
		Maintenance Section Officers			2	1	1*	1*	1*		2*	1	1	1					
	Radiomen	Advanced Course Maintenance Enlisted Trainees			1	4	4	2	2	2	2	4	2	1	2	2	2	2	
		Ordinary Course Maintenance Enlisted Trainees			1	4	4	2	2	2	2	4	2	1	8	8	8	8	
	Radar Personnel	Advanced Course Maintenance Enlisted Trainees				4	2	2		2	2	2			2	2	2	2	
		Ordinary Course Maintenance Enlisted Trainees				6	2	2		2	2	2			6	6	6	6	
Wire Telephone Maintenance Personnel															10	5	3	3	

Authorized Strength of Base Air Force Communications Department (cont'd)

Chart 20-d

KEY

- A   Air Fleet Headquarters
- B   Air Squadron Headquarters

"KO" Air Force (Air)
- C   Headquarters
- D   Bombers
- E   Fighters, light bombers and medium attack planes
- F   Reconnaissance planes
- G   Flying boats
- H   Reconnaissance seaplanes
- I   Transport planes
- J   Fighters and interceptors
- K   Night fighters

"OTSU" Air Force (Ground)
- L   Headquarters
- M   Base A
- N   Base B
- O   Base C
- P   Base D
- Q   Base E

NOTES

1. The authorized strength for "KO" Air Force is to be determined on the basis of its air units.

2. Types and number of assigned bases will be the basis for determining the authorized strength for "OTSU" Air Force.

3. The various bases will be used as follows:
   - Base A: By Air Fleet Headquarters
   - Base B: By Air Squadron Headquarters
   - Base C: For permanent stationing or as a mobile base for attack units or reconnaissance air units.
   - Base D: For permanent stationing or as a mobile base for fighter units.
   - Base E: To be used as a shelter base.

4. The main strength of radar maintenance personnel will be assigned to "KO" Air Force.

5. Advanced course radio enlisted trainees (air equipment) will be temporarily assigned as advanced course maintenance enlisted trainees.

6. Personnel for the column "Warrant officers and above" will be assigned from inter-plane communications.

7. Figures with asterisks indicate specialists for radar maintenance.

143

industry of Japan was so overburdened that there was no means for time to manufacture new equipment. There was no alternative but for the air bases to use low-power sets which were originally to be installed on ships.

Base Communications Equipment

The standard for communications equipment supply to occupied bases and mobile land-based air forces was determined after the outbreak of hostilities (Chart 21).

The base construction policy had undergone great changes since the start of the Inner South Seas Operations. The changes meant that bases were maintained as a group of bases and that base installations were dispersed and converted into bombproof installations. As a result, all communications equipment was moved into the bombproof installations. The standard for communications equipment supply was reestablished in consideration of the speedy execution of this type of large scale conversion work and of the need for increasing medium-frequency transmissions.

Standard for Naval Air Base Communications Installations and Equipment (established in September 1944) entailed dividing the air base installations into the following four categories: (Chart 22).

Chart 21

Standard Communications Equipment for Mobile Land-Based Air Force

Communications Equipment		Permanent Base	Mobile Base
Transmitter	Low and Medium Frequency	1	1
	High Frequency	4	2
Receiver		8	8
Radio Direction Finder		1	1
Mobile High-Frequency (or 'AGS' type)		2	4
Power Source		60 Kilovolt Ampere High Frequency 40 x 1 60 Kilovolt Ampere High Frequency 3 x 1	
Description		This standard shows per base communication equipment supply; actually, from half to several times the number of per base communication equipment listed herein were supplied in proportion to the strength and mission of the base force.	

Classification	Transmitter			Receiver
	High Freq	Med Freq	Low Freq	
(A) Air Fleet Hq	6	2	2	20 (later changed to 30)
(B) Air Flotilla Hq	5 (some with medium-frequency transmission)		1	10
(C) Air Gp at large base	5 (some with medium-frequency transmission)		1	7 (later changed to 9)
(D) Air Gp at small base	3 (some with medium-frequency transmission)			5

Chart 22

1. Major Air Base Communications Equipment Maintained in 1937 (Chart 23).

2. Major Air Base Communications Equipment Maintained from 1938 to 1940 (Chart 24).

3. Major Air Base Communications Equipment Maintained from 1941 to 1943 (Chart 25).

4. Major Air Base Communications Equipment Maintained in Japan at Termination of War (Chart 26).

Communications of Air Squadrons

General Situation

The concept of the air squadron communications system and its application, taking into consideration the battle experiences of the

Chart 23-a

Major Air Base Communications Equipment Maintained in 1937

No	Name of Base	Transmitter							Receiver	Emergency Power Source	Description
		Low Frequency		Medium Freq		High Frequency					
		1 KW	0.5 KW	250 W	2 KW	1 KW	0.5 KW	250 W			
1	Kazan	1									At first provided with no communications equipment. Maintained as a transport plane base
2	Ominato (Mizukami)						2		8	40 X 1	
3	Tsukuba		1				2		8	100 X 1	Maintained as a training plane base
4	Hyakurigahara		1				1		4	100 X 1	Same as above
5	Kasumigaura	1	2		1	2	2		18	350X1 100X1 60 X1	Same as above
6	Kashima		1				2		8		Same as above
7	Kisarazu	2	2		1	2	3		24	250X1 100X1	Maintained as a central base for land medium bombers
8	Tateyama	1	2		1	2	2		18	100X3	Maintained as a combat aircraft base
9	Yokohama	1	2		1	2	2		18	40 X 2	Maintained as a central base for large flying boats
10	Yokosuka No 1	2	1	1	1	3	3		24	250X1 100X1	Maintained as a training plane base
11	Oi	1	2			2	2		18	100X2 250X1	Same as above
12	Suzuka No 1	1	2		1	2	2		24	250X1 100X1	Same as above

Chart 29-b

Major Air Base Communications Equipment Maintained in 1937 (Cont'd)

No	Name of Base	Transmitter Low Frequency 1 KW	Transmitter Low Frequency 0.5 KW	Medium Freq 250 W	High Frequency 2 KW	High Frequency 1 KW	High Frequency 0.5 KW	High Frequency 250 W	Receiver	Emergency Power Source	Description
13	Maizuru		1			1	2		8		Maintained as a combat aircraft base
14	Kure		1			1	2		8	250X1 60X1	Same as above
15	Saeki	1	1		1	2	2		18	100X2	Same as above
16	Sasebo	1			1	2	2	1	18	100X2	Same as above
17	Omura	2				1	3	1	18	100X2	Same as above
18	Kanoya	2			1	3	3		24	100 X 2	Maintained as a central base for land medium bombers
19	Chinhae		1			1	2		8	100 X 2	Maintained as a combat aircraft base
20	Takao	2			1	5	6		32	100 X 3	Maintained as a central base for land medium bombers
21	Saipan	1	1		1	2	2		18	250 X 2	Same as above
22	Koroku		1				2		8	100 X 3	Maintained as a staging base

Note: The information contained herein is based mostly on memory since records were scattered and lost. In some cases, the amount of communications equipment is based on the originally formulated plan; transmitters of 250-watt or less, except those recalled from memory, are not included in this table. A considerable number of medium-wave transmitters besides those listed herein were installed after the middle phase of the war. Generally, a considerable amount of communications equipment was removed while in use or moved to some other area in keeping with the progress of operations.

Chart 24-a

Major Air Base Communications Equipment Maintained from 1938 to 1940

No	Name of Base	Transmitter								Receiver	Emergency Power Source (KVA)	Remarks
		Low Frequency		Medium Frequency		High Frequency						
		1 KW	0.5KW	250W	100W	5 KW	2 KW	1 KW	0.5KW	250 W or less			
25	Shisuka	1						2	2		13	250 x 1 200 x 1	The communications equipment listed herein was installed after the transmitting-receiving station and night landing equipment.
26	Matsuwa	1						2	1		10	100 x 2	
27	Tennei	1						3	2		10	100 x 2 200 x 1	
28	Mihoro No 1	1	1			1	1	5	2		24	250 x 2 100 x 2	Maintained as a central bases for medium bombers
29	Nemuro								1		7		Maintained as an emergency landing base
30	Chitose No 1	1	2			1	1	4	5		32	250 x 2	Maintained as the Hokkaido Area Central Base Equipped with radio landing device
2	Ominato	1	1				1	1	2		18	100 x 2 40 x 1	Reinforced
31	Misawa	1	1				1	3	3		18	100 x 2	Maintained as a medium weather base
32	Matsushima	1	1			1	1	3	3		18	100 x 2	
5	Kasumigaura	3	2				2	2	7		60	350 x 1 100 x 1 60 x 1	Expanded as a training plane base

Chart 24-b

Major Air Base Communications Equipment
Maintained from 1938 to 1940 (Cont'd)

No	Name of Base	1 KW	0.5KW	250W	100W	5 KW	2 KW	1 KW	0.5KW	250 W or less	Receiver	E P S (KVA)	Remarks
33	Tsuchiura												Used jointly with the Kasumigaura Base by primary training planes
34	Mohara	1 (2KW) 1							3		18	250 x 2	Maintained as a medium bomber base
7	Kisarazu	3	2				4	3	4		60	250 x 2 100 x 2	Maintained as a central base for medium bombers
8	Tateyama	1	3				1	7	4	1	24	100 x 3	Expanded as an amphibious base
35	Hachijojima		1					1	2	2	9	60 x 2	
9	Yokohama	1	2			1	1	2	2	1	24	100 x 2 40 x 2	Reinforced as a central base for large flying boats
10	Yokosuka No 1	2	1	1	2		1	5	6		42	250 x 2 100 x 2	Reinforced as a training plane base
36	Toyohashi	1	1			1	2	3	2	1	32	300 x 1 100 x 2	Maintained as a central base for medium bombers
37	Meiji	1						2	2		8	100 x 2	Maintained as a fighter plane base
38	Mineyama		1					2			8	60 x 1	Same as above
39	Otsu							1			6	250 x 1	Maintained as a training plane base
40	Miho	1	1			1	1	3	3		18	250 x 2	Maintained as a medium bomber base (The communications equipment was later removed)
41	Iwakuni	1	1					3	4		32	100 x 2	Maintained as a training plane base
42	Tokushima	1	1				1	2	1		18	100 x 2	Maintained as a combat aircraft base

Major Air Base Communications Equipment
Maintained from 1938 to 1940 (Cont'd)

No	Name of Base	1 KW	0.5KW	250W	100W	5 KW	2 KW	1 KW	0.5 KW	250 W or less	Receiver	E P S (KVA)	Remarks
43	Komatsujima	1	1					3	2		18	100 x 2	Maintained as a combat aircraft base.
44	Kochi	2	3				1	3	5		18	100 x 1 250 x 1	
45	Sukumo		1						1		6		Maintained as an emergency landing base
46	Tsuiki	1	1					3	2		18	250 x 1 100 x 1	Maintained as a combat aircraft base
47	Usa	2						4	3		24	250 x 1 100 x 1	Maintained as a combat aircraft base as well as a training plane base
48	Oita	1	1					2	2		24	250 x 1 100 x 1	
49	Tomitaka	1						3	2		18	250 x 1 100 x 1	Maintained as a combat aircraft base
50	Hakata	2	1					4	3		24	250 x 1 100 x 1	Maintained as a training plane base
51	Izumi	1	1				1	3			18	100 x 2	Most of the communications equipment was removed after the base was established as a medium bomber base
52	Kagoshima	1						2	2		18	250 x 1 100 x 1	Maintained as a combat aircraft base
53	Kessanohara		1					1	2		18	50 x 1 15 x 1	

Chart 24-c

Chart 24-d

Major Air Base Communications Equipment Maintained from 1938 to 1940 (Cont'd)

No	Name of Base	1 KW	0.5KW	250W	100W	5 KW	2 KW	1 KW	0.5KW	250 W or less	Receiver	E P S (KVA)	Remarks
18	Kanoya	3				1	3	6	13		42	100 x 3	Reinforced as a central operational base
54	Kikai									6	8		Temporarily established as an emergency landing base
55	Koniya									3	6		
22	Koroku		1					1	1		8	100 x 2	Later underwent many changes with progress of operations
56	Minamidaito									6	4	60 x 2	Temporarily established as an emergency landing base
57	Ishigaki No 1									6	4		Same as above
58	Chichijima		1					1	2		8	100 x 2	Maintained as a small aircraft base
59	Saishu-to		2					3	2		18	100 x 2	Maintained as a staging base; the communications equipment was later removed
60	Genzan		2				1	3	3		24	250 x 1 100 x 1	Maintained as a medium bomber base
61	Taihoku	1 (1)						2	2 (1)	(2)	8 (4)		Civilian installations were reinforced to use the airport as a medium bomber base
62	Shinchiku	1	1				1	3	3		24	250 x 2	Maintained as a medium bomber base
63	Taichu		1					1	1		8	100 x 2	The communications equipment was later removed
64	Tainan		2				1	2	2		18	100 x 2	Maintained as a fighter base

Chart 24-e

Major Air Base Communications Equipment Maintained
from 1938 to 1940 (Cont'd)

No	Name of Base	1 KW	0.5KW	250W	100W	5 KW	2 KW	1 KW	0.5KW	250 W or less	Re-ceiver	E P S (KVA)	Remarks
20	Takao	2	2			1	2	5	8	6	72	250 x 1 100 x 2	Reinforced as a central operational base
65	Toko	1	1				1	9	3		18	250 x 1 100 x 1	Maintained as a large flying boat base
66	Mako												Installations of the communications unit were utilized
67	Tinian	1	1			1	1	3	2		24	250 x 1	Maintained as a medium bomber base
68	Truk	1	2			1	2	3	2		32	100 x 3	Overall amphibious installations
69	Pagan												Emergency landing field
70	Woleai									5	6		
71	Jaluit	1	1			1	1	2	2		18	250 x 2	Maintained as a medium bomber base
72	Wotje	1	1			1	1	2	2		18	250 x 2	
75	Shanghai		2				2	2	4		32	100 x 2	Total communications equipment for several Shanghai area bases are listed herein. Maintained as an operational base.

Chart 24-f

Major Air Base Communications Equipment Maintained from 1938 to 1940 (Cont'd)

No	Name of Base	1 KW	0.5KW	250W	100W	5 KW	2 KW	1 KW	0.5KW	250 W or less	Re-ceiver	E P S (KVA)	Remarks
73	Tsingtao		1						1		8		The communications equipment was originally earmarked for supply to the Chiangkou Base
76	Nanking		1					1	1		8	100 x 2	Maintained as a base
77	Kiukiang							1	1		8	100 x 2	
80	Hankow	1					1	2	2		18	150 x 2	
83	Santsaotao	1	1				1	2	2		18	150 x 2 100 x 1	
81	Amoy									1	6		
74	Chiangkou									1	8		
78	Anking		1					1	1		8	150 x 2	
79	Nanchang	1	1				1	2	2		18	100 x 2	
82			1					1	1	1	18	100 x 2	
84	Haikow		1						1	1	8		
85	Samah	1					1	2	2		18	250 x 1 100 x 1	

Chart 25-a

Major Air Base Communications Equipment Maintained from 1941 to 1943

| No | Name of Base | Transmitter ||||||||| Receiver | Emergency Power Source (KVA) | Emergency Electrical Device for Night Landing | Remarks |
| | | Low Freq || Med Freq || High Frequency |||| Others | | | | |
		1 KW	0.5 KW	250 W	100 W	2 KW	1 KW	0.5 KW	250 W	100 W					
101	Shumushu No 1	2	1		2	1	2	2				26	60 x 1	1	Maintained as an operational base
102	Shumushu No 2				1							13		1	Same as above
103	Paramushiro No 1	1			1		2	2				26		1	Same as above
104	Paramushiro No 2		1					2				10		1	Same as above
105	Minoro No 2	1		1	2		1	1				18	100 x 2	1	Same as above
106	Akeshi									2		7		1	Maintained as an emergency landing base
107	Chitose No 2	3	2			1 (5 KW .1)									
30	Chitose No 1			1	4		4	5				88	250 x 2	1	Reinforced as a central base
108	Yatabe									2		3		1	Maintained as a training plane base
109	Konoike	1					3	2		7		8	100 x 2	1	Maintained as a combat aircraft base

155

Major Air Base Communications Equipment
Maintained from 1941 to 1943 (Cont'd)

Chart 25-1

No	Name of Base	1 KW	0.5 KW	250 W	100 W	2 KW	1 KW	0.5 KW	250 W	100 W	Others	Receiver	EPS (KVA)	EDNL	Remarks
110	Katori	2	1		2	2	4	2		4		18	100x2 250x1	1	Maintained as a central base
111	Tokyo									2		2		1	Maintained as a training plane base
112	Yokosuka No 2	2	1	1	3	1	4	5		6		42	250x2 100x2	1	Maintained as a training plane base
10	Yokosuka No 1													1	Reinforced as a training plane base and as an operational base
113	Atsugi	1	1		1		2	4		5		20	250x1 100x1	1	Maintained as a combat aircraft base
114	Sagamino									1				1	Maintained as a training plane base
115	Nagoya	1			1	1	2	1				9	100x2	1	Maintained as a combat aircraft base
116	Yamato		1		1				1	1		4	250x1	1	Same as above
117	Komatsu	1		1	2	1	2	2		2	10		100x2	1	Same as above
118	Kushimoto		1				1	1		1	7		8x1	1	Same as above
119	Takuma	2	1		3	1	2	2		3	16		250x1 100x1	1	Same as above
120	Saijo	1	1	1	2	1	2	2	1	1	14			1	Maintained as a fighter base
121	Matsuyama	1	1	1	3	1	2	2		1	10		100x2	1	Maintained as a combat aircraft base

Chart 25-c

Major Air Base Communications Equipment
Maintained from 1941 to 1943 (Cont'd)

No	Name of Base	1 KW	0.5 KW	250 W	100 W	2 KW	1 KW	0.5 KW	250 W	100 W	Others	Receiver	E P S (KVA)	E D N L	Remarks
122	Miyazaki	1		1	2	2	1	1			6		100 x 2	1	Maintained as a combat aircraft base (Most of the communications equipment was later removed)
123	Isahaya									5	3		100 x 1	1	Maintained as a primary training plane base
124	Kokubu			1				1		5	6		100 x 1	1	Maintained as a training plane base and later as a combat aircraft base
125	Ibusuki				2	1	3	2		1	15			1	Maintained as a combat aircraft base
126	Tanegashima				2		2	2		1	12		250 x 1 / 100 x 2	1	Maintained as a combat aircraft base (The communications equipment was later removed)
127	Nawa		1		2	2				6	18		100 x 2	1	Reinforced as a combat aircraft base
128	Karenko															Although the plan was formulated previously for providing the bases with communications equipment, the local Naval Construction and Repair Section apparently did not install communications equipment; nothing is known definitely due to lack of records.
129	Taito															
130	Ulithi		1		1					3	6		60 x 1		Maintained as a staging base
131	Palau	1	1	1	2	2	2			5	18		150 x 2	1	Maintained as an amphibious base
132	Mortlock		1		1					3	6				Maintained as an emergency landing field
133	Ponape		1			1	2			2	8		100 x 2	1	Maintained as a combat aircraft base
134	Eniwetok		1		1	2	2			5	18		150 x 2	1	

Chart 25-d

Major Air Base Communications Equipment
Maintained from 1941 to 1943 (Cont'd)

No	Name of Base	1 KW	0.5 KW	250 W	100 W	2 KW	1 KW	0.5 KW	250 W	100 W	Others	Receiver	E P S (KVA)	E D N L	Remarks
135	Kusaie		1		1		2			3	6				Maintained as a staging base
136	Rongelap		1		1	2	2			5	18		150 x 2	1	Maintained as a combat aircraft base
137	Maloelap		1		1	2	2			5	18		150 x 2	1	Same as above
138	Majuro		1		1	2	2			5	18		150 x 2	1	Same as above
139	Mili	1			1	1	2	2		5		18	100 x 2 250 x 2	1	Same as above
140	Makin	1			1		1			3		18	150 x 2	1	Same as above
141	Tarawa	1			1		1	1		3		8	100 x 1	1	Same as above
142	Toulon														
143	Nhatrang														
144	Camranh														
145	Thu Dau Mot														Communication equipment for five permanent bases was dispersed and maintained by the local commanders.
146	Saigon														
147	St. Jacques														
148	Soctrang														

Communication equipment for five permanent bases was dispersed and maintained by the local commanders.
Details are unknown.

Chart 25-e

Major Air Base Communications Equipment
Maintained from 1941 to 1943 (Cont'd)

No	Name of Base	1 KW	0.5 KW	250 W	100 W	2 KW	1 KW	0.5 KW	250 W	100 W	Others	Receiver	E P S (KVA)	E D N L	Remarks
149	Port Blair		1					1	3	3		6			Details unknown
150	Car Nicobar		1				1		3	3		6			
151	Sabang														
152	Koetaradja														
153	Penang														
154	Seletar														
155	Bataan														Communication equipment for 15 permanent bases and 10 mobile bases was dispersed and maintained by the local commanders.
156	Jakarta														
157	Jogjakarta														
158	Madang														
159	Soerabaja														
160	Labuan														
161	Bandjermasin														

Chart 25-f

Major Air Base Communications Equipment
Maintained from 1941 to 1943 (Cont'd)

No	Name of Base	1 KW	0.5 KW	250 W	100 W	2 KW	1 KW	0.5 KW	250 W	100 W	Others	Receiver	E P S (KVA)	E D N L	Remarks
162	Palikpapan														
163	Makassar														
164	Kendari														
165	Menado														
166	Ternate														
167	Kace						Communication equipment for 15 permanent bases and 10 mobile bases was dispersed and maintained by the local commanders.								
168	Amboina														
169	Waingapoe														
170	Koepang														
171	Delhi														
172	Soron														
173	Manokwari														
174	Kavieng														
175	Rabaul														

Major Air Base Communications Equipment
Maintained from 1941 to 1943 (Cont'd)

Chart 25-g

No	Name of Base	1 KW	0.5 KW	250 100 W	2 KW	1 KW	0.5 KW	250 W	100 W	Others	Receiver	E P S (KVA)	E D N L	Remarks
176	Buka													Communication equipment for 15 permanent bases and 10 mobile bases was dispersed and maintained by the local commanders.
177	Buin													
178	Wake													
179	Heitaku		1	2	1	2	2				8	100 x 2	1	Maintained as an operational base
180	Reisui		1	2	1	1	1				8	100 x 2	1	
181	Pusan		1	2	1	1	2				12	100 x 2	1	

Chart 26-a

Major Air Base Communications Equipment Maintained in Japan at Termination of War

Name of Base	Transmitter									Receiver	Remarks: (The figure in parenthesis indicates the quantity of equipment which was not completed)
	Low Frequency		Medium Frequency		High Frequency						
	1 KW	0.5 KW	250 W	100 W	2 KW	1 KW	0.5 KW	250 W	150 W		
Shisuka (Shikuka)	1			1 (1)		2	2 (1)			13	Hardly used
Odomari	1		1			2	2 (1)	1	2	7	The communications equipment was shipped but apparently was not installed
Shumushu No 1	2	1		2 (2)	1	2	2 (2)			26	Bombproof construction was completed
Shumushu No 2				(1) 1						17	The transmitting station was to be used jointly with Shumushu Base No 1
Paramushiro No 1	1			1 (1)		2	2 (1)			26	The communications equipment in the Chishima area was removed and shipped to Hokkaido
Paramushiro No 2		1					2 (2)			10	
Matsuwa	1					2	1 (1)			10	
Tennei	1					3	2 (2)			10	
Mihoro No 1	1	1		2 (2)	1 (5KW) 1	5	2 (1)			18	The ground bombproof construction was converted into the underground type
Mihoro No 2	1		1	2 (2)		1	1 (1)		2 (1)	10	Bombproof construction completed

Major Air Base Communications Equipment Maintained in Japan at Termination of War (cont'd)

Chart 26-b

Name of Base	1 KW	0.5 KW	250 W	100 W	2 KW	1 KW	0.5 KW	250 W	150 W	Receiver	Remarks
Mihoro No 3	1		1				2	1	1 (1)	7	Bombproof construction completed
Shibetsu No 1	1	1	1			1	2	2	2	14	Same as above
Shibetsu No 2	1	1	1			1	2	2		14	Same as above
Nemuro							1		1	7	The same construction as the Mihoro Base No 2 was planned, but actually a smaller base was constructed
Chitose No 1											Converted to underground bombproof construction with headquarters installations
Chitose No 2	3	2		4 (4)	1(5 KW) 1	4	5		9 (4)	88	
Chitose No 3											
Kabayama	1					1	2	2		10	Construction work discontinued
Ominato	1		1	2 (1)			2 (2)		1 (1)	14	Maintained also as an agency for the communications units
Masawazawa	1	1			2	3	2 (1)			22	
Matsushima		1			1 (5 KW) 2	3	2 (1)		1	10	Conversion to bombproof construction completed

Major Air Base Communications Equipment Maintained in Japan at Termination of War (cont'd)

Name of Base	1 KW	0.5 KW	250 W	100 W	2 KW	1 KW	0.5 KW	250 W	150 W	Receiver	Remarks
Koriyama				1 (1)					4 (4)	11	Conversion to bombproof construction completed
Koriyama No 3	1		1				2	2		13	The planned construction of a "RENZAN"-type bomber base was under way
Tsukuba		1		1 (1)		1	1		7 (4)	8	Bombproof construction was completed
Hyakurigahara		2		1 (1)		2	2		6 (3)	16	Same as above
Kasumigaura	3	2	2	3 (3)		2	7		8 (4)	38	Bombproof construction with headquarters installations completed
Yatabe				1 (1)			2 (2)		2 (2)	12	Bombproof construction completed
Kashima	1	2				2	2		4	10	Same as above
Konoike	1					3	2		7 (3)	8	Same as above
Katori	2	1		2 (2)	2	4	2 (1)		4	14	Same as above
Mohara	1(2KW) 1			2 (2)	2	3	2 (2)			13	Same as above
Kisarazu	3	1			4	7 (2)	2 (2)		6 (3)	41	Bombproof construction with headquarters installations completed; the receiving station moved again

Chart 26-d

Major Air Base Communications Equipment Maintained in Japan at Termination of War (cont'd)

Name of Base	1 KW	0.5 KW	250 W	100 W	2 KW	1 KW	0.5 KW	250 W	150 W	Receiver	Remarks
Tateyama	1	3	2		1	4	2 (2)	1		20	
Hachijo	1	1	1			1	2 (2)	2	6	21	Provided with communication equipment which was not included in the plan; bombproof construction completed
Tokyo									2	2	
Yokohama	1	1	1		1	2				9	Hardly used. Part of the communications equipment transferred to the Igaueno base
Yokosuka No 1	2	1	1	3 (3)	1	4 (1)	5 (1)		6	25	Bombproof construction completed
Yokosuka No 2	1			1 (2)			1		2	5	Construction work under way
Atsugi	1	1		1		2	4 (2)		5 (5)	20	Bombproof construction completed
Fujisawa								1	3 (1)	8	Same as above
Fujieda	1					2	3 (1)			12	Same as above
Oi	2	1	1	2		3	4		2	12	The communications equipment for training was removed and transferred to the Yamato Base and others
Toyohashi	1	1		2 (2)	1(5KW) 2	3	2	1	1 (1)	13	Bombproof construction completed

Major Air Base Communications Equipment Maintained in Japan at Termination of War (cont'd)

Name of Base	1 KW	0.5 KW	250 W	100 W	2 KW	1 KW	0.5 KW	250 W	150 W	Re-ceiver	Remarks
Okazaki						1			1	4	Bombproof construction completed
Meiji	1		1 (1)	3 (3)		2 (2)	2 (2)			13	Bombproof construction completed; headquarters installations were being established
Nagoya	1			1 (1)		2	1 (1)			9	Bombproof construction completed
Kowa		1		1 (1)				1	1	4	Same as above
Suzuka No 1	1	3		1 (1)		4	5 (1)			9	Bombproof construction completed; the training equipment was rearranged to be used at other locations
Suzuka No 2	2		1			4 (1)			3 (1)	12	Bombproof construction was completed
Igaueno	1		1			2	2		3 (2)	16	Construction work under way; headquarters installations under construction
Jimmachi				2 (2)		1	1		3 (1)	8	A request was received for the construction of headquarters installations, but no decision had been made
Komatsu	1		1	2 (2)	1	2	2 (2)		2 (1)	10	Bombproof construction completed
Otsu							1		1 (1)	5	Same as above
Yamato	2					6 (4)	8		2	30	Headquarters installations were prepared and completed

Chart 26-e

Chart 26-f

Major Air Base Communications Equipment Maintained in Japan at Termination of War (cont'd)

Name of Base	1 KW	0.5 KW	250 W	100 W	2 KW	1 KW	0.5 KW	250 W	150 W	Receiver	Remarks
Maizuru	2	1				1	3			16	Bombproof construction completed
Mineyama		1					1 (1)			6	Same as above
Fukuchiyama				1 (1)			1	2	6 (5)	11	Construction work under way
Miho	1		1	1 (1)	1(5KW) 1	2	2			18	Same as above
Kushimoto		1				1	1		1	7	Bombproof construction completed
Naruo	1		1	2 (2)		4			4 (3)	12	Bombproof construction completed; conducted part of the antiaircraft defense communications of the Osaka Security Unit
Itami										5	Bombproof construction completed
Himeji		1	1	2 (2)		2 (1)	1		4 (3)	13	Same as above
Kurashiki									4 (3)	6	Same as above
Fukuyama	1		1				1		4	9	Same as above
Kure	1	1	1	2 (2)		3	2 (1)		2 (2)	24	Bombproof construction completed; planned as the reserve for the Kure Communications Unit

Major Air Base Communications Equipment Maintained in Japan at Termination of War (Cont'd)

Chart 26-g

Name of Base	1 KW	0.5 KW	250 W	100 W	2 KW	1 KW	0.5 KW	250 W	150 W	Receiver	Remarks
Iwakuni	1	1	1	3 (3)		3	4		1 (1)	29	Bombproof construction completed
Tokushima	1	1			1	2	1		3 (2)	15	Bombproof construction completed; training installations partially moved elsewhere
Tokushima No 2									3	4	Construction work under way
Komatsujima	1	1	1	2 (2)		3	2			10	Being converted to bombproof construction
Takuma	2	1		3 (3)	1	2	2		3 (1)	16	Completed
Kannonji	1		1	2 (2)	1	2	2		1 (1)	14	Completed
Saijo	1		1	2 (2)		2	1 (1)			8	
Matsuyama	1	1	1	3 (3)	1	2	2 (2)			20	
Taisha	1						1 (1)		3 (3)	9	A request was received for the construction of headquarters installations, but the construction was not effected
Nanao									2 (1)	2	
Kochi	2	3	1	2 (2)	1	3	5 (2)			15	Completed

Major Air Base Communications Equipment Maintained in Japan at Termination of War (cont'd)

Name of Base	1 KW	0.5 KW	250 W	100 W	2 KW	1 KW	0.5 KW	250 W	150 W	Receiver	Remarks
Sukumo		1					1			3	
Tsuiki	1	1	1	3 (3)		3	2 (2)		2 (2)	12	Bombproof construction completed
Usa	2		1	3 (3)		4	3 (1)		2 (2)	20	Same as above
Oita	1	1	1	1 (1)		2	2		11 (4)	40	Bombproof construction completed; headquarters installations established
Saeki	1	1	1	3 (3)	1	3	2 (2)			16	Bombproof construction completed
Tomitaka	1		1	2 (2)		3	2 (1)		1 (1)	10	Same as above
Miyazaki	1	1							1 (1)	6	Same as above
Hakata	2	1	1	1 (1)		4	3 (1)		9	22	Bombproof construction completed; headquarters installations established
Fukuoka									2	11	Bombproof construction completed
Sasebo	1		1	2 (2)	1	3	2 (1)		3	14	Bombproof construction completed; can be used as auxiliary to the Sasebo Communications Unit
Omura	2					1	6		4	10	Bombproof construction completed

Major Air Base Communications Equipment Maintained in Japan at Termination of War (cont'd)

Chart 26-1

Name of Base	1 KW	0.5 KW	250 W	100 W	2 KW	1 KW	0.5 KW	250 W	150 W	Re-ceiver	Remarks
Isahaya									5	3	Bombproof construction completed
Tomie							1 (1)	1	2	10	Same as above
Amakusa							1		2	9	Same as above
Izumi	1		1	1 (1)			1		3 (3)	6	Same as above
Kokubu			1				1		1 (1)		Same as above
Kokubu No 2			1	1 (1)			2 (1)		6 (2)	7	Same as above
Kagoshima	1		1	3 (3)		2	2 (1)		1 (1)	14	Same as above
Iwakawa			1	1 (1)			2 (1)		2 (1)	7	Same as above
Shibushi			1	1 (1)		2	2 (2)		1	12	Same as above
Kushira	1			2 (2)		1	1 (1)			101	Same as above
Kasanohara				1			1 (1)		2 (1)	7	Same as above

170

Major Air Base Communications Equipment Maintained in Japan at Termination of War (cont'd)

Name of Base	1 KW	0.5 KW	250 W	100 W	2 KW	1 KW	0.5 KW	250 W	150 W	Receiver	Remarks
Kanoya	3		4	2 (2)	1(5KW) 3	6	13 (4)		5	36	Bombproof construction completed; headquarters installations established
Ibusuki	1			2	1	3	2 (1)		1 (1)	15	Bombproof construction completed
Tanegashima	1			2		2	2 (1)		1 (1)	12	Same as above
Kikaigashima									6 (3)	7	Same as above
Koniya									3 (1)	5	Same as above
Minamidaito-jima									6 (5)	10	Same as above
Miyakojima									6 (5)	10	Same as above
Ishigakijima									6 (4)	8	Same as above
Ishigakijima No 2									3 (1)	6	Same as above
Koroku	1	1				2	3		3 (2)	15	Same as above
Okinawakita	1	1	1			2	4		4 (4)	20	Bombproof construction completed; headquarters installations established

171

China Incident, was more or less stabilized before the outbreak of the Pacific War. There was no noticeable improvement in aircraft equipment after the outbreak of war, but instead there was a definite trend in which the quality as well as quantity dropped as the supply of materials became scarce. Moreover, the skill of flight radiomen dropped in proportion to the increase in casualties and consequently, the air communications system had to be simplified according to the capabilities of the available personnel.

Intensive training in telegraphic communications with fighter planes had been carried out prior to the outbreak of war. The use of the radiotelephone in communications with fighters was the most advantageous and suitable method. However, since it was necessary for the fighters to coordinate with the attack unit and for security reasons, there was no alternative but to utilize telegraphic communications to cover the 200-mile range. This placed a considerable burden upon the flight personnel of fighter planes in operations, but they successfully overcame these difficulties and showed satisfactory skill in operational actions, at least during the early phase of the war.

Frequency System

Frequencies used by the forces committed to an operation were classified into three types, that is, A, B and C, according to the usages (Chart 27) (See Charts 28 and 29 for Frequency Assignment Standard and Organization of Communications Net respectively).

Chart 27

Frequency Classification

Classification	Usages
Type-A air communications frequency	This will be used for communications of important operational matters and matters concerning the entire fleet.
Type-B air communications frequency	1. Operational communications concerning the flotilla (or unit corresponding to the above in strength). 2. Communications in case each flotilla attacks a different target.
Type-C air communications frequency	1. Communications between air flotillas and the base or aircraft carriers. 2. Communications for securing homing flight.

Chart 28

Frequency Assignment Standard

Unit	Type A High Frequency	Type B High Frequency	Type C High Frequency	Type A Low Frequency	Type B Low Frequency	Type C Low Frequency	Very-high Frequency
Search Force Attack Unit	Regular 1 Auxiliary 2	Regular 1 Auxiliary 1	Regular 1 Auxiliary 1	Regular 1 Auxiliary 1	Regular 1	Regular 1	Regular 1
Patrol Force	Regular 1 or Auxiliary 1	Regular 1	Regular 1 Auxiliary 1	Regular 1	Regular 1	Regular 1	
Air Control Unit	Regular 1	Regular 1					
Antisubmarine Direct Escort Unit			Regular 1				
Combat Air Patrol			Regular 1				
Interception Patrol Force			Regular 1				
Notes	1. The Type C low frequency will be used in homing direction finding. 2. The Type A high frequency for fighter plane (attack unit) use may also be used by the plane of the attack unit commander.						

Organization of Communications Net

Chart 29-a

Classification	Communicating Ship, Station or Aircraft	Frequency	Radio Control Ship or Aircraft	Communications Procedure
General Aviation Communications	Plane unit (attack, search, reconnaissance, patrol and tracking) and aircraft carrier	(High) or (Medium), or (Low) depending on the situation	Aircraft carrier	Free and direct exchange of communications or controlled communications as occasions demand.
Communications between Flying Squadrons and Others	Between plane unit and ship, aircraft carrier, radio station and aircraft of other units	(High) or (Medium)	Aircraft carrier	Aircraft carrier will be the relay ship and no direct exchange of communications will be made.
Communications within Attack Unit	Between planes	(Very-high)	Unit communications plane	Free and direct exchange of communications
Air Control Unit Communications	Between fighter planes; guide plane, unit commander's plane	(High) (Telephone)	Unit communications plane	Free and direct exchange of communications; communications between aircraft carrier and fighter planes will be relayed, as a rule, by guide plane.

175

Organization of Communications Net (cont'd)

Chart 29-b

Classification	Communicating Ship, Station or Aircraft	Frequency	Radio Control Ship or Aircraft	Communications Procedure
Combat Air Patrol Communications	Between fighter plane and ship escorted by fighter plane	(High)(Telephone)	Ship escorted by fighter plane	Free and direct exchange of communications
Antisubmarine Direct Escort Communications	Between antisubmarine escort plane and ship escorted by antisubmarine escort plane	(High)(Telephone) (Very-high wave) (Telephone)	Ship escorted by antisubmarine escort plane	Same as above
Communications between Plane and Submarine	Between plane and submarine	(High) or (Medium)		Communications by time (as per agreement)
Radio Direction Finding Communications (Low frequency Radio Direction Finding)	Between plane and aircraft carrier	Exchange of communications (High) Radio direction finding (Low)	Aircraft carrier	Controlled communications
Radio Direction Finding Communications (High Frequency Radio Direction Finding)	Between plane and aircraft carrier	Both exchange of communications and radio direction finding (High), (Medium) or (Low)	Aircraft carrier	Same as above
Radio Homing (Aircraft Radio Direction Finding)	Between plane and aircraft carrier		Aircraft carrier	One-way communications

176

Radio Equipment

1. The standard radio equipment for various types of aircraft is shown in Chart 30, and spare equipment equivalent to 30 per cent of each item was supplied to each air squadron.

2. Changes in radio equipment

   a. First Phase Operations

      The types of aircraft radio equipment in late 1941 were as shown in Chart 31. Every item of equipment was produced in rapid succession and every type of aircraft was, in general, properly equipped. The breakdown of equipment was quite rare and flight radiomen were skillful enough to repair and maintain the equipment. Consequently, in the battles of various areas in the early phase of the war, there were rarely any occurrences of poor liaison or difficulty of communications due to breakdowns of equipment to hinder combat efficiency. Moreover, one radio maintenance man was assigned to each air squadron and he successfully discharged duties in cooperation with the flight radiomen. Meanwhile, the Central Agency decided to carry out manufacture of experimental new equipment (Chart 32) to improve quality and to effect standardization and mass production of equipment in order to meet the growing demands of the expanded operational zone and improved aircraft performance.

   b. Second Phase operations

      The First Phase operations had progressed very satisfactorily and the operations zone was greatly expanded. In parti-

Chart 30

Standard Radio Equipment for Various Types of Aircraft
(Excluding Radar)

Type of Aircraft	For Communications with Units Outside the Air Force	For Communication within the Air Force	Radio Direction Finder
Large-size planes	N3-type (R3) 2 sets	U4-type 1 set	1
Medium-size planes	N3-type (R3) (2) 1 set	U4-type 1 set	1
Two or three-seater planes	N3-type (R3, N2) 1 set	U3-type 1 set	1
Single-seater fighter	N1-type 1 set		1
Remarks	Guide plane of fighter plane unit had an additional N1-type set.		

Communications Equipment in Actual Use at Start of War

Equipment	Type of Aircraft Carrying Communication Equipment	Frequency in Kilocycles	Power in Watts	Weight in Kg	Radio Range Plane to Ground (Miles)	Remarks
Type-96 Aircraft Radiotelephone Set No 1, Improved Model No 1	Single seater	4,200-5,500	15	18	50	This is an improved model of Aircraft Radiotelephone Set No 1, using the aircraft generator instead of dry cell battery.
Type-96 Aircraft Radio Set No 2	Two-seater	High... 5,000-10,000 Low... 300 - 500	100	45	600	Possible to change three transmission frequencies in a single motion; devised mainly for observation communications use; for radio-telegraph and radiotelephone communications use:
Type-96 Aircraft Radio Set No 3	Three-seater Multiseater	High... 5,000-10,000 Low... 300 - 500	150	52	700	
Type-96 Aircraft Radio Set No 4	Multiseater	High... 5,000-10,000 Low... 300 - 500 (Receiving)	300	76	1,200	Low frequencies are used only in receiving; transmitter is remote-control type.
Type-1 Aircraft Radiotelephone No 3 for communications within the unit	Two or three-seater	30 - 50 Megacycles	10	18	Plane-to-plane, 5 miles	Both transmitter and receiver are crystal controlled; capable of transmitting musical sound.

Chart 31-a

Communications Equipment in Actual Use at Start of War (cont'd)

Equipment	Type of Aircraft Carrying Communication Equipment	Frequency in Kilocycles	Power in Watts	Weight in Kg	Radio Range Plane to Plane to Ground (Miles)	Remarks
Type-98 Aircraft Radiotelephone No 4 for communications within the unit	Multiseater	30 – 50 Megacycles	40	35	Plane-to-plane, 20 Miles	Same as above.
Type-1 Aircraft Radio Direction Finder and Homing Device No 3	Light Aircraft	170–1,200		28	60	Modelled after the American radio direction finder.
Type-0 Aircraft Radio Direction Finder and Homing Device No 4	Large-type and medium-type aircraft	165–1,000		58	200	Improved model of the German TELEFUNKEN radio direction finder.
Notes	1. Both crystal-controlled and automatic transmissions can be conducted (except radiotelephone communications within the unit). 2. Only automatic reception is conducted (same as above). 3. 75-meter trailing antenna is used in all low frequency transmissions.					

Chart 31-b

Experimental Communications Equipment at Start of War

Equipment	User	Frequency in Kilocycle	Power in Watt	Weight in Kg	Remarks
Type 3 Aircraft Radiotelephone Set No 1	Fighter Plane	5,000-10,000	100	30	Improved model of the Type 96 Aircraft Radiotelephone Set No 1
Type 1 Aircraft Radio Set No 3	Three-Seater Aircraft	High 5,000-20,000 Low 300 - 500	300	70	Superior aircraft radio set with characteristics of both the Type 96 Aircraft Radio Sets No 2 and No 3.
Type 3 Aircraft Radio set No 5	Air Base	2,500-20,000	300x3	150	Mobile radio set for exclusive use of air bases.
Type 96 Aircraft Radio Set No 2, Improved Model No 1	Two-Seater Aircraft	High 5,000-10,000 Low 300 - 500	100	45	Standard vacuum tubes used.
Type 96 Aircraft Radio Set No 4, Improved Model No 1	Multi-Seater Aircraft	5,000-15,000	300	76	Frequency bands magnified.
Type 1 Aircraft Radiotelephone No 3, for communications within the unit. Improved Model	Two or Three-Seater Aircraft	30 - 50 Megacycle	15	13.5	Standard vacuum tubes used.
Notes	Types of vacuum tubes were decreased as much as possible and the vacuum tubes made interchangeable. Namely: Transmitting Tubes: Master Oscillator Tube, FZ-064A, Amplifier Tube, & FE-325A. Receiving Tube: FM-2A05A				

Chart 32

cular, when the Solomons area became the main theater of operations, radio frequency unexpectedly became an important problem as data was lacking on the frequency range in this area. In night communications, high frequency was ineffective and this greatly hindered operations. Although it was known that high frequency is less effective at night than daytime, this was not considered a matter of great importance in Japan. However, for air operations in the southern areas in which night flying was frequently conducted, the frequencies of 5,000-10,000 kilocycles ordinarily used in the past turned out to be extremely ineffective. In many cases, a search plane's report on the sighting of the enemy failed to reach its destination and frequently hindered the execution of operations. Therefore, research and experiments were started immediately on the utilization of the medium frequency band.

Towards the end of 1942, the medium frequency band (2,500-5,000 KC) was first added to the Type-96 No 3 aircraft radio set and sent to the forces in operations (excluding fighter planes). As a temporary measure, part of the trailing antenna for low frequency was used for this modified set. As the adjustment of this medium frequency attachment was more complicated than that of the high frequency and as its handling was not thoroughly understood, the peak performance in medium frequency was not realized.

With the Guadalcanal campaign as a turning point, the Japanese realized that war production was too slow to meet the counteroffensives of the enemy. Therefore, standardization of the materials and products and simplification of design was [were] attempted in order to facilitate mass production.

Principal improvements realized from the manufacture of experimental equipment were as follows:

1. Experimental manufacture of the Type-43 experimental equipment (equipment experimentally manufactured in the fiscal year 1943) for various types of aircraft.

2. Elimination of covers to various radio sets for protection from dust and water.

3. Decrease in number of relays in various radio sets.

4. Restricting the use of neon tubes by using Argon tubes.

5. Use of iron and wood as substitutes for aluminium and copper.

The above were tested and successively put into practice after 1943 (Chart 33).

c. The beginning of the Third Phase operations (February 1943 - October 1944).

As a result of the widespread war covering the entire Pacific Ocean, the greater part of the highly-trained, skilled flight personnel was lost and they were replaced by those who had undergone mass-training in a shortened period. Therefore, interior communications technique as well as poor handling and maintenance of equipment became apparent. Furthermore, carelessly manufactured equipment was supplied to the front line forces without being tested. Consequently,

Chart 33

Summary of the 1943 — Experimental Equipment
(Excluding Radar)

Equipment	Use	Frequency in Kilocycles	Power in Watts	Weight Kg	Range Nautical miles	Remarks
Type-43, No 1, Aircraft Radiotelephone Set	Fighter planes	5,000-10,000	100	30	500	Construction and operation simplified; tone quality improved.
No 3, Experimental Aircraft Radio Set, modified 1943	Various types of aircraft except fighter planes	2,500-10,000 300 - 500	300	45	1,500	Remote control and common use for various types of aircraft possible. Manufacturing process of Type-2, No 3 Aircraft Radio Set simplified.
No 5, Experimental Aircraft Radio Set, modified 1943	Bases	100-20,000 (All wave)	300	?	1,500	Six tuning units used in plug-in method; plywood used.
Experimental Radio Homing Direction Finder, modified 1943.	Various types of aircraft	300 - 500	—	35	200	Two kinds of loop antenna used for large and small planes.
No 8, Experimental Aircraft Radio Set, modified 1943	Parachute forces	2,500-10,000	60	20	300	
Experimental Interphone, modified 1943.	Three-seater planes	—	—	7.5	—	When completed, to be installed in other types of aircraft.

184

every unit was plagued with frequent breakdowns of equipment and complaints were received from a number of units that the failure of messages reaching the destination and improper functioning of communications equipment hindered the execution of operations. The practical and experimental equipment manufactured in this period is shown in Chart 34.

    d. The latter period of the Third Phase operations (November 1944 - August 1945).

        In order to meet the rapidly mounting enemy counter-offensives, the role of operational communications became increasingly important. The most urgent problems were the need for strict supervision over the increasing output of carelessly manufactured equipment and the need for immediate use of experimental equipment. By March 1945, such equipment had undergone some improvement and was ready for practical use (Chart 35).

When enemy air attacks by B-29's increased in intensity, the plants manufacturing vacuum tubes and other various parts of equipment were successively destroyed. In addition, due to the drop in productive capacity resulting from the dispersal of plants, the manufacture of equipment was insufficient to meet the requirements of front line forces. Later, in anticipation of the Homeland operation in which all-out suicide attacks were to be carried out, the need for simplified communications equipment for special attack planes was envisaged and efforts were directed to the experimental

Radio Communications Equipment in Actual Use
(Jan 43 – Oct 44)

Equipment	Equipped on	Frequency in Kilocycles	Power in Watts	Weight in Kg	Transmitting Range Miles	Remarks
Type-3 Aircraft Radio-telephone Set No 1, Improved Model No 1	Fighter planes	5,000-10,000	100	20	To plane, 100 To ground, 300	Standardized Type-18 Experimental Aircraft Radiotelephone Set No 1.
Type-96 Aircraft Radio Set No 2, Improved Model No 2.	Two-seater planes	2,500-10,000 300 - 500	100	46	600	Further developed Improved Model No 1 with additional medium frequency band, however receiver went out of order frequently.
Type-96 Aircraft Radio Set No 3, Improved Model No 1.	Three-seater planes	2,500-10,000 300 - 500	150	52	700	Improved with additional medium frequency band.
Type-2 Aircraft Radio Set No 3, Improved Model No 1	Three-seater & Multi-seater planes	2,500-20,000 300 - 500	300	74	1,500	Weight and capacity increased with additional medium frequency band.
Type-1 Aircraft Radiotelephone No 3 for communications within the unit.	Two or three-seater planes	30 - 50 Megacycle	15	18.5	To plane, 10	Went out of order frequently due to faulty wiring in plane.
Type-98 Aircraft Radiotelephone No 4 for communications within the unit	Multi-seater planes	30 - 50 Megacycle	40	35	To plane, 10	Many defective vacuum tubes.
Homing Device	Same as that in initial phase of war.					Hardly used by the units towards latter phase of the war.

Chart 34-b

Improved Models of Radio Communications Equipment in Actual Use

Equipment	Equipped on	Frequency Kilocycles	Power Watts	Weight Kg	Transmitting Range Miles	Remarks
Type-3 Aircraft Radio-telephone Set No 1, Improved Model No 2	Fighter planes	5,000-10,000	100	30	To plane, 100 To ground, 300	Equipped with auxiliary controller for send-receive switching.
Type-3 Aircraft Radio-telephone Set No 1, Improved Model No 3	Fighter planes	5,000-10,000	100	32	To plane, 100 To ground, 300	All receiving-tubes changed with "SORA"-type.
Type-19 Experimental Aircraft Radio Set No 3	Two or three-seater planes	2,500-10,000 300 - 500	300	50	1,500	Improved experimental model of the Type-18 Experimental Aircraft Radio Set No 3; rebuilt because of numerous defects.
Type-19 Experimental Aircraft Radio Set No 4	Multi-seater aircraft	2,500-10,000 300 - 500	300	55	1,500	Remote control transmitter, improved model of the transmitter of the Type-19 Experimental Aircraft Radio Set No 3.
Type-19 Experimental Aircraft Radio Set No 9	Life raft	4,528	About 6	About 5	100	Hand-operated transmitter designed for telegraphing emergency landing; no receiver.
Type-19 Experimental Aircraft Radio Transmitter No 10	Transmitter parachuted over enemy fleet	950	About 60	About 60	?	Special radio wave radiation transmitter parachuted to determine the radio direction of enemy fleet.
Type-18 Experimental Aircraft Radiotelephone for communications within the unit	Three-seater aircraft			7.5		Provided with "SORA"-type vacuum tubes replacing those of the Type-18 Experimental Radiotelephone for communications within the unit.

Chart 35

Experimental Radio Equipment

Equipment	Equipped on	Frequency in Kilocycles	Power in Watts	Weight in Kg	Range plane to ground	Remarks
Type 96, No 4 Aircraft Radio Set, Improved Model No 3	Multi-seater planes	2,500-10,000 300- 500	300	80	High freq 1,500 Low freq 300	Modification with low frequency bands attached to the improved models, No 1 and No 2
Experimental Aircraft Radio Set, No 1 Modified 1944.	Fighter planes	4,000- 8,000	100	30	Telephone 350	Modification of frequency bands; Modification of Type 3, Aircraft Radio Set No 1 for mass production.
Receiver for Shusui-type planes	Shusui-type planes	5,000-10,000		9	100	Receiver removed from Type 3, Aircraft Radio Set No 1
Radio Set for suicide planes	Special attack planes	4,000- 8,000		More than 20	100	Short-range communications stressed.
Experimental radio-telephone for intra-unit communication, modified 1945.	Two-seater planes; three-seater planes	30,000-50,000	15	22	40	Acron tubes used; strength and clarity greatly improved.

Note: Of those listed above, only the Type 96, No 4 Aircraft Radio Set was in practical use.

manufacture of small-type radio sets for these planes.

The improvement and experimental manufacture of principal equipment was carried out during the period just prior to the end of war. On the other hand, manufacture of much of the other equipment had to be suspended due to lack of vital parts:

1. Suspension of manufacture of Type-96, No 2, aircraft radio set, improved model No 2.

2. Suspension of manufacture of Type-96, No 3, aircraft radio set, improved model No 1.

3. Suspension of manufacture of Type-2, No 3, aircraft radio set, improved model No 1.

4. Improvement of Type-96, No 4, aircraft radio set, improved models No 1 and No 2 (adding low and high frequency bands to the equipment turned in for replacement).

5. Suspension of experimental manufacture and test of the No 10, experimental aircraft radio transmitter, modified 1944 (because its practical value was questionable).

6. Experimental manufacture of No 1 experimental aircraft radiotelephone, modified 1944 (improvement and modification of Type-3, No 1, aircraft radiotelephone for mass production).

7. Acceleration of mass production of No 3 experimental aircraft radio set, modified 1944.

8. Experimental manufacture of radio set for special attack planes (small-size sets less than 20 kg in weight).

9. Experimental manufacture and test of the receivers exclusively for the Shusui (interceptor plane).

10. Experimental manufacture and test of experimental radiotelephone for inter-unit communications, modified 1945 (measures taken to increase the power of inter-unit telephone communications).

11. Acceleration of experiments on experimental aircraft radio homing direction finder, modified 1944.

Communications Procedure

Since the establishment of the Naval Radio Communications Regulations in 1937, all the naval communications were carried out in accordance with these regulations. At that time, these regulations were considered satisfactory in carrying out the general communications and were disseminated to all units to effect uninterrupted communications. The contents of these regulations were divided into two classes—general communications and special communications procedures.

The general communications procedure entailed communications between two or more ships or stations under ordinary conditions. Such communications were considered complete after receiving acknowledgment from the ship or station at the other end.

The special communications procedure entailed the following: (1) Unilateral broadcasting in that acknowledgment was not required from the radio receiving ship or station; (2) indirect communications by intercepting telegraph messages from a third party instead of directly from the receiving ship or station; (3) collation of messages received; (4) ship or station controlled communications instead of permitting free and direct communications; (5) transmission on a certain frequency or that designated by the radio ship or station can be either curtailed or changed; (6) transmission of emergency signal in case of distress; (7) time synchronization; (8) and a means to calibrate to standard frequency.

These communications regulations were also applied to aircraft communications. However, as they were originally established for use by ships and local radio stations, they caused some barriers when strictly applied to aircraft communications and steps were taken to permit a more flexible application of the regulations.

Aircraft communications were different from other general ship or land communications on various points, particularly in regards to the following factors:

1. There were many instances requiring emergency communications.

2. Large number of aircraft used one common frequency. This was in contrast to ship-to-ship or ship-to-station communications.

3. Radio equipment used in aircraft was not as reliable as that used for ground communications.

4. Compared with general communications, there were more tactical communications which required simple procedures.

5. The range of communications changed suddenly and greatly in

a short period.

6. There were rarely any relay communications to be conducted.

7. Where there were no skilled radio operators, communications had to be conducted to verify if equipment was functioning. This had to be done even at crucial periods when strict radio silence was mandatory.

8. Codes used in headings were required to be brief as possible or omitted.

When special communications procedures were initially formulated as required for aircraft communications, they were not standardized by the Central Agency and their implementation was left up to each unit as it saw fit. Some of the disadvantages which became apparent were:

1. Special communications procedures could not be applied to the communications other than that of the unit concerned.

2. Whenever a unit operated in concert with other units, prearrangement was necessary.

3. When the communications of other units were intercepted, the headings of the monitored messages could not be identified in many cases.

4. It was necessary for aircraft radiomen and ground radiomen to learn quickly the special communications procedures of the new unit whenever they were transferred.

From about the end of 1943, heavy demands were placed on the Central Agency to establish a standard communications regulations suited to the actual circumstances required in aircraft communications. Consequently the establishment of the new communications regulations for aircraft became the responsibility of the Communications Counter-Planning Committee which was comprised of authorities from the 9th Section of the Naval General Staff, the Naval Communications School and the Yokosuka Naval Air Group.

The new communications procedures were centered on the broadcast communications system. There were actually five classifications of communications procedures and one of these was for aircraft communications. The principal changes effected in the new communications regulations for aircraft communications were completed in January 1945 and were as follows:

1. The aircraft communications were simplified by distributing an extract of the communications regulations to aircraft communications personnel. By this means, they were fully able to conduct communications in spite of their unfamiliarity with other complicated ground communications procedures.

2. A standard reply signal was designated for plane units.

3. Call signals for communications control stations were made uniform.

4. The merits of the special communications procedures of various units were adopted. Communications dispatch forms were standardized to facilitate usage.

Communications Plan for Homeland Air Defense Operation

The air defense of the Homeland was undertaken by the Army, and the Navy was in charge of the air defense of the Naval districts and naval guard districts. Consequently, each naval district or guard district functioned as a central organ for the air defense operations, and the communications structure was planned and maintained along this line in accordance with the air defense program of each naval district and guard district.

As the war progressed and the Homeland was subjected to incessant bombings by B-29's, a partial change was made of the air defense structure, but no change was made in general principles. The Army expressed earnest desire to effect Army-Navy unification of intelligence agencies, especially the unified command of search radars. However, the Navy was opposed to the Army proposal because of the difficulty in unification of communications and for fear of serious setback to communications capacity. By compromise, an agreement was made to merely maintain closer contact with each other and this was observed until the war ended.

The communications plan for the Homeland air defense operation was as follows:

Policy

    1. The establishment of the new communications system will conform to the objectives of the Homeland antiaircraft defense operations. Judging from the disposition of the main enemy air bases in the south (Iwo Jima and Marianas), and in the light of

the enemy air raid tactics upon the Homeland in the past, a rough estimate can be made as to the directions from which the enemy will attack.

2. The air raid information and warning system will be newly established to cope with the potential directions of the enemy air attacks in order to locate their approach and spread the warning to the necessary organs as early as possible. The command communications system should also be adequately equipped to expedite communications with the interceptor planes for interception operations.

Plan

1. An air defense intelligence center will be placed in each naval district and guard district, and auxiliary centers will be established within the command center of the interceptor fighters according to the area of the assigned defense sector and the disposition of the interceptor fighter units.

2. The intelligence center and the interception command center will be combined.

3. Both wire and radio communications will be used, and radio broadcasting in plain language will be carried out to the fullest extent.

4. Telephone communications will be established between adjacent radar stations for mutual use of intelligence gathered by the Army and the Navy.

5. The intelligence report procedures of the Army and the Navy lookout posts will be unified, while the information notification procedure will be revised to facilitate use of information reports by the various quarters.

Intelligence and Air Defense Command Centers

The principal centers will be: Ominato, Yokosuka, Yamato, Maizuru, Kure, Sasebo and Kanoya.

The auxiliary centers will be: Chitose, Kisarazu, Meiji, Osaka (for intelligence only), Matsuyama and Oita.

Lookout Communications Net

Policy:

In establishing a communications system for lookout posts,

the main assault directions of the enemy air attack force upon the mainland will be taken into consideration and presumed to be as follows: Attack from the Marianas bases; attack from the Philippines and Okinawa; attack from the bases in China; and attack from the bases in the Aleutians.

Preparations:

In view of the installations and current assignments of air defense tasks, an intelligence center will be established in the headquarters of each naval district and guard district. Kanoya and Yamato will be added; the former will be the center of southern Kyushu and the latter will be the center of the area consisting chiefly of the Kinki District.

A principal center will organize one intelligence system by placing under its control lookout posts deployed within an approximate 120-mile range.

Organization:

As a rule, the operational communications net will be separated from the administrative communications net. In the operational communications net, the report communications net must be completely separate from the command communications; and although the common use of one communications net for report and administrative purposes may be permitted depending upon the installation, the communications net for command must always be separate for exclusive use.

Wire communications, as a general rule, will be established to connect lookout posts with the centers to which they belong and with adjacent air bases.

Communications Nets: (See Chart 36)

Transmission of Air Defense Intelligence

The object will be to notify promptly each department of any information collected and collated at the intelligence center in order to enable each department to make prompt and effective use of the information for operational purposes or its own defense.

The transmission of information will be effected by radio or wiretelephone broadcasting and the chief of the department will make possible the direct use of these information reports.

Chart 36

Lookout Communications Nets

Communications Net	Details
Report Communications Net	1. The communications of mutual stations is ideal, but due to the lack of communications facilities and personnel and the difficulty of assigning frequencies in the center, two or three separate lookout stations within approximately the same distance from the center will be included in the same frequency as a standard, and each organization will establish three or four different report nets. 2. This communications net will be used exclusively for reports from lookout stations in which the broadcast method will be used. 3. In case of lack of facilities, this communications net will be used for daily administrative communications, depending on the situation.
Communications Net for Controlling Lookout Activities	1. This net will be subdivided into two or three communications nets according to the specified areas. (anticipated directions of enemy invasion). 2. As a rule, telephone broadcasting will be carried out, but the report communications net will be employed to control remote stations which are difficult to reach by telephone broadcasting. 3. This net will be used exclusively for controlling lookout activities. 4. The simultaneous command issuing apparatus will be attached to wire communications.
Daily Administrative Communications Net	1. As a rule, all lookout agencies stationed in the district under administrative assignment will be included in one communications net, but, especially, in case a different frequency is required because of the distance, two communications nets will be provided. 2. As a rule, this will be provided independently of other communications nets, but it will be employed as the report net, depending on the situation.

The method of indicating the target is prescribed as follows: The target will be indicated by the bearing and distance from the principal center. (Example): Target number, bearing and distance (in degrees and kilometers); altitude, course.

Medium frequency will be employed in telephone broadcasting in order to permit radio receiving sets to be repaired or completed for use. To supplement the lack of communications capacity resulting from the above measure, the auxiliary center and the low frequency telegraph broadcasting will also be used.

Communications nets:

Communications Net	Details
Telephone net for broadcasting air defense intelligence	1. Medium frequency radiotelephone broadcasting will be carried out. 2. The air defense center will monitor the intelligence broadcasts of adjacent sectors and include the necessary data in its own broadcasts.
Communications net for broadcasting air defense intelligence	1. The existing communications net for the air defense intelligence broadcast will be used. 2. Frequencies of adjacent sectors will differ to facilitate the mutual interception of information broadcasting.

Chart 37

Organization of command communications nets:

Communications Net	Details
Communications net for commanding air defense operations	1. This will be used exclusively for the transmission of operational orders to the interceptor fighter units. 2. Broadcasting method will be used generally, but ordinary communications procedure will also be adopted depending on the situation.
Wiretelephone communications net	As a wire communications net, only a telephone net is adopted and used chiefly, but it will also be used for wire telegraphy, depending on the situation.
Telephone net for commanding air defense operations	1. This net will be used exclusively for the transmission of operational orders to the interceptor fighter units. 2. One-way telephone communications will generally be carried out, but the exchange of talk is possible, depending on the situation.

Chart 38

Ground Control of Interceptor Fighters

A new communications net for intelligence broadcasting will be established with the view to facilitate the actions of a small number of interceptor fighters. The intelligence center of each sector will broadcast the information necessary for interception operations and the fighter planes operating in the sector will maneuver in accordance with the information monitored.

A special command-communications net other than the one mentioned in the preceding paragraph will be established for command with unit and for ground control of interceptor fighter planes.

Communications net:

Communications Net	Details
Communications net for broadcasting intelligence	1. This will be used exclusively for the transmission of intelligence to fighter planes in flight or waiting in readiness, but can also be used for ground control, depending on the situation. 2. As a rule, telephone broadcasting by Type-A high frequency will be adopted. 3. Classification of frequencies will correspond to that of the disposition of units and the assigned districts.
Command telephone net	1. This net will be used exclusively for ground control of the fighter plane units and for intra-unit command by the fighter plane unit commander. 2. Type-B and C high frequencies will be adopted.

Chart 39

Summary of Installation Work

In November 1944, when large-scale enemy air attacks upon the Homeland became imminent, it was decided to implement the plan for completing the communications system for the Homeland Air Defense Operation. The preparations were started immediately after the formulation of the plan, and, by May 1945, the work was nearly completed.

Later as air attacks by B-29's grew in intensity and attacks were launched from higher altitude (above clouds), there was a pressing need for hastening the establishment of a radar net and fighter homing device. Meanwhile, warning was used at air bases, because there was practically no reserve of the new equipment and partly because the air defense of the Homeland was originally assigned to the Army.

Communications Between the Army and Navy

From the outbreak of war, joint operations of the Army and Navy Air Groups were frequently carried out, but communications were always conducted by prearrangement and were never operated by direct mutual communications between plane units because of the different systems used.

The Army used mainly the numerical code for aircraft communications and the Navy used Japanese characters. Therefore, despite the fact that direct communications between the services would have been very expedient, nothing was done about standardizing the systems.

The Army and the Navy established communications regulations for joint operations after consultations in Tokyo (in 1943), but as these regulations were found to be inapplicable to the actual conditions of operational forces, they were not enforced. When the war situation became adverse, direct joint operations between the Army and the Navy became vitally necessary. This was particularly evident when elements of the Army Air Force (98th Air Regiment and 7th Air Regiment) were placed under the command of a naval force (762d Naval Air Group) for training in torpedo bombing. Therefore, the Naval Communications Regulations were taught to the Army personnel, and in about four months they reached the point where operations could be carried out somewhat satisfactorily. Thereafter, the necessity for direct communications between the Army and the Navy became even greater, but the war situation worsened day by day and precluded any efforts towards establishing standard regulations.

Radio Navigation

In accordance with the demands from the standpoint of security and operations, research and improvement of the radio direction finder and the guide apparatus had been carried out even before the outbreak of war. After the outbreak of war, the United States invented many effective navigational devices such as the radar, the high frequency directional beam transmitting set and the long-range radio aid to navigation. These contributed much to their capability in air navigation, whereas Japan made little progress from the time of the outbreak of war until its termination.

As far as Japan's capability in radio navigation was concerned, the planes could not fly through even slightly inclement weather. When on a mission, they missed the enemy which should have been sighted, or lost a tactical opportunity for attack and allowed the enemy to take the initiative. From about the end of 1943, forced landings became very frequent because they could not return to their carriers or bases due to the incapability of the navigator. Actually, if the radio equipment which was supplied at that time had been fully utilized, a number of the forced landings would have been generally avoided. However, with the low caliber of flight and communications personnel, nothing could be done to prevent losses as radio navigation was hardly comprehensible. Moreover, since the equipment in itself was very inferior as compared to American equipment, the Japanese operational forces had no confidence in the equipment.

Utilization of the Radio Direction Finder

The utilization of the high frequency radio direction finder on ships was impossible owing to the polarization and turbulence phenomena. Thus, high frequency radio direction finders were established only as fixed equipment at land bases, and ships were equipped exclusively with low frequency direction finders. Some of the ground high frequency radio direction finders were used mainly for the interception of enemy radio communications, but very few were utilized for navigation. Low frequency radio direction finders were actually used only by carriers and naval vessels carrying seaplanes. These ships reported only the direction of a plane, and although the reporting of a plotted position by cross-bearing method was specified in various communications regulations, it was not actually carried out because the cross-bearing coordination by radio direction finder stations was difficult to execute. Generally, the base air forces did not use direction finders for the following reasons:

1. The flight personnel preferred simple ground navigation and avoided use of radio aid navigation because it was not necessary when the visibility was good.
2. Low frequency radiation was much too complicated to be conducted on aircraft.
3. Communications authorities were generally indifferent toward this problem.

The carrier forces often conducted training in radio navigation by direction finding from ships and utilized it in actual battles. This method was deemed particularly necessary for aircraft in returning to the carrier. The drawback was that it was necessary to trail the antenna about 70 meters from the plane in order to radiate low frequency, and this slowed down the plane considerably. Moreover, with the improvement of aircraft and the increase of aircraft speed, a trailing antenna often broke during high speed. Therefore, the use of high frequency equipment for ordinary communications as direction finding from ships was advocated and this was first installed on the task force aircraft carrier Taiho in March 1944. The results were very favorable as this equipment kept the mean margin of error within five degrees, although compared with the automatic radio direction finder, it was still unsatisfactory.

At the outbreak of war almost all combat aircraft had radio

direction finders, the range of which was approximately 150 to 200 miles for large aircraft and approximately 50 to 100 miles for the small aircraft.

With the huge expansion of air strength, the number of aircraft which were to be equipped with radio direction finders increased greatly. However, since this equipment required precise adjustments at the time of manufacture and vacuum tubes of excellent quality, production could not meet the demand. Moreover, as production was boosted, defective equipment was supplied successively to the operational forces due to failure to inspect the finished products. Consequently, confidence in the equipment was gradually lost. In particular, since the pilots of small land-based aircraft felt that radio direction finders were useless and only increased the weight of aircraft, the radio direction finders were stored away in warehouses.

The carrier task force had radio direction finders to the very end because of the necessity for aircraft homing, but there were many radio direction finders which could not be used because of poor functional capacity.

There was a gradual increase in accidents in which planes were listed missing due to poor navigation. The Central Agency, therefore, encouraged the use of the homing device, and at the same time established a plan to facilitate navigation by installing powerful low frequency transmitters at well known capes and bases to radiate induction waves regularly as necessary.

Radio Beacon

Before the war, there had been a considerable number of radio beacon stations under the jurisdiction of the Transportation and Communications Ministry, and they were utilized for civil aviation and by some of the military aircraft. However, after the outbreak of the war, nearly all the radio beacon radiating devices were removed and these stations were used merely as short wave radio stations.

From the time the decisive battle on the mainland was advocated due to the critical war situation, the importance of the beacon was emphasized again in order to prevent navigation accidents which would occur because of the deterioration in skill of flight personnel. The officials of the Navy, the Army and the Transportation and Communications Ministry met and advocated the restoration and utilization of existing equipment, but because of the protracted disuse, its restoration could not be effected as anticipated. Also, experiments were carried out on a portable medium frequency beacon but it proved impractical. Thus the beacon was not used during the war.

CHAPTER VI

Communications in Escort Operations

General Situation

The communications in the operations for protecting surface traffic varied with the change of system for escort operations. For purpose of analysis, the conduct of communications can be divided into two periods: the period in which each naval district executed the operations for protecting traffic at the outbreak of the war; and the period in which unified operations for protecting surface traffic was executed by the establishment of the General Escort Command (15 Nov 43).

At the beginning of the war, the naval districts and guard districts took charge of the protection of surface traffic within their respective sea areas. Consequently, the communications for the operation of protecting a convoy or an individual ship which sailed through two or more sea areas necessitated the use of as many communications nets.

After the establishment of the General Escort Command, this situation was improved. Later however, with the increase in shipping losses due to enemy submarines, coordinated operations of the air groups were carried out and a great improvement resulted chiefly in the aircraft communications system. Moreover, as the minelaying operation by the enemy B-29's became intensified, additional lookout posts were newly established to watch for the laying of mines, and this added a new burden to the General Escort Command's communications.

The Communications Plan of the General Escort Command

The communications of forces under the General Escort Command were conducted in accordance with the Naval Communication Regulations, Combined Fleet Communications Regulations, the communications regulations of the General Escort Command, the communications regulations of various escort units, shipping communications regulations and the Convoy Movement and Communications Regulations. The foregoing regulations were supplemented with the following instructions:

The communications of the surface escort units and traffic protecting organs which are located in the same sector will be executed jointly, except under unavoidable circumstances.

1. Ship communications

    a. The communications net will be divided into three categories: escort unit communications net, broadcast net, and the specially established communications net in the Japan Sea area (Chart 40).

    b. Monitoring by units and ships will be prescribed as shown in Chart 41.

    c. The ship or station which is the central communications unit in each communications net will promptly broadcast necessary communications to the escort unit by the broadcast net (Consecutive numbers will be given to each message). The above communications ship or station will also monitor the wave of the broadcast net of the neighboring unit and endeavor to transmit immediately the messages concerned.

    d. Escort units and transport vessels will always exercise radio silence during their movement except when special

Escort Unit Communications Net — Chart 40-a

Communications Net	Central Station	Stations of Communications Net	Frequency Used			
			Low freq	Med freq	High freq	Very-High Freq
Ominato Escort Unit Communications Net	Ominato Communications Unit	Ominato Surface Escort Unit Wakkanai Communications Unit 903d Air Group Hq.				41,350 (TE-TA1)
1st Escort Unit Communications Net	Maizuru Communications Unit	1st Escort Unit 901st Air Group Hq. Rashin Base Force Hq.				
Seventh Fleet Escort Unit Communications Net	Seventh Fleet Hq. (Moji)	Seventh Fleet Escort Unit Chinhae Communications Unit				

Chart 40-b

Surface Escort Unit Broadcast Communications Net

Communications Net	Abbreviation	Broadcasting Station	Broadcast Time	Frequency
Ominato Surface Escort Unit Broadcasting Net		Ominato Communications Unit	Regular	
1st Surface Escort Unit Broadcasting Net		Maizuru Communications Unit	Regular	
Seventh Fleet Escort Unit Broadcasting Net		Seventh Fleet Hq. (Moji)	Regular	
Remarks	Broadcasting stations or ships will always monitor communications of the broadcasting net of adjacent sea areas.			

Japan Sea Area Special Communications Net

Communications Net	Central Station	Stations of Communications Net	Frequency
Japan Sea Area Special Communications Net	Maizuru Communications Unit	Tokyo Communications Unit, Wakkanai, Ominato, Niigata, Rashin, Chinhae, Moji.	

210

Monitoring by Surface Escort Unit or Ship — Chart 41

Comm Net	Fleet-level Flagship (Communications Unit)	Division-level Flagship	Single Ship or Unit	Single Vessel, or Escort	Office of Resident Naval Officer
Escort Unit Frequency	X	X	X	X	Z
Escort Unit Broadcasting Net	X	Y	Y	Y	Y
Tokyo Broadcasting Net No 1	Y	Y			
Aircraft Frequency	Y	Y	Y	Z	
Air Base Comm Net	Z				
Japan Sea Special Comm Net	X	Z			
Submarine Information, (Weather)	Y	Y	Y	Y	Y
500 Kilocycles	Y	Y	X	X	Y
Adjacent Broadcasting Net	Y				

Key

X..... Exchange of communications

Y..... Monitoring

Z..... Monitoring, depending on the situation

orders are issued.

e. The communications of a convoy with the units outside the convoy will be the responsibility of the ship carrying the commanding officer, except as noted in paragraph f.

f. All the ships in the convoy will normally monitor through the 500 kilocycles net and will broadcast to the proper party by the same channel and by the frequency designated by the escort unit when it positively sights the enemy or when attacked by enemy submarines.

g. For communications within the convoy, each vessel will use the frequency prescribed by the Convoy Movement and Communications Regulations and also the 41,350 kilocycles band unless special orders are issued. While antisubmarine patrol planes are escorting in the air, special precaution must be taken regarding this frequency.

h. Communications between escort vessels and transports within a convoy will be conducted by the visual communications method. Such communications will be completed by sundown except in unavoidable cases. Night communications will be avoided.

i. As for communications of ships at anchor in the harbor, the direct radiation of waves by vessels will be avoided except under special orders, and the ships will dispatch communications through the nearest land-based communication unit or by wire.

2. Air communications

a. The communications net will be classified as the air base communications net and the aircraft communications net, and will be designated as in Chart 42.

b. Monitoring by the groups will be designated as in Chart 43.

c. When an aircraft sights the enemy, it will broadcast the sighting immediately, and the central air base will broadcast this report by the same frequency and also on the frequency of the surface escort unit.

d. While an aircraft is in flight, it will maintain strict

Air Base Net
Chart 42

Communications Net	Abbreviation	Central Base	Bases of Air Base Net
901st Air Group 1st Base Net		Maizuru Air Base	Noshiro, Nanao, Komatsu, Mineyama, Miho, Tamatsukuri, Chinhae Air Group, 903d Air Group
901st Air Group 2d Base Net		Chinhae Air Base	Rashin, Genzan, Oura, Hakata, Pusan, Yosu
903d Air Group Base Net		Ominato Air Group	Akeshi, Noshiro, Otaru, Wakkanai, Bihoro, Chitose, Odomari

Frequency for Escort Plan

Air Group	Abbreviation	Frequency		
		Low	High	Very-high
901st Air Group				
903d Air Group				41,350 (TE-TA 1)
958th Air Group				

Monitoring by Aircraft   Chart 43

Communications Net	(KO) A - Base	(OTSU) B - Base	(HEI) C - Base
Air Base Communications Net	X	X	X
Aircraft Frequency	X	X	X
Tokyo Broadcasting Net No 1	Y		
Escort Unit Broadcasting Net	Y	Y	
Escort Unit Frequency	X	Z	
500 Kilocycles	Y	Y	
Submarine Information, (Weather)	Y	Y	Y
Air Defense Communications	Z	Z	Z

Note: 1. A-Base (where the C in C is located)

      2. B-Base (where a base commander is located)

      3. C-Base (where a squadron commander is located on a mission)

Key: X ... Exchange of communications.

      Y ... Monitoring.

      Z ... Monitoring, depending on the situation.

radio silence, except for the transmission of enemy contact reports, emergency dispatches and other important information. Special precautions must be taken regarding the radiation of waves.

e. When an aircraft engaged in antisubmarine patrol sights a friendly convoy, the plane will report the name, position, course, speed and the time the convoy is sighted to the base. The base will relay the message to the adjacent air base scheduled to take over the patrol and at the same time report to the local surface escort unit. In this instance, wave radiation above the convoy must be avoided as much as possible.

f. While an aircraft is patrolling above a convoy, it will monitor on 41,350 kilocycles (radiotelephone frequency which is used within the convoy), and will try to maintain close contact with the convoy. If the aircraft locates an enemy submarine, it will immediately report to the convoy by the abbreviations specially prescribed in the communications regulations of the General Escort Command, and by the signals prescribed in the Convoy Movement Regulations and Communications Regulations.

3. Communications of ship protecting facilities

   a. Communications between a naval district or a guard district and the office of the Resident Naval Officer will be carried out by wire, but the radio communications net prescribed by the commandant of the naval district or the guard district will be used additionally in an effort to report accurately and quickly.

   b. Besides the above, the officer of the Resident Naval Officer will endeavor to receive directly antisubmarine information, weather reports and monitor the broadcast net for the sea area under the charge of the local naval district or guard district.

   c. The Resident Naval Officer will closely analyze air defense information, establish close contact with the air defense intelligence headquarters and harbor guard unit stationed in his jurisdictional area, and endeavor thereby to obtain promptly reports on enemy air raids and minelaying. He will send such reports immediately to the ships at anchor in the harbor under his jurisdiction.

e. The commandants of naval districts, guard districts and the C in C of the Seventh Fleet will establish anti-mine lookout communications nets in their respective sea areas.

4. Intelligence communications

   a. The General Escort Command will broadcast antisubmarine information prescribed in the shipping communications regulations.

   b. The General Escort Command will broadcast battle situation reports (serially numbered) to the forces under the General Escort Command whenever antisubmarine reports are broadcast. The reports will also be broadcast to ships which are directly concerned, using the call sign directed to all ships (including the forces under the General Escort Command).

   c. The commandants of naval districts, guard districts and the C in C of the Seventh Fleet will broadcast anti-mine reports for their respective sea areas. Also, the General Escort Command will broadcast a comprehensive anti-mine report (based on the above anti-mine reports), to all vessels (including the forces under the General Escort Command) whenever the anti-mine reports are broadcast.

   d. The force under the General Escort Command will always pay attention to air defense information and endeavor to receive it directly in order to be on the alert against enemy air attack.

5. Interception of enemy communications

   a. The General Escort Command will maintain close contact with the Special Duty Section (radio intelligence) of the Navy General Staff and other organs concerned and promptly notify the necessary quarters the battle situation reports or warnings.

   b. All naval districts, guard districts and the First Escort Fleet headquarters will order the intercepting and radio direction finder organs under their command to concentrate on enemy communications to determine enemy locations and movements and promptly notify the authorities concerned of any enemy activity.

   c. The commandants of all naval districts, guard districts

and C in C, First Escort Fleet may conduct jamming and radio deception against enemy communications if necessary.

   d. In accordance with the order of the commanding officer, the enemy communications interception section attached to each escort convoy will endeavor to intercept on the frequency of enemy submarines and enemy patrol planes maneuvering in the vicinity.

6. Code books and cipher tables

   a. Besides the present code books and cipher tables, the abbreviations and signals prescribed in the communications regulations of the General Escort Command will be used.

   b. For communications from surface escort units to transports, special attention must be paid to the code books and call sign list in possession of the other party.

Communications of the General Escort Command

Before the General Escort Command was established, the Japanese Navy was without a standard system for its surface escort and anti-submarine operations. Instead, these operations were carried out under separate systems by the commander of each unit responsible for escort. This made it difficult to maintain mutual liaison and the convoy escort forces operating in their respective sea areas under such conditions experienced great difficulty. Moreover, as these escort forces were organized with various types of escort craft assembled each time for each convoy trip, no unified conception of the communications system existed among them. The equipment used by these vessels was generally worn out and the communications personnel were of low caliber. Under such conditions, it was impossible to carry out operational communications smoothly, skillfully and rapidly.

After the General Escort Command was established, the gradual unification of the system and reorganization of the facilities and personnel were planned. However, the importance of safeguarding transport routes by surface escort was not generally recognized and by the time its necessity was realized, it was too late to take any effective measures.

Ship Communications

Since communications between the various escort units were not carried out smoothly at the time the General Escort Command was established, convoy escort proved weak at the boundary of sea areas where escort transfers took place (an escort unit operated up to the limits of a designated sea area only, whereby another unit took over for the next area). Therefore, the through-escort system was adopted wherever possible and the communications systems were revised and unified. The frequencies for the communications over the routes from Yokosuka to Ominato, Osaka and Saipan respectively were unified with those of the Yokosuka Surface Escort Force, and the frequencies for the route between the Kyushu area and Formosa were unified with those of the Surface Escort Force of the Sasebo Naval District.

Communications units in the South China Sea monitored the frequency of the 1st Surface Escort Unit and conducted scheduled communications. As for the communications of the 1st Surface Escort

Unit (with its center at the Takao Communications Unit) which was in charge of the through-escort on the special route between Majo and Singapore, the following communications units rendered assistance to the escort forces in order to offset the limited capacity of the Escort Unit (by monitoring on the frequency of the 1st Surface Escort Unit and conducting scheduled communications): Sasebo Communications Unit, 11th Communications Unit (Saigon), 30th Communications Unit (Manila) and 10th Communications Unit (Singapore).

After the American forces landed at Lingayen Gulf in the Philippines in early January 1945, the special route between Moji and Singapore, for which the First Escort Fleet (1st Surface Escort Unit was deactivated 10 December 1944) activity and traffic became difficult over the transport route in the South China Sea. Therefore in February 1945, the First Escort Fleet headquarters moved to Moji where it became the communications relay point for the transport routes to north and central China areas.

As escort ships were often required to use low and high frequencies simultaneously, it was repeatedly requested that each escort ship be equipped with one transmitter solely for low frequency and another one for high frequency instead of one transmitter then in use for both low and high frequency. Requests were also made for the high frequency capacity to be increased to that of high frequency No 4 transmitter to meet the needs of the expanded operating sea areas. However, none of these requests were ever brought to realization.

The communications personnel were also few in number. Each coast defense ship engaged in extensive operations under the 1st Surface Escort headquarters had only six radiomen (including maintenance) and one code clerk, while the old-type destroyers each had only four radiomen for every five receiving sets. Since it was extremely difficult to carry out extensive escort communications under these conditions, a request was made to increase the personnel at least to the extent where three receiving sets could be in operation continuously. As a result, a temporary increase of the radio crew by two persons and the code personnel by one was authorized for each coast defense ship and destroyer.

Up to autumn of 1944, escort vessels had not been organized into the escort divisions and destroyer divisions. The escort units had been comprised of various types of vessels which had but few opportunities for training and had no unified plan or system. As it was difficult for such escort units to carry out inter-unit communications (with telephones such as Type-90 very-high frequency telephones and No. 2 telephones), it was decided to use the handy crystal-controlled aircraft radiotelephones designed for communications within the unit. Thus, all vessels except for a very limited number of converted vessels were equipped with these telephones and contact with aircraft was improved by standardizing the frequencies (41,350 KC) for communications within the escort forces so as to be applicable to both surface craft and aircraft. With a view to equipping ships in important convoys with telephones of this type, the training of telephone crews was started. This plan did not materialize since the American forces had launched the Okinawa operations and disrupted transport routes from the southern areas.

In early 1945, many of Japan's shipping lanes were in enemy hands and after May, only the Japan Sea was safe for transport purposes. Therefore, efforts were made to strengthen the communications facilities in the Japan Sea area with Maizuru as the relay base and Niigata as the central port of discharge.

Aircraft Communications

From May 1944, a part of the Army Air Force began to cooperate in the antisubmarine operations. However, the differences in the communications systems, code books and techniques were great hindrances to communications. Contact by wire communications was attempted but this also proved inadequate. As an expedient measure, a communications system with call signs and a code book common to both parties was established and an emergency frequency (7045 KC) was selected and used from July for important communications such as reports of the sighting of enemy forces. However, even this did not prove satisfactory because of the complicated nature of the method and therefore was rescinded.

The various frequencies used for communications within the air forces under the General Escort Command were unified at 41,350 KC.

Moreover, with the aim to maintain close contact between convoy escort planes and escort ships, the frequencies for telephone communications within air forces under the General Escort Command were also unified at 41,350 KC.

In February 1945, the air forces under the General Escort Command were reorganized into four air groups: The 901st, 903d, 936th and 951st Air Groups; and the base communications net was divided into the East and West Base Communications Nets with continuous contact maintained between them. With the invasion of Okinawa by the American forces, however, part of the air communications nets were destroyed, and until the end of the war, air communications were virtually limited to the small sea areas of the Okhotsk Sea and the Japan Sea with only the 901st and the 903d Air Groups in operation.

Radio Intelligence

Enemy communications intercepting organs along the routes for which the surface escort forces were responsible were Tokyo, Yokosuka, Sasebo, the 30th Communications Unit (Manila) and the 10th Communications Unit (Singapore). However, these organs were not adequate for utilization by the surface escort forces. In particular, the 30th and 10th Communications Units, with their main objectives directed toward the east, left the areas of the South China Sea and the Formosa Strait in a very uncertain state. In view of this situation, it was urgently necessary to strengthen the organs in the South China Sea which provided an important route for the transport of vital commodities from the southern areas. Therefore, a demand was made for the establishment of a new radio direction finding net composed of Samah (reactivated), the 11th (Saigon) and 10th (Singapore) Communications Units with their relay point at Takao. The 1st Surface Escort Unit headquarters (Takao) was authorized the full utilization of the net.

Up until 1944, the foreign communications interception organs on the Japan Sea coast were directed at the Soviet Union and had personnel for intercepting Soviet communications only. Thereafter, when it became difficult to prevent American submarines from entering the Japan Sea, additional personnel were assigned to the foreign communications intercepting organs for intercepting American and British communications.

From March 1944, foreign communications interception teams, each consisting of one petty officer and three seamen, were assigned to flagships in important convoys and also to escort aircraft carriers for the purpose of avoiding enemy submarines and detecting enemy patrol planes. Moreover, the 1st Surface Escort Unit headquarters was reinforced with six teams and each naval district (except Maizuru) and each guard district with two to six teams respectively. These teams achieved considerable results but the commanders could not utilize them to the fullest extent because the ships lacked high frequency radio direction finders.

When it became apparent that the enemy would increase air raids over Formosa and the Homeland, foreign communications interception teams were assigned to major air groups in an effort to predict enemy air raids and detect patrol activities of enemy planes over transport routes.

The General Escort Command, in close liaison with the Special Duty Group of the Navy General Staff, issued intelligence reports and warnings at appropriate times concerning enemy movements, and at the same time, issued the Submarine Intelligence Report every ten days. The distribution of the latter report, however, was discontinued as enemy submarines roamed throughout the home waters in 1945. Thereafter, the General Escort Command radioed its estimates of attacks by enemy task forces, made forecasts of any large-scale air attacks on the Homeland and issued warnings for the retirement of convoys and the dispersal of ships.

Office of the Resident Naval Officer and Communications

To prevent confusion in communications likely to be created by the activities of enemy submarines swarming in home waters and by the intensification of air raids over the Homeland, the communications capacity of the Office of the Resident Naval Officer was strengthened as follows:

1. The wire communications net between each naval district or guard district headquarters and the Office the Resident Naval Officer which had been left almost in total disuse was restored as much as

possible.

2. Each Office of the Resident Naval Officer was additionally provided with one or two portable high frequency radio sets, and one to three receiving sets, together with the personnel required to operate them to effect communications by radio as well as by wire.

3. Each Office of the Resident Naval Officer was provided with intelligence receiving sets of Type-2 and special Type-2-A. These were used in connection with directing the dispersal and retirement of ships at anchor in case of an air raid.

CHAPTER VII

Operational Communications of Submarines

Irrespective of the mission, whether it be destruction of ships or cooperation in fleet operations, a submarine frequently undertook independent missions covering a long distance. Such being the case, it had to facilitate its operational movement by speedy receipt of orders as well as be informed of the numerous intelligence reports on the area concerned. In expediting submarine warfare from the communications point of view, the formulation of the communications plan had to be based on the following characteristics inherent in submarine operations:

1. Submarines cover extensive areas and thus require long-distance communications. In particular, great longitudinal distances adversely affect communications.

2. As submarines cruise underwater a great part of the time, suitable communications measures must be conducted to assure liaison.

3. Movements and dispositions of submarines must be under constant secrecy.

4. Limited space in submarines restricted number of radio personnel.

Summary of Communications Plan

With reference to communications over long distances and of great longitudinal distances, it was necessary to assign suitable day and night frequencies according to propagation characteristics of wave frequencies. However, with the limited radio personnel, this was not easily undertaken; furthermore it was definitely restricted with respect to the number of radio waves as well as to the wave frequency itself due to the antenna problem.

The time of change-over between day and night frequencies was set at sunset in approximately the central area of a submarine's operating area. In the period a few hours before the change-over time, dual employment of day and night frequencies was prescribed.

A suitable frequency was selected according to the nature of the ocean and the latitude of the area in which a submarine was located. In the frequency band, a relatively lower frequency was more suitable for both day and night frequencies in the Pacific Ocean, while a higher frequency was suitable in the Indian Ocean.

In order to insure the transmittal of messages to a submarine in submerged cruising, the following were taken into consideration:

1. Scheduled communications were conducted in order to regulate the time for a submarine to raise the high frequency wave antenna or attain the very-low frequency reception depth. The communications time was selected at every even or odd-numbered hour; and for security purposes, communications were to start, not at the beginning of the designated hour, but at the same numbered minutes past the designated hour, or a few minutes added to those minutes.

2. Messages were broadcast twice (once during the day and once at night), and messages which were broadcast during the day were broadcast collectively at night. As to the time of collective broad-

casting, the usual starting time was at about two hours after sunset on the longitudinal line on the western extremity of the submarine's operating area.

3. Broadcast messages were numbered serially to check any messages not received by a submarine.

4. As for dispatches from a submarine, a central communications unit repeated messages received from a submarine for acknowledgement as well as for collation.

5. Except in special cases, submarines did not communicate mutually but depended upon relay broadcasts by the central communications unit.

In order to afford greater protection to the secrecy of submarines, the following matters were taken into consideration:

1. In daytime, the time was held to a minimum for very-low frequency wave reception while completely submerged as well as the time for reception with the high frequency wave antenna up.

2. In transmitting from a submarine, the time was minimized by making the messages concise and the transmitting power was adjusted so as to minimize the communications range.

3. The submarine special communications procedure (radiating radio waves for about five seconds at suitable time intervals) was used to avoid detection by enemy radio direction finders.

4. Through employment of several combinations of day and night

frequencies shifted irregularly at about one hour intervals, efforts were made to avoid enemy interception and radio direction finders.

In order to maintain secrecy of the position of a submarine, the following were considered in conducting communications:

1. A submarine had to prepare all outgoing dispatches and transmit them after surfacing and having moved to another position at night. On completion of the transmission, the submarine was permitted to return to its former position.

2. A submarine was required to move to a new position after completing transmittal from its former position.

3. When a submarine started for, or withdrew from an operational sea area, it was permitted to transmit messages from a position which would not betray its movement.

Summary of Submarine Communications Operations

As high frequency and very-low frequency waves were used jointly for broadcasting to submarines, there was no particular concern over broadcasts failing to reach their destination during the war. Percentage of broadcast reception by submarines with the high frequency wave antenna up or the very-low frequency wave reception while completely submerged was about 30 percent in the daytime, and generally 90 to 100 percent at night; and as collective broadcasting of all messages was conducted at night, the receiving of most broadcasts was ensured.

The high frequency radio range with the high frequency wave antenna during submerged cruising in the daytime was 800 to 1,000 miles (transmitting range), while in reception it was about equal in comparison with that of other antennae; and while surfaced, day or night, no great difference was observed either in transmission or in reception as compared to other antennae.

As to a submarine's submerged cruising depth capable of reception in the Pacific Ocean, it was 15 to 17 meters in the Hawaiian area, while off the west coast of the United States it was about one meter less than in the above-mentioned area.

Radio Direction Finder

A submarine was capable of utilizing medium frequency as well as high frequency radio direction finders, and this capability was an effective asset for antiaircraft warning against enemy targets at the beginning of war in the Indian Ocean as well as in the Australian area; but after a submarine was equipped with radar (from 1943), opportunities for the use of the direction finder gradually decreased. Radio direction finders were utilized with particularly effective results by the 2d Submarine Squadron in intercepting and attacking the US aircraft carrier Lexington.

Submarine Communications Bases

Communications bases used for submarine operations from the outbreak of the war were as follows (Chart 44):

Pacific Ocean Area (Sixth Fleet)		Indian Ocean Area (8th Submarine Squadron)	
Period	Location	Period	Location
Outbreak of war to August 1942	Kwajalein: (6th Communications Unit and CL Katori)	Outbreak of war to capture of Singapore	Submarine Squadron Flagship
August 1942 to May 1944	Truk: (4th Communications Unit and CL Katori)	Capture of Singapore to April 1942	Singapore: (10th Communications Unit)
June 1944 to July 1944	Saipan: (5th Communications Unit)	April 1942 to end of war	Penang
July 1944 to end of war	Kure: (Kure Communications Unit and Tsukushi Maru)		

Chart 44

Development of Principal Equipment for Submarines

Transmitter

The Type-99 Special No 3 (4) transmitter, which was capable of shifting three low frequency waves and three high frequency waves in a single motion, was completed in 1940 and installed in the new submarines. Old submarines were gradually equipped with this transmitter.

Very-low Frequency Wave Receiving Set

Very-low frequency wave reception was made possible by means of an amplifier attached to the Type-92 special receiving set re-modelled after the all-wave receiving set in German submarines and the test for reception while completely submerged was completed several months before the outbreak of war. The receiving radio wave by this amplifier (with which all submarines were equipped immediately before the outbreak of the war) was of a fixed frequency in most cases, but later in 1944, a very-low frequency wave receiving set which was capable of changing the receiving frequency was manufactured and installed in the new submarines.

Very-low Frequency Wave Transmitter

As very-low frequency wave reception became possible by a submarine completely submerged, the 17.44 KC, 850 KW transmitter (installed at the International Communications Company, Ltd, Isami Machi in Aichi Prefecture, and which had been in use for communications to Europe in winter time) was used in broadcasting to submarines by remote control from Tokyo. (From Kure after July 1944).

Radio Direction Finder

Besides low frequency radio direction finding, a submarine was capable of medium and high frequency radio direction findings which were quite impossible by any other type of naval vessel. A Type-92 special receiving set connected through an interstage transformer with a Type T No 4 radio direction finder was used for this purpose.

Standard medium and high frequency radio direction finders were developed about 1944, and several of the large submarines were equipped with them, but they were not put to practical use before the war ended.

Very-low Frequency Wave Receiving Antenna

The effectiveness of using the Type-T No 4 radio direction finder's loop antenna as a very-low frequency wave receiving antenna was recognized, but as the same radio direction finder's antenna shaft came to be used as the antiaircraft radar antenna, an iron-dust core antenna fixed on the bridge canopy came into use as a very-low frequency wave receiving antenna from the end of 1944. As to the submarine's submergible depth capable of all-wave reception with this antenna, no marked difference was observed when the radio direction finder's loop antenna was used.

CHAPTER VIII

Communications in First Phase Operations

Operational Plan

Policy

The operational communications of the Combined Fleet will be conducted in accordance with the following procedure which will also be in accordance with the Combined Fleet Radio Communications Regulations and the Army-Navy Central Agreement on Communications in the Southern Operations (See Charts 45 & 46 for communications instructions at commencement of hostilities. The time chart for operation is given in Chart 47).

Communications Procedure

1. The internal communications of the operational force will be conducted chiefly by means of broadcast. In case it is uncertain that the broadcast has been received or when an important message is broadcast, confirmation of having heard the broadcast will be required.

2. Each force will be attached to the short distance communications net (long distance communications net if necessary) of the nearest land-based communications unit as designated by its commander. The communications concerning transportation, supply, personnel and other matters which do not require immediate attention from the operational standpoint will be conducted through this communications net. However, task forces and commerce raiding units which conduct long-range operations for special duty will be attached to the special communications net and communicate with the Tokyo Communications Unit after leaving the standby base.

3. Each land-based communications unit will relay the communications of the operational force in the area concerned to the proper parties as stipulated in Chart 48. As a standard procedure, the relay will be conducted by broadcast and the acknowledgment of the messages will be required when confirmation of transmission is necessary. Communications with higher priority than emergency will be relayed immediately. Other important matters will be broadcast according to the time given in paragraph 4.

4. Each force will broadcast radio messages of operational importance in accordance with Chart 49. In order to conduct the communications in the area concerned, each force commander will utilize

Chart 45

Ship, Aircraft and Submarine Communications

Comm Net	Communications Assignment	Notes
Ship Comm	2d Strategic Communications (2 SE-TSU-HA) 3d Frequency System (3 TE-SO) 2d Communications (2 KU-UN) (Ship or force joint communications)	1. The frequencies of flagship communications nets are used mainly by the flagship of each fleet and special squadron. 2. General high frequencies are used by vessels when necessary and by flagship of each squadron. 3. The frequencies for ship communications are used mainly by the Southern Force and other forces closely concerned. All other forces are authorized the use of said frequencies only in case of emergency. However, in case the Combined Fleet is deployed for interception, the Southern Force accedes the above priority. 4. The communications area of the Southern Force is called the 3d Area.
Aircraft Comm	4th Frequency System (4 TE-SO)	
Submarine Comm	3d Frequency System (3 TE-SO)	The advance force submarine communications will be designated by its commander.

Remarks:

The use of day and night frequencies will be in accordance with the Combined Fleet Radio Communications Regulations. Furthermore frequencies will be used in accordance with the following:

The night frequency will be mainly used; however, in case the transmission by night frequency alone is inadequate, the day frequency also will be used.

Chart 46-a

Communications Unit (Base) Communications

Comm Net	Assigned Unit	Frequencies (KC)				Notes
		First Assignment		Second Assignment		
		Primary	Reserve	Primary	Reserve	
1st Comm Net	Tokyo Comm Unit; Takao Comm Unit 5th Comm Unit	6505 (RE56) 13010 (RE57)	5550 (RE51) 11100 (RE52) 7590 (RE72) 15180 (RE76)	6505 (RE56) 13010 (RE57) 5550 (RE51) 11100 (RE52)	7590 (RE75) 15180 (RE76)	
2d Comm Net	Takao Comm Unit; 3d Comm Unit 8th Comm Unit	6760 (TA25) 13320 (TA26)	7155 (TA27) 14310 (TA28) 7750 (RE77) 15500 (RE78)	6760 (TA25) 13520 (TA26) 7155 (TA27) 14130 (TA28)	7750 (RE77) 15500 (RE78)	
3d Comm Net	Tokyo Comm Unit; 3d Comm Unit 8th Comm Unit	4745 (TO17) 18980 (TO19)	7855 (NA35) 15710 (NA34) 7315 (RE73) 14630 (RE74)	4745 (TO17) 15710 (NA34) 8610 (RE81) 17220 (RE82)	7315 (RE73) 14630 (RE74)	The Communications unit will be placed in this communications net in accordance with the special order.
4th Comm Net	5th Comm Unit; 3d Comm Unit 4th Comm Unit 6th Comm Unit	5180 (NA14) 10360 (NA15)	7290 (NA31) 14580 (NA32) 7655 (NA18) 15310 (NA19)	5180 (NA14) 10360 (NA15) 7290 (NA31) 14580 (NA32)	7655 (NA18) 15310 (NA19)	
5th Comm Net	Takao Comm Unit; Hainan Comm Unit 81st Comm Unit	7010 (RE71) 14020 (RE72)	6260 (RE61) 12520 (RE62)	7010 (RE71) 14020 (RE72)	6260 (RE61) 12520 (RE62)	
6th Comm Net	5th Comm Unit; Chichijima Comm Unit Marcus Is. Comm Unit	5725 (RI14) 11450 (RI15)	4925 (RE41) 9850 (RE42)	5725 (RI14) 11450 (RI15)	4925 (RE41) 9850 (RE42)	

Communications Unit (Base)
Communications (Cont'd)

7th Comm Net	Tokyo Comm Unit: (Yokosuka Comm Unit) Ominato Comm Unit (Paramushiro) Chichijima Comm Unit	5925 (YO17) 11350 (YO18)	6300 (TA23) 12600 (TAN23)	5925 (YO17) 11850 (YO18)	6300 (TAN23) 12600 (TAN223)
8th Comm Net	Tokyo Comm Unit Ominato Comm Unit Maizuru Comm Unit Chinkai Comm Unit	4320 (MA11) 8640 (MA12)	6695 (O25) 13390 (O26)		These Communications nets will be established by special orders.
9th Comm Net	Tokyo Comm Unit Wakkanai Comm Unit Ominato Comm Unit Rashin Comm Unit Maizuru Comm Unit	2015 (O11) 8030 (O12) 16060 (O13)	4775 (TAN28) 9435 (TAN24)		Same as above

Remarks:
1. Unless otherwise specified, communications will be continuous.
2. In case communications are impossible between ships and places within the same communications net, the intermediate communications unit will take charge of relay.
3. Unless there is a special order, the first disposition will be used. Thereafter, the frequency changes will be designated by the commander of the 1st Combined Communications Unit.
4. Communications Unit (Base) communications in the occupied areas will be decided separately and will be designated by each force commander.
5. Reserve frequencies.

```
5085    10650    4205    4030    6820    9330
10170    5225    3410    8060   13040   18660
 5325   10430   16820   16120    4665    6150
                                        12360
```

Communications Net

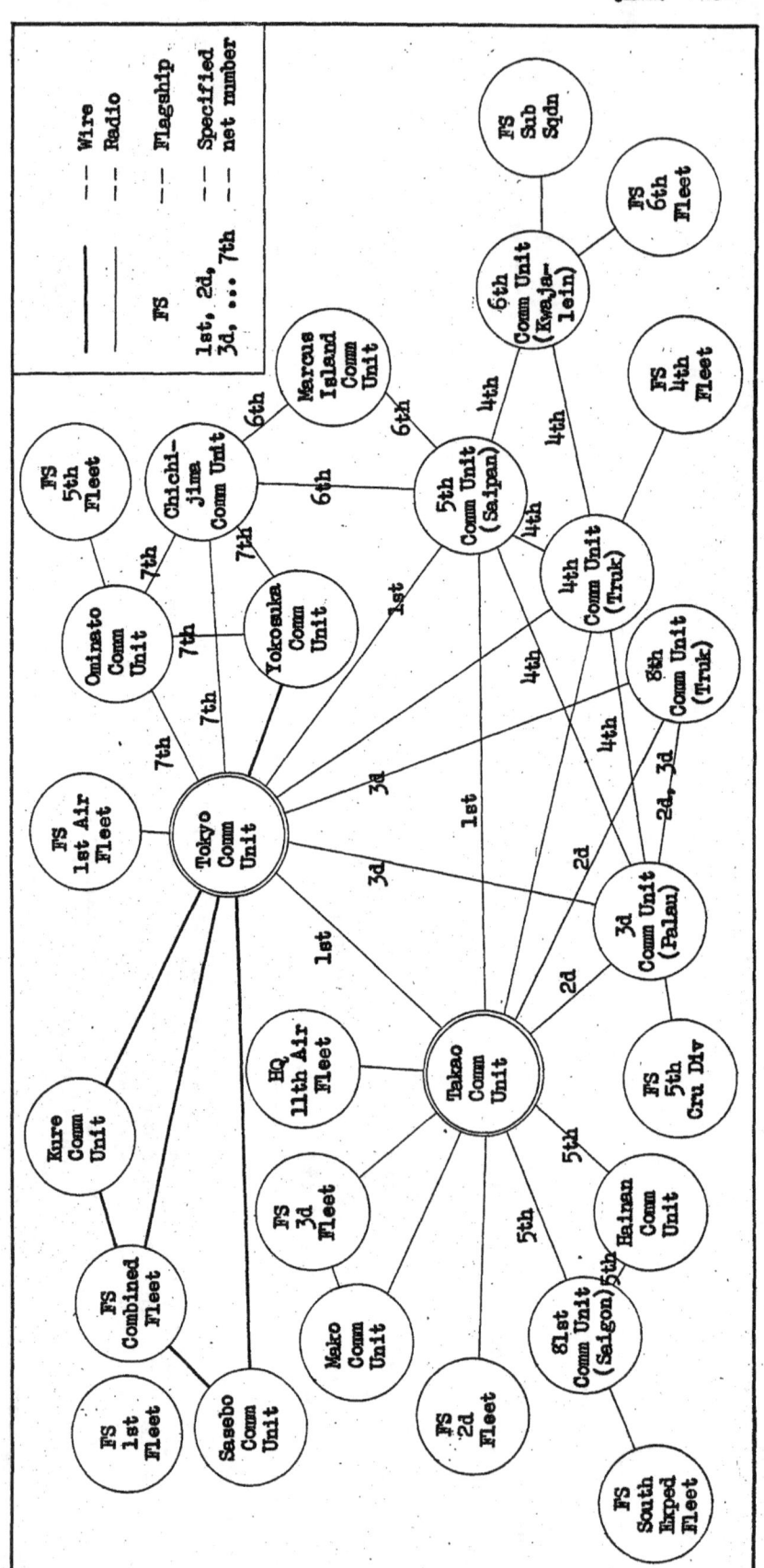

Chart 46-c

Chart 47

Communications Operations Time Chart

Classification of Communications	Commencement Time
Communications Unit Communications	0000 hours X minus 7 day
Ship communications Submarine communications	0000 hours X minus 5 day
Aircraft communications	0000 hours X minus 2 day
Special force communications	Special order

Note:

After 0000 hours X minus 2 day, the Second China Expeditionary Fleet and the Hainan Guard District will be assigned to the ship communications net until further notice.

Remarks:

1. When a force is required to commence communications disposition before the date shown in this chart, the commander of the force concerned will designate the date and notify the proper parties.

2. Commencement time of part of the force will be changed by special orders.

Communications Relay

Chart 48

Communications Unit	Communications to be relayed
Tokyo Communications Unit	The communications of the forces such as task force and commerce raiding unit which join the special communications net.
Takao Communications Unit	The communications of submarines and aircraft assigned to the Southern Force.
3d Communications Unit	The communications of 5th Submarine Squadron of the Southern Force and of aircraft based in the Palau Area.
81st Communications Unit	The communications of submarines and aircraft operating in the South China Sea.
5th Communications Unit	The communications of submarines and aircraft assigned to the South Seas Forces.
6th Communications Unit	The communications of submarines of the advance submarine force.
Remarks:	If there is no fear of interference in the operational communications of the operational force, the ship frequency will be used.

Broadcast Specifications

Chart 49-a

Comm Unit	Broadcast hours	Frequency	Message
Tokyo Comm Unit	Continuous	4175 KC (TO 14) 8350 KC (TO 15) 16700 KC (TO 16)	To the entire operational forces. 1. Important messages transmitted from the flagship of the Combined Fleet. 2. Important messages transmitted from the Central Agency. 3. General situations.
	0100 to 1600 Latter half of every odd numbered hour 1600 to 1800 Latter half of every even numbered hour	17.44 KC	The foregoing also applicable to the advance submarines and 4th and 5th Submarine Squadrons.
Takao Comm Unit	Continuous	7155 KC (SA 27) 14310 KC (SA 28)	Operationally important communications to the Southern Force.
	For 30 minutes from last quarter of each hour	Frequencies used by the 5th and 6th Submarine Squadrons.	Important communications to submarine forces of the Southern Force.
3d Comm Unit	From the half hour of every hour	7280 KC (NA 31) 14560 KC (NA 32)	Operationally important communications to the Southern Force and the Middle East Area Force.
81st Comm Unit	From the quarter of every hour	7315 KC (RE 73) 14830 KC (RE 73)	Operationally important message to the South China Sea Area Force.

Broadcast Specifications (Cont'd)　　　　　　Chart 49-b

Comm Unit	Broadcast hours	Frequency	Message
81st Comm Unit	For 20 minutes from the last quarter of every hour	Frequency used by the 4th Submarine Squadron	Important communications to the Submarines of the 4th Submarine Squadron.
6th Comm Unit	From the last quarter of every hour	5950 KC (NA 11) 11900 KC (NA 12)	Important communications to the advance force of the South Seas Force.
5th Comm Unit	From the Second quarter of every hour	4860 KC (NA 61) 9720 KC (NA 62)	Important communications to the South Seas Force and the force operating in the Nansei Islands Area.

Remarks:

1. Each communications unit will relay high frequency broadcasts of the Tokyo Communications Unit.

2. The serial numbers will be given to the broadcast communications after X minus 2 day.

3. When confirmation is necessary, the acknowledgment will be dispatched. (with pro sign 15 minutes after the receipt of the broadcast.)

4. The Tokyo Communications Unit and the Takao Communications Unit will transmit broadcast with the designated frequencies. Other units will broadcast with one night frequency but, between 1000 hours and 1600 hours, they will also use the day frequency depending upon the situation.

5. When necessary, the time of broadcast will be changed in accordance with the request (designation) of the operational force commander in the area.

6. Each communications unit will be authorized to change the frequencies according to the circumstances. In such cases, however, it will be reported in advance to the proper party.

the broadcast communications of the land-based communications unit. Each force will receive the broadcast as designated by its commander.

   5. When the main force is located within Japanese waters, the flagship of the Combined Fleet will conduct remote control of the transmitters of the Tokyo Communications Unit (or the Kure Communications Unit), or will direct the Tokyo Communications Unit to conduct communications in the name of the flagship, Combined Fleet.

   6. With the exception of special emergency messages, communications with other forces will be conducted through the communications net of the nearest land-based communications unit.

Communications Security

   1. Frequency security:

      a. The Combined Fleet Top Secret Order No 177 (Standing order for radio silence during operations) will be applicable.

   2. Message security:

      a. Code books and call signs will be based on the following orders:

         Combined Fleet Top Secret Order No 171
            (Guide for Use of Code Books)

         Combined Fleet Top Secret Order No 52
            (Combined Fleet Wartime Special Call Sign Chart)

         Combined Fleet Top Secret Order No 169
            (Strategic Communications Abbreviation Codes)

         Combined Fleet Top Secret Order No 179
            (Combined Fleet Special Operation Communications Priority Classification Code Chart)

      b. Message authentication and categorized deceptive message system will be based on:

         Combined Fleet Top Secret Instruction No 49
            (Combined Fleet Categorized Deceptive Message Security System)

  c. Date indication system will be based on:

    Combined Fleet Top Secret Instruction No 51
     (Combined Fleet Special Military Date Indication
     Code Chart)

  d. Place Indication System: See Chart 50.

Radio Intelligence

  1. The radio intelligence group assigned to the fleet will utilize enemy communications in accordance with the directives of the C in C of each fleet.

  2. The radio intelligence group assigned to the land-based communications unit will utilize enemy communications as shown in Chart 51.

  3. Unless otherwise ordered, the interference of enemy communications will be conducted in accordance with the directives of the unit commander.

  4. When known to be effective, the unit commander (the 1st Combined Communications Unit commander) will direct the nearby communications unit (subordinate communications unit) to carry out interference of enemy communications.

Army-Navy Communications Agreement for Southern Operations

The main objective of the Army-Navy Communications Agreement for the Southern Operations was to avoid radio interference by both services. Although there had been a peacetime radio frequency agreement, it had not been enforced since the power output used by the Army was not strong and the Navy had not recognized the necessity for adjustment. Because of the possibility of radio interference during the Southern Operations, the Army and Navy agreed upon a plan to avoid using frequencies which caused radio interference between the

Place Indication System

Chart 50-a

Indication System	Abbreviation	Reference	Purpose
Place Indication System No 1	CHI-HE 1	Navy Air Strategic Point Code Chart (Navy Ministry Secret No 167) will be used in accordance with the direction of Operational Communications Abbreviations and Cryptographic Book G.	Will be used in emergency for ship and aircraft communications.
Place Indication System No 2	CHI-HE 2	The reference specified in Navy Operational Communications Abbreviations A, B and Navy Cryptographic Book G.	
Place Indication System No 3	CHI-HE 3		
Place Indication System No 4	CHI-HE 4		
Place Indication System No 5	CHI-HE 5	Regulations concerning the Use of Pacific Strategic Point Map (Navy Top Secret No 585) and Pacific Strategic Point Map (Navy Top Secret No 347).	For general operations (ship communications)
Place Indication System No 6	CHI-HE 6	Navy Air Strategic Point Code Chart (Navy Ministry Secret No 167). (Paragraph 3 will be the guide for the use of Code Chart)	For aircraft communications
Place Indication System No 7	CHI-HE 7	Directions for the use of Special Strategic Point Map (Navy Ministry Top Secret No 123) and Special Strategic Point Map.	1. For Army-Navy joint operations. 2. For local operations.
Place Indication System No 8	CHI-HE 8	District Indication Map for trade security (Navy Ministry Secret No 165).	For trade security

Place Indication System (Cont'd)　　　　　　　　　　　　　Chart 50-b

Indication System	Abbreviation	Reference	Purpose
Place Indication System No 9	CHI-HE 9	Combined Fleet Wartime Emergency Strategic Point System (Combined Fleet Confidential Order No 175)	For the emergency use of CHI-HE 5. Will be used by special order.
Place Indication System No 10	CHI-HE 10	Special Point Abbreviation Chart (A), (Naval General Staff Secret No 144).	For indicating points mentioned in the messages.
Place Indication System No 11	CHI-HE 11	Combined Fleet Temporary Name of Key Point Abbreviation Chart.	For emergency use of CHI-HE 10. Will be used by special order.

Utilization of Navy Air Strategic Point Code Chart
(Navy Ministry, Secret No 167)

Type Classification	Period of Use
A	From 1 to 15 of odd-numbered month.
B	From 16 to the end of odd-numbered month.
C	From 1 to 15 of even-numbered month.
D	From 16 to the end of even-numbered month.
E	Substitutes for A B C D (By Special Order).

Chart 51

Radio Intelligence

Communications Unit	Procedure
Tokyo Communications Unit	The radio intelligence group will plot primarily the movements of the United States fleet and aircraft, and secondarily, the forces of the Soviet Union. Details will be determined by the commander of the 1st Combined Communications Unit.
Takao Communications Unit	1. The radio intelligence group will plot mainly the movements of the United States, British and Dutch vessels and aircraft. Details will be determined by the commander of the 1st Combined Communications Unit. 2. In accordance with the situation, an element will be placed under the command of the Eleventh Air Fleet commander. 3. The unit will advance to occupied areas in accordance with the progress of the Southern Operation.
Other Communications Unit	Operations data will be obtained in accordance with the direction of the 1st Combined Communications Unit commander.

two.

The agreement provided that when an Army force embarked on a naval vessel, communications were to be conducted as designated by the naval commander, and communications between the naval escort and the Army transports were to be conducted, as a rule, by direct liaison. When necessary, an element of the Navy's communications unit was to be placed aboard the ship of the ranking Army commander of the landing force to conduct the communications. During movement under surface escort, communications between the landing force and its headquarters were to be conducted under the control of the Navy escort commander. Also, the Navy was to be responsible for communications between the landing force (advance force) and its headquarters until the landing force was ashore, and, assist in the communications between the landing force and its headquarters until just after the landing. When necessary, the Navy was to provide communications between the landing force headquarters and the main headquarters in the area after the landing.

The Navy was to be responsible for providing communications for those Army forces which were directly under the command of Imperial General Headquarters and lacked communications facilities of their own.

Communications between the Army and Navy commanders in Formosa and French Indo-China were to be conducted by wire. With the exception of those facilities used exclusively by the Navy, the facilities were to be equipped and maintained by the Army. Communications between the Army and Navy Air Forces were to be conducted by radio after the Army Air Force commander's advance to Malay and the Philippines. The Navy was responsible for their radio communications, and when necessary, liaison officers and communications facilities were to be exchanged between the Army and Navy Air Forces. The Army and Navy commanders were to conclude necessary local agreements on the use of frequencies to avoid radio interference.

Under further provisions of the agreement, the Army was to cut off the submarine cables between Shanghai and Manila, Hongkong and Saigon, and Saigon and Singapore, and complete the submarine cable between Takao and Manila for the joint use of both services. The Navy was to cut off the submarine cable between Hongkong and Manila, Hongkong and Singapore, Hongkong and Labuan, and Shanghai and Hongkong. The disposition of other submarine cables were to be decided later.

Special Measures Adopted for Southern Operations

Every effort was made to expand the Takao Communications Unit as the operational communications center for the Southern Force. In addition, the 1st Combined Communications Unit headquarters was recommended to be moved to Takao to facilitate its operations but this move did not materialize. After the occupation of southern French Indo-China, the 81st Communications Unit was established at Saigon. This became the communications center for the Malay Force in the Southern Area invasion operations. Since this communications unit had an important role in the operations of the Malay Force, the communications staff of the Malay Force commander was assigned the additional duty of taking charge of this unit. Plans were also made for the strengthening of the 4th Communications Unit at Truk to serve as the operational communications center for the Inner South Seas Force (Nucleus--Fourth Fleet).

For the invasion operations, mobile communications units were activated, and, in addition to the 81st Communications Unit which was attached to the Malay Force, the 1st Communications Unit was attached to the Philippines Force in order to assure communications liaison with the Army forces as well as to maintain communications with the base forces. The broadcast capacity of the Tokyo Communications Unit had been strengthened in order to handle the increased wartime communications and to immediately transmit important operational communications to all combatant forces.

Communications in Hawaiian Operation

Communications prior to and during the Hawaiian operations were conducted in accordance with the Combined Fleet Communications Plan for First Phase Operations. Each commanding officer concerned in communications was responsible for controlling the various frequencies utilized (Chart 52).

Inasmuch as the success or failure of the operations depended

Ship Communications Nets

Chart 52

Communications Net	Frequency	Control Ship	Assigned Ship Station	Personnel on Duty
General Communications Net	Low frequency	Flagship of Air Fleet	Each vessel	Continuous
General Telephone Communications Net	Very-high frequency	"	All warships	"
First flagship telephone communications net	"	"	Each flagship and carriers	By a special order or without orders when meeting enemy
Second flagship telephone communications net	Medium frequency	"	"	Special order

Aircraft Communications Nets

Mission of Plane	Type of Frequency	Control Ship
Attack Search Local rcn	A-type high frequency	Air fleet flagship
Air control unit	A-type high frequency used by fighters	2d Carrier Division flagship
Combat air patrol	C-type (special) high frequency used by fighters	Air fleet flagship
Antisubmarine patrol	B-type low frequency	Air fleet flagship

Note: After making battle report, switch to C-type frequency.

heavily upon the effectiveness of the concealment of the plan, it was necessary to prohibit all radio transmissions after any force left its base. Transmitters were carefully checked and all possible efforts were exerted to maintain them in good condition. Some of the aircraft carriers removed a part of the transmitter circuit to prevent any unnecessary radio transmission.

In the communications between the Tokyo Communications Unit and the First Air Fleet (the carrier striking force for the assault on Hawaii), the Tokyo Communications Unit used the General Communications Net while the First Air Fleet transmitted on a special frequency. The acknowledgment to transmission was done by means of rebroadcast by the Tokyo Communications Unit. For this means, abbreviations and call signs used in the signals were similar to those used by merchant ships. Transmission conducted by special cipher was used mainly when messages of significance were transmitted such as the decision for war or peace in connection with the result of the Japanese-American negotiations just prior to the outbreak of World War II.

When the First Air Fleet departed from its training area off southern Kyushu in the middle of November 1941, the forces stationed at the air bases conducted radio deception to feign that the First Air Fleet was still training in this area. By the end of the month, the Fleet had rendezvoused at Hitokappu Bay and all communications from Etorofu Island were placed under strict control to prevent any exposure of its movements. During this period, all communications were sent to the Ominato Communications Unit by aircraft and were handled by that unit.

The flagship of the 3d Battleship Division was designated as the communications ship for the Combined Fleet and all communications with other forces were controlled by this ship. Messages to the Fleet were sent via the 1st Broadcast Net of the Tokyo Communications Unit and messages originating within the Fleet were sent via the Special Communications Net of the same unit.

Communications with fighter planes were conducted by radiotelephone. However, when fighter units advanced 200 miles or more in conducting joint operations with the attack planes, radiotelegraph was used. All fighter pilots had been trained in aircraft radiotelegraph communications so that even air patrol command was executed by telegraphic communications.

Fighter planes operating within 100 miles of their carriers were brought home by the homing device. Planes operating beyond 100 miles of the carrier returned by means of navigation or were guided back by the carrier bombers.

For communications with submarines in operation, transmission was by very-low frequency (17.5 KC). The low frequency transmitter at Yosami, controlled by the Tokyo Communications Unit, was used for this purpose and broadcast was conducted as the 4th Broadcast of the Tokyo Communications Unit.

Communications in the Indian Ocean Operation

The communications plan of this operation was similar to the communications plan of the Hawaiian operation. Instead of the Tokyo Communications Unit, the 10th Communications Unit (Singapore) and the 21st Communications Unit (Soerabaja) served as the communications centers for this operation.

Before the commencement of attack, one destroyer was dispatched to Ten Degree Channel from the waters west of Sumatra to report by radio the attack plan and subsequent movements of our force. These radio messages were handled by the broadcast net of the 10th Communications Unit via the local communications net of this unit and the 1st Broadcast Net of the Tokyo Communications Unit.

The day before the first attack on Colombo, the Japanese force was contacted by an enemy flying boat. However, the flying boat was shot down while it was transmitting information. It was confirmed by the interception of the enemy communications that the enemy had received no important information on the approach of the Japanese force.

CHAPTER IX

Communications in Second Phase Operations

Communications Plan for Midway Operation

The communications plan of the Combined Fleet during the Midway Operation will be conducted in accordance with the following procedures as well as in accordance with the Second Phase Operations Communications Plan of the Combined Fleet.

1. Fleet communications:

    a. Apply the third frequency system of the ship communications, second strategic communications assignment; second frequency system of the aircraft communications; very strict radio silence for high and medium frequencies; strict radio silence for low and very-high frequencies.

    b. Communications between the invasion force, task force and screening force will be conducted by the Combined Fleet common high frequency or the flagship high frequency.

    c. The Tokyo Communications Unit will receive and broadcast the messages from the Midway Operation forces and relay them to forces as required.

2. Radio intelligence:

    a. The main objective of radio intelligence by the 1st Combined Communications Unit is to pick up information concerning the movements of the enemy task force and to detect what the enemy knows of our force's movements.

    b. Jamming will be conducted as designated by each force commander.

    c. Radio deception will be conducted according to the plan of the Kure Naval District commandant. It will be conducted by elements of the forces stationed in Japan with the objective of leading the enemy to believe that the bulk of the Combined Fleet is deployed and training off southern Kyushu and in the western part of the Inland Sea. The C in C, Combined Fleet will give special orders for all other matters.

(See Chart 53 for Combined Fleet Communications Net)

Communications Plan for 1st Task Force

The communications plan for the 1st Task Force will be in accordance with the Communications Plan of the Combined Fleet Midway Operation as well as in accordance with the following:

1. Communications within the force:

    a. Communications among the screening force, invasion forces and the task force will be conducted by the Combined Fleet common high frequency and the Combined Fleet flagship high frequency.

    b. Each ship will be tuned in continuously on the broadcast of the Tokyo Communications Unit.

2. Radio intelligence:

    a. The main objective will be to intercept enemy aircraft and submarine communications and derive information about the enemy.

    b. Jamming will be conducted by special order. However, each division commander will conduct it whenever the division flagship recognizes it to be expedient.

3. Visual communications:

    Visual communications will be used chiefly for communications during cruises.

4. Emergency communications:

    a. In case the communications capacity of the fleet flagship is decreased or is lost, one ship of the 3d Battleship Division will conduct the flagship communications in place of the fleet flagship.

    b. In case of a decrease in the communications capacity, the Priority of manning will be as follows:

Chart 53

Communications Net for Midway Operation

- Air Units
- Air Units
- Submarines
- 4th Carrier Division
- 1st Air Fleet
- 6th Comm Unit (6th Fleet) (Kwajalein)
- 1st Fleet
- 2d Fleet
- 5th Fleet
- Combined Fleet
- Wake Is Base
- Chichijima Comm Unit
- Marcus Is Comm Unit
- 4th Comm Unit (Truk)
- 5th Comm Unit (Saipan)
- Shumushu Comm Unit
- Yokosuka Comm Unit
- 3d Comm Unit (Palau)
- Ominato Comm Unit
- Tokyo Comm Unit
- Takao Comm Unit
- Sasebo Comm Unit
- Kure Comm Unit
- Radio deception
- Air Base
- Vessels

Legend:
- ―――― Wire
- ────── Radio
- ━━━━━ 1st Combined Comm Force
- *

257

(1) Communications within force
(2) The Tokyo broadcast
(3) Communications with other forces
(4) Aircraft communications
(5) Submarine communications
(6) Radio intelligence

Communications in the Midway Operation

The 1st Task Force and the screening force sailed out of the Inland Sea on 27 May 1942 while the invasion force left Saipan on the evening of 28 May. Maintaining strict radio silence, they reached the waters northwest and west of Midway.

The Task Force encountered dense fog from approximately 1000 hours of 2 June to 2300 hours 3 June. Visual communications were impossible during these hours. According to the interception of enemy aircraft communications, the range of the enemy patrol planes from Midway Island was 500 miles. Since it was believed that air reconnaissance by the enemy was being conducted very thoroughly, the force changed its course to the north. However, it was still very foggy and there was no promise of its lifting in that vicinity. Consequently the only alternative was to return to the first course. At 1030 hours on 3 June, an order was transmitted with the common low frequency which read:

"At 1200 hours, change to course 100 degrees."

Thus, a large force changed its course in the fog. Soon after the change in course, the fog began to lift and visual communications became barely possible.

The Task Force reached a point approximately 200 miles northwest of Midway on 5 June and launched an attack unit at 0130 hours and finished its bombing run on Midway between 0345 and 0410 hours, after which the attack unit commander sent an important dispatch at 0400 hours stating:

"There is a need of second attack on Midway."

The Task Force commander received this dispatch four and a half minutes later. For the second attack, the attack unit was alerted with the order, "Equip attack planes for land bombing." This dispatch was acknowledge by the other carriers at 0415 hours. At 0500 hours, the force received the following dispatch from No 4 plane of the Tone:

"Ten vessels which appear to be enemy sighted at a position 240 miles, bearing 10 degrees from Midway; course 150, speed 20 knots, 0428 hours."

There was no subsequent report concerning the type of vessels and an order was transmitted immediately to the contact plane, asking the type of vessles. In reply, the force received the dispatch as follows at about 0530 hours:

"The enemy has what appears to be a carrier in the rear of the column, 0520 hours."

This was the first report concerning an enemy carrier. Then one "Judy" from CV Soryu sighted at 0530 hours an Enterprise-class carrier in the north. However, because of the malfunctioning of the transmitter, this was reported after the bomber returned to the carrier. This was the second report on the enemy carrier.

By this time, attack units of every carrier had been alerted. Meanwhile the first attack unit, which had been committed to Midway, returned at about 0600 hours, and was then ordered to launch the attack on the enemy carrier. However, the planned attack on the enemy fleet did not materialize as the enemy took the initiative at this critical moment. At approximately 0730 hours, the CV's Akagi, Kaga and Soryu were hit by bombs almost simultaneously and set afire. As a result, their communications became impossible, and even when the emergency communications plan was undertaken, communications remained temporarily in a state of considerable confusion. The fleet headquarters was then transferred at 0746 hours to the CL Nagara, which took command and placed communications under control. However, signal communications and radio communications were not efficiently executed due to shortage of equipment and personnel.

The invasion of Midway was suspended as all the carriers suffered heavy damage and the Japanese force was ordered to withdraw. In order to expedite the retreat of the operational force, the C in C, Combined Fleet made plans for the nucleus of the 5th Cruiser Division to lure the enemy pursuit force within the range of the land-based air strength on Wake. The nucleus of the 5th Cruiser Division conducted radio deception to indicate that a large force was operating in that area. However, no information was obtained on the effectiveness of this radio deception.

The aircraft communications were, on the whole, efficiently conducted from the time of the initial Midway attack. After the <u>Akagi</u>, <u>Kaga</u> and the <u>Soryu</u> were hit by bombs, the carrier <u>Hiryu</u> took over their entire aircraft communications. However, its communications capacity was too limited to control the planes of other carriers. Attack units were launched twice from the <u>Hiryu</u> but considerable confusion resulted due to maladjustment of the transmitters and poor tuning.

Operations of the 1st Combined Communications Unit

During this operation, the 1st Combined Communications Unit intercepted information on the movements of enemy air forces and submarines. It detected signs of the enemy task force's plan to sortie from Hawaii; however, no further information was available on the enemy's subsequent movements. It also detected and reported to friendly forces the intensification of enemy patrols in the Midway area. Information regarding enemy submarine activities was obtained to some extent. On one specific occasion when the screening force and the 1st Task Force left Bungo Channel for the attack, the communications unit intercepted a long dispatch from an enemy submarine. From this interception, it was surmised that the enemy had gained knowledge of the Japanese movements. It was further ascertained that the enemy knew of the Japanese invasion force from

Saipan and that later two or three enemy submarines were tracking this force.

On 3 June a plain message was intercepted and its source was presumed to have been from an enemy patrol boat. On 4 June, further enemy plain messages were intercepted, the text of which indicated that enemy aircraft were flying by radio homing device. Every time an enemy attack plane unit took off (5 June), aircraft radio messages were intercepted. Although the messages were not clear, the closing-in of the enemy planes was determinable by the increases of sensitivity in interception and this information was utilized by the antiaircraft defense commands. Also on 5 June, enemy aircraft communications were intercepted by the carrier <u>Akagi</u> and simultaneous jamming was conducted in accordance with the prearranged plan.

Northern Force Communications Plan

The communications plan of the Northern Force will be in accordance with the Midway Operation Communications Plan of the Combined Fleet as well in accordance with the following:

1. Communications within the force

    a. Ship communications:

    (1) Very strict radio silence will be maintained for high and medium frequencies and strict radio silence for other frequencies. Complete radio silence will be maintained before the commencement of air attacks.

(2) Communications assignment: (Chart 54)

Communications Net	Frequency	Manning Standard
Common Communications Net	High frequency	In encounter with enemy or by a special order
Common Communications Net	Low frequency	Continuous
Common Radio-telephone Communications Net	Medium frequency	Continuous (secondary use during day)
Common Radio-telephone Communications Net	Very-high frequency	Continuous
Flagship Communications Net	Medium frequency	Continuous (primary use during day)

Chart 54

(3) The minimum range promulgating frequencies covering the distance between each force will be used for the communications between forces. The use of long range promulgating frequencies, especially high frequencies, will be restricted.

(4) Every possible effort will be exerted to utilize relay broadcasts by the Ominato and the Shumushu Communications Units.

(5) The force flagship (CA Nachi) will serve as intermediary between the Shumushu Communications Unit and the operational force in the Kiska area. It will be responsible for the relay of the low frequency communications and for the prevention of the operational force from using high frequencies prematurely.

b. Aircraft communications:

This will be conducted in accordance with the decision of the 2d Task Force commander.

c. Submarine communications:

    Details will be initiated by the submarine force commander. The communications from the submarine force will be broadcast by the Tokyo and the Ominato Communications Units. However, each unit will endeavor to receive directly all communications concerning its own operations. As a standard procedure, the communications to the submarines will be conducted through the flagship of each squadron concerned.

2. Communications with other forces:

    a. The communications with the 1st Task Force and the screening force will be conducted with the common high frequency of the Combined Fleet or the high frequency of fleet flagships.

    b. The Ominato and the Shumushu Communications Units will cooperate mainly with the Northern Force concerning the operational communications.

3. Communications with the Occupation Forces:

    Communications detachments will be assigned to both the Kiska and Attu Occupation Forces. One ship from each occupation force will be assigned as the communications ship.

4. Radio intelligence

    The main targets of interception will be radio transmissions from enemy submarines and enemy land-based aircraft. The details of the operation will be set forth by each force commander.

Communications Plan for 2d Task Force

This will be conducted in accordance with the operational communications plan of the Northern Force as well as in accordance with the following:

1. Ship communications:

    a. Very strict radio silence of frequencies other than the very-high frequency will be observed.

b. Visual communications will be used mainly during cruise. In case visual communications are impossible, communications will be conducted mainly with the very-high frequency of the common radiotelephone communications net of the force. However, before the commencement of attack, the use of the radiotelephone will be controlled as much as possible except when tactically unavoidable or necessary for safety. In case communications are impossible with these procedures, the Northern Force common communications net (low frequency) will be utilized.

c. Communications Nets (Chart 55)

Communications Net	Frequency	Manning Standard
Common Radiotelephone Communications Net of the Northern Force	Very-high frequency	Continuous
Common Communications Net	Medium frequency	Continuous

Chart 55

d. As a standard procedure, each ship (unit) will obtain the operational information of the Northern Force by monitoring the broadcasts of the Ominato and the Shumushu Communications Units and by directly receiving the information from the Northern Force common communications net.

e. The flagship of the 4th Carrier Division will control the communications within the force, and if necessary, will be responsible for the relay of the messages to all ships.

f. Important information will be notified or relayed by the force flagship.

g. In order to avoid the force flagship's failure of receiving an important message, the second carrier of the 4th Cruiser Division will ascertain whether the flagship received it.

h. The flagship of the 4th Cruiser Division will be in charge of the communications with other forces.

i. The communications from other forces will be received as follows:

>Tokyo broadcast: Each ship to receive communications.

>Communications from submarines operating along the northwest coast of North America: One ship of the 4th Carrier Division will be responsible as the communications ship in charge. The messages will be relayed and broadcast by the Ominato and the Shumushu Communications Units.

>Other communications: The warships (carriers and the 2d Subdivision of the 4th Cruiser Division) will receive communications by combined monitoring system.

j. As a rule, air combat communications will not be relayed.

2. Aircraft communications: (Chart 56)

Communications Net	Frequencies	Control
Search plane	A-type high frequency	Flagship of 4th Carrier Division
Attack plane	A-type high frequency	Flagship of 4th Carrier Division
Fighter group	Fighter plane A-type high frequency	Flagship of 4th Carrier Division
Air patrol	Fighter plane A-type high frequency	Flagship of 4th Carrier Division
Antisubmarine patrol plane	A-type low frequency	Flagship of 4th Carrier Division
Homing low frequency	B-type low frequency	2d Carrier of 4th Carrier Division

Note:
　　1. After the command plane makes the battle report, the attack plane group will switch to B-type high frequency. However, in case the control over the homing communications of the flagship of the 4th Carrier Division is difficult, switch to the C-type frequency of the planes of the second carrier.
　　2. For homing communications, the carrier bombers and attack planes will primarily use high frequency for communications and low frequency for direction finding. Homing device will be used as a secondary means.
　　3. As a rule, the fighter planes will be guided home by carrier bombers. However, in case of independent flight, they will utilize the homing device.

Chart 56

3. Radio intelligence:

 a. Special attention will be directed toward the utilization of the data of the 1st Combined Communications Unit.

b. The main targets of interception to be conducted by each carrier will be radio transmissions from enemy patrol planes and submarines. The second carrier of the 4th Carrier Division will be in charge of interception.

c. The communications from the enemy observation posts on the Aleutian Islands will be monitored. Jamming will be conducted by special order.

Communications in the Aleutians Operation

Since this operation was planned and conducted in concert with the Midway operation, its communications plan was formulated in accordance with the Combined Fleet Communications Plan mentioned previously.

Great emphasis was placed on the concealment of the plan and it was necessary to minimize the use of long promulgating frequencies. With the expectation of dense fog, it was necessary to secure radiotelephone communications by very-high frequency because of difficulty of visual communications.

The operational force was comprised of various units which were hastily assembled on the very day of departure for attack. Therefore, it was not expedient to adopt a special communications method other than the one generally used in the Combined Fleet. Also in order to be thoroughly familiar with the battle progress of the Midway operation, it was necessary to monitor the radio traffic of the friendly forces concerned through the main communications net of the Midway operational force.

The flagship of the Northern Force operated between Kiska and Paramushiro and took charge of the operational command by the low frequency communications net via the Shumushu Communications Unit. It also relayed low frequency communications between the Shumushu Communications Unit and the forces engaged in operations in this area.

The 2d Task Force sailed from Ominato on 26 May. The main body and the Attu Occupation Force left Ominato on 27 May while the screening force left the western part of the Inland Sea on 28 May. They all operated according to schedule, maintaining strict radio silence. The 2d Task Force advanced to the waters south of Dutch Harbor on 4 June. It launched the first attack unit at 0107 hours for a successful surprise attack. The air squadrons of CVE Junyo (second carrier) turned back, unable to locate their targets due to heavy fog. Only the air squadrons of the CV Ryujo were able to make a successful attack and conducted communications as planned. As a result, most planes of the second attack squadron had to return individually owing to encounters with enemy interceptors. Moreover, as the bulk of the carrier bombers assigned as guides for the fighter planes lost their positions, a considerable number of the fighters returned by aid of the homing device. Even some of the carrier bombers returned to the carriers guided by fighter planes flying by the aid of the homing device.

One carrier bomber lost its position and its low frequency

transmitter was inoperative because of flak hits. When it was learned that it had no homing device, the carrier guided the bomber's return by high frequency, but it did not sight the carrier due to heavy fog and crashed after running out of fuel. The carrier, being unaware of this, had continued transmitting on high frequency risking detection by the enemy.

On the following morning just before the third attack squadron was about to launch an attack on Dutch Harbor, the 2d Task Force received the following dispatch from the C in C of the Combined Fleet:

> "The 2d Task Force will head southward immediately and join the 1st Task Force."

Thus, the launching of the attack squadron was cancelled. Soon after the force headed southward, it was ordered:

> "Rendezvous with the 1st Task Force is cancelled. The 2d Task Force will continue support of the Kiska and Attu occupation operations."

The force reversed course and launched the attack squadron to attack the air base on Adak Island. The attack was a success and all aircraft, both carrier bombers and carrier fighters, returned to their carriers mainly by the aid of the homing device.

In regard to radio intelligence, each carrier had clearly intercepted the communications of enemy patrol planes which were searching for the 2d Task Force in the heavy fog. As the enemy conducted radiotelephone communications, approach of the enemy planes was detected beforehand by the details of the message and the increase in sensitivity. This enabled the Japanese to alert combat patrol planes and antiaircraft stations. In one instance, antiaircraft guns shot down an enemy torpedo bomber approaching at low altitude through heavy fog. In another instance, the communications officer made the following analysis:

> "The sensitivity of the radiotelephone from the enemy flying boat is maximum. It is certain that the enemy plane is circling overhead."

Three fighter planes were alerted, took off and as soon as these fighters got above the fog, the enemy aircraft was contacted and shot down.

After the Kiska and Attu occupation operations were practically completed, the Northern Force commander on 19 June ordered the screening force and the main body of the Northern Force as well as the 2d Task Force to return to Ominato. They returned to Ominato on 23 June and immediately took on supplies and commenced preparations for the next mission.

During this period, the 1st and 2d Submarine Squadrons, a flying boat unit and a subchaser division remained in the battle theater. In order surface force had returned to Ominato, the Northern Force commander ordered the Kiska and the Attu Communications Detachments, the Ominato Communications Unit and the submarine division stationed there to conduct radio deception. Its effect was not confirmed.

From the day before the return of the surface force to Ominato, a considerable volume of communications in regards to supply and repair were conducted by the short-distance communications net of the Ominato Communications Unit. The radio wave frequency was not far reaching but the enemy may have had intercepted the communications.

Communications in the Solomons Area Operation

The plan was mapped out for the invasion operation of Port Moresby and Tulagi after the capture of New Britain, New Ireland, Lae, Salamaua, Bougainville and the Admiralty Islands. The purpose of this operation was to isolate strategic areas of the British territory of Eastern New Guinea and the Solomons from Australia and gain command of the Coral Sea. In May 1942, the Japanese forces made successful landings at Tulagi and Gavutu.

On 7 and 8 May, the Japanese surface force engaged in battle with an enemy task force in the Coral Sea. The engagement developed into a major sea battle which ultimately resulted in heavy Japanese losses. The C in C, Combined Fleet therefore ordered on 10 May the postponement of the Port Moresby operation to July in consideration of the forthcoming operation. The C in C, Fourth Fleet made preparations to capture Nauru and Ocean with elements of his Fleet. However, he cancelled this operation upon receiving information that an enemy task force had been located to the east of the Solomons. On 18 June, in accordance with the directive of Imperial General Headquarters, the C in C, Combined Fleet postponed the slated Port

Moresby operation and ordered the C in C, Fourth Fleet to conduct a study to capture Port Moresby by land. At the time, the enemy strength in the Port Moresby area was gradually being increased while Japanese forces rushed the construction of air bases in the Solomons, Bismarck, Lae and Salamaua areas.

In view of the prevailing circumstances in these areas, the Eighth Fleet was activated on 14 July to take over from the Fourth Fleet the operations of the Bismarck, Solomon and New Guinea areas. The Eighth Fleet reorganized the 8th Communications Unit stationed at Rabaul to effect flagship communications. (Details of Eighth Fleet communications are discussed in later section of this chapter)

In the early morning of 7 August, the enemy task force and assault force attacked Tulagi and Guadalcanal and commenced landing operations. Immediately the entire Japanese air strength available in the Rabaul area was alerted to counterattack this enemy. Surface units also participated by engaging in a night attack. However, Tulagi and air bases on Guadalcanal were lost, although considerable damage was inflicted on the enemy.

In the meanwhile, the Eleventh Air Fleet headquarters advanced to Rabaul from Tinian on 7 August to direct land-based air operations. From this time on, the enemy's counteroffensives from the Solomons and Eastern New Guinea were gradually intensified.

On 24 December, the Southeast Area Fleet composed of the Eleventh Air Fleet and the Eighth Fleet was activated at Rabaul and the post of C in C of this newly activated Area Fleet was assumed concurrently by C in C, Eleventh Air Fleet. Paralleling the organizational change, its operational communications center was also established at Rabaul. What actually resulted was that both the Eleventh Air Fleet and the Eighth Fleet had communications centers at Rabaul independently. The possibility of a merger of these two had often been discussed, but because of their respective special operational duties, they remained as separate entities and such a merger was not realized until the Rabaul area was entirely isolated.

Communications Plan of the South Seas Force for Port Moresby Operation

This plan will be based on the Second Phase Operations Communications Plan of the Combined Fleet and supplemented with the following details:

1. Ship communications:

    a. Apply the second strategic communications disposition: Very strict radio silence for high frequency, medium frequency (day) and strict radio silence for other frequencies.

    b. The 4th and 8th Communications Units will give their fullest cooperation to operational communications.

2. Air communications:

    a. Air communications will be as designated by the commander of the Port Moresby Operation Task Force.

    b. Important communications in the air operations of the 25th Air Flotilla, which will cooperate in this operation, will be broadcast by the 4th and 8th Communications Units.

3. Submarine Communications:

    a. Radio messages from submarine units will be received and relayed by the 8th Communications Unit.

4. Communications with occupation forces:

    a. Communications detachments (dispatched from the 8th Communications Unit) will be assigned to the Moresby Occupation Force and its Support Force.

    b. Immediately upon the occupation of Moresby and other strategic points, each communications detachment will set up a land communications base and join the local communications net of the 8th Communications Unit.

    c. Communications liaison with the occupation force on Tulagi will be decided by the 8th Base Force commander.

5. Communications with forces other than the occupation forces:

    a. This will be handled by the 4th Communications Unit. Communications through the ship communications net will be the standard procedure for communications between the 4th Communications Unit and the Moresby Occupation Force. However, the Combined Fleet and the Moresby Occupation Force communications net will receive directly and relay communications. The 8th Communications Unit will cooperate in such communications.

6. Radio intelligence:

    a. Utilization of enemy communications: The radio intelligence groups of the 4th and 6th Communications Units will cooperate in this operation. Their main duty will be to detect the movements of the enemy task force and land-based air forces.

    b. Jamming will be conducted as designated by each force commander.

<u>Port Moresby Occupation Force Communications Plan</u>

    This will be based on the following as well as in accordance with the Communications Plan of the South Seas Force for Port Moresby Operation.

1. Ship communications:

    a. Communications nets (Chart 57)

Communications Net	Frequency	Manning Standard	
Common Communications Net	High frequency & Low frequency	By special order or when encountering enemy	
Common Radiotelephone Communications Net	Medium frequency	Primary use for day	Continuous
	Very-high frequency	Primary use for night	
Flagship Radiotelephone Communications Net	Medium frequency	Continuous	

Chart 57

   b. The Combined Fleet common communications net will be used for communications between forces.

   c. The 4th and 8th Communications Units will cooperate in the communications of this operation.

   d. Visual communications will be used mainly for communications with a unit within sight.

   e. Each force will strive for direct reception of radio from land-based aircraft.

   f. Communications from submarines will be relayed by the 4th and 8th Communications Unit. However, each force will also endeavor to receive the communications directly as designated by its commander.

2. Communications with the Occupation Force:

   a. Immediately upon landing at Tulagi, the land combat force will join the local communications net of the 8th Communications Unit. Until liaison is completely established with this net, communications must be secured with the flagship (CM <u>Okinoshima</u>) of the Occupation Force.

b. The communications detachment of the 8th Communications Unit assigned to the Port Moresby Occupation Force and its Support Force will join the local communications net of the 8th Communications Unit immediately upon landing. However, until liaison is completely established in this net, communications must be secured with the flagship for the Occupation or the Support Force.

3. Radio intelligence:

a. The target of interception of each force will be enemy air force and submarines.

b. Jamming will be conducted by special orders. However, when considered effective, each force commander is authorized to conduct jamming according to his own decision.

Communications Plan of the Port Moresby Task Force and Air Force
(29 April 1942)

The communications of the Port Moresby Task Force and Air Force will be conducted in accordance with the following as well as in accordance with the South Seas Force Top Secret Operations Order No 13 and the Port Moresby Task Force Top Secret Operation Order No 1:

1. Ship communications:

   a. Ship communications in group movement will be conducted by visual signal.

   b. Special orders will be issued for manning the radio frequency for communications within the force.

   c. Any vessel maneuvering outside the limit of visibility will utilize the common medium frequency (if necessary the Fourth Fleet common high frequency) without specific order.

   d. The 5th Carrier Division flagship will relay important aircraft communications to the South Seas Force by the common high frequency of the Fourth Fleet (or Combined Fleet common high frequency or the flagship high frequency, depending upon situation).

2. Aircraft communications:

   a. The standard procedure for communications from aircraft to ship will be by broadcast (repeating the entire message two times) except very important dispatches.

   b. (See Chart 58)

   c. When a search plane succeeds in maintaining contact with the enemy fleet, the contact plane will transmit on low frequency, and utilizing the homing device, the attack planes will assemble over the enemy. If circumstance requires, the flagship of the 5th Cruiser Division will find the direction of the contact plane while the second vessel of the same division will find the direction of the attack squadron and guide the attack squadron toward the enemy fleet.

   d. Radio wave transmission for a plane's homing (or assembling) will be conducted as shown in Chart 59.

   e. When planes are overdue, they may transmit low frequency to be calibrated on board the ship and utilize the bearing in homing. In this case, however, the homing frequency should be the C-type low frequency (for CV Zuikaku, HI-76; for CV Shokaku, HI-7) and the C-type high frequency of each ship.

3. Communications with other forces:

   The receiving of communications of those forces other than the Occupation Force will be conducted as designated by each commander and as stipulated in Chart 60.

4. Call sign list:

   This will be based on the designation of the Combined Fleet as well as on the following:

   a. Special call signs of the 5th Carrier Division are applicable only at the time of air attack against land targets. (F-10, RI-SA-B will be used in case of air attack against enemy vessels).

   b. The First Air Fleet special call signs may be applied only for communications using Type-B frequencies. This is limited to communications of carrier bomber units and inter-unit communications.

Aircraft Communications   Chart 58

Aircraft	Frequency	Notes	
Reconnaissance seaplanes of 5th Cruiser Division	TA-HI 740 (7035 KC)	Intra-unit communications plan (4th Air Communications assignment)	
Carrier attack planes and bombers of the 5th Carrier Division			
Carrier bombers and fighters of the 5th Carrier Division or Reconnaissance seaplanes of 5th Cruiser Division	HI 7 (359 KC)		
Reconnaissance seaplanes of 5th Cruiser Division	TA-HI 740		
Fighters of 5th Carrier Division	TA-HI 743 (4660 KC)	In charge of communications	2d Subdivision of 5th Carrier Division
	TA-HI 744 (4285 KC)		5th Carrier Division Flagship

Reference

1. In the event of contact with enemy ships, consecutive dashes will be transmitted without orders, (inserting one's own call sign properly) and use the following low frequency in order to guide the attack unit:
    Reconnaissance seaplanes of the 5th Cruiser Division -- "HI 22" (423 KC); carrier attack planes and bombers of the 5th Carriers Division -- "HI 7" (359 KC).

2. In the event the attack unit returns to the assembly point after completing the attack (or when the search unit completes its duty), it will switch to the designated C-type high frequency of its ship.

Chart 59

Homing Procedure

Transmitting ship (or plane)	Call sign	Frequency	Transmitting procedure
Shokaku	SE	(23)	Transmit dashes consecutively, inserting this call sign properly. Transmit when necessary
Aircraft of CV Zuikaku	SU 1	HI 7	Transmit when necessary
Aircraft of CV Shokaku	SE 1		
Reconnaissance seaplanes (Cover unit)	E	HI 7	1. (HO-TE-HI-7) for commencement of transmission and (HO-TE-YA-ME) for ending will be ordered specially. 2. Transmit dashes consecutively inserting this call sign properly.

Receiving of Communications

Chart 60

No	Communications Classification	Frequency	5th Carrier Division Flagship	2d Sub-Div of 5th Carrier Division	27th Destroyer Div
1	4th Communications Unit Broadcast	4860 9720			
2	Fourth Fleet General high frequency	TA-UN 16 TA-UN 216	*		
3	Fourth Fleet Flagship	TA-UN 17 TA-UN 217	*		
4	Combined Fleet general high frequency				
5	Re-transmission of Sixth Fleet Headquarters	TA-UN 51 TA 325	*		
6	8th Submarine Squadron (3d and 14th Submarine Divisions) Class A	TA-UN 52 TA-UN 325	(0400) (1600)	*	
7	7th Submarine Squadron (21st Submarine Division) Class A	TA-UN 60	*		
8	Fourth Fleet (planes of 6th and 19th Cruiser Divisions, Kamikawa Maru and Kiyokawa Maru)	TA-HI 4		"	
9	Eleventh Air Fleet (planes of 5th Air Attack Force)	TA-HI 16	*		
10	Tokyo Communications Unit			*	

Notes: 1. * Indicates communications control ship. This ship will relay communications within the 5th Carrier Division by means of visual signals when necessary.

2. Receiving of communications of the 81st, 82d and 83d Communications Nets will be done by special orders.

    c. Interception of enemy communications will be conducted by special orders.

Communications of the Tulagi Occupation Force

The bulk of the Tulagi Occupation Force made its operational preparations at Rabaul and Truk. It completed rendezvous at Rabaul on 29 April and made arrangements for operational communications. The Occupation Force sailed from Rabaul on the 29th and the 30th. Maintaining strict radio silence, the force advanced according to schedule and at dawn of 3 May, it conducted successful landing operations at Tulagi and Gavutu Islands and completely occupied these islands without meeting any hostile opposition. The Occupation Force immediately established a temporary communications station and commenced communications with CM <u>Okinoshima</u>, the flagship of the Occupation Force. By evening of the same day, it commenced communications with the 8th Communications Unit. In these communications, high frequencies were used, but night communications from about 2300 to about 0400 hours were unsatisfactory.

The Japanese force on 4 May. At the time of this enemy raid, the lookout communications net had not been completed. The Japanese had depended upon the patrol of flying boats based on Shortland Island and was unable to obtain any other information beforehand.

At 1200 hours on 4 May, a change in task organization was ordered which deactivated the Tulagi Occupation Force, and its surface strength was allotted to the Port Moresby Occupation Force, the

Bismarck Area Force and the Ocean-Nauru Occupation Force.

Communications of the Port Moresby Occupation Operation
(Battle of the Coral Sea)

The Port Moresby Task Force sailed from Truk on 1 May, maintaining strict radio silence, and proceeded southward toward the east side of the Solomons. Upon receiving a report on 4 May that enemy carrier planes attacked Tulagi, the Task Force immediately headed south toward Tulagi. The Port Moresby Occupation Force sailed from Rabaul on 4 May. On 5 May, the main body of the Port Moresby Occupation Force was attacked by enemy land-based aircraft. A wide search for the enemy was conducted by land-based attack planes and flying boats of the 25th Air Flotilla but no information on the enemy was obtained. At 0810 hours, 6 May, a flying boat reported the sighting of an enemy task force composed of one carrier, one battleship, three cruisers and five destroyers (course 190 degrees, and speed 15 knots) at a point 420 miles, bearing 192 degrees from Tulagi. This was the first dispatch of information on an enemy carrier. The flying boat maintained contact with the enemy but lost it at 0900 hours. The opportunity was lost in maintaining contact and attacking the enemy before sunset. The same day, the Japanese convoy was detected by enemy B-17's. Consequently, the enemy had obtained an overall picture of the whole Japanese force.

In the early morning of 7 May, the enemy's large type land-based planes attacked the convoy. Search planes were launched at

0400 hours, and at 0530 hours, one of the planes detected a large tanker 163 miles, bearing 182 degrees from the Japanese carrier. The plane had mistakenly identified it as an enemy carrier, but as a result of the original report, the entire attack squadron was immediately launched at 0610 hours. At 0640 hours, a seaplane from CA Kinugasa detected a task force comprised of one carrier, two battleships, two cruisers and seven destroyers at a point 82 miles, bearing 170 degree from Rossel Island. However, as change of the attack objective was impossible due to the limited range of the attack squadron, it attacked the large tanker and one destroyer between 0930 and 0940 hours. Aircraft communications were conducted without any trouble.

Upon receiving a report of sighting an enemy task force, the Occupation Force retired temporarily at 0700 hours to the northwest. While making attack preparations, the CVL Shoho received concentrated attacks by enemy carrier planes between 0910 and 0935 hours and was sunk.

As the Japanese Task Force had missed the chance of attacking in the morning owing to the erroneous report of a search plane, night fighters took off to attack the enemy task force. However, they failed to locate the enemy due to inclement weather prevailing in the vicinity and instead encountered enemy fighters. After waging a short dogfight, they broke formation and returned to the carrier. Communications during this attack were effected very smoothly as the operators concerned were of superior caliber. In another report, a seaplane of CA Kinugasa sighted an enemy task force and immediately, land-based attack squadrons took off at 0750 and 0900 hours and attacked the enemy between 1230 and 1244 hours. The communications of these attack squadrons were also conducted smoothly and efficiently.

With the plan for a night action, the 6th Cruiser Division and the 6th Destroyer Squadron advanced toward the enemy. However, since the search plane lost contact with the enemy, the plan was dropped, thus ending the 7 May action. During that night, each force maintained strict radio silence.

On 8 May, the Japanese Task Force launched search planes at 0400 hours. At 0624 hours, the planes sighted the enemy and transmitted the first dispatch. All attack squadrons took off at 0715 hours.

At 0740 and 0750 hours, the search planes of CV Shokaku reported that a large number of enemy planes were coming in for an attack. The carrier fighters were immediately alerted and sent up to meet them. Between 0850 and 0940 hours, a squadron of enemy aircraft attacked and the CV Shokaku received bomb hits and was set afire. Subsequently, landing or take-off operation was impossible on this carrier although the carrier maintained communications in spite of damages.

Meanwhile at 0920 hours, the attack squadron attacked and inflicted heavy damages upon the enemy task force. The communications of this attack were also conducted successfully.

The Task Force abandoned its pursuit action due to heavy damages inflicted upon the planes, and in view of the overall situation, C in C, Combined Fleet ordered the suspension of the Port Moresby Operation.

The Task Force subsequently concentrated its effort upon the interception of enemy aircraft radio communications and gathered considerable information which contributed to the whole operation. Aircraft radio communications of the enemy land-based air force and carrier aircraft were picked up; and furthermore, since most of the enemy communications were conducted in plain language, it was possible to keep informed of the enemy command communications to their fighter planes as well as keep tab on the presence of enemy search planes. Moreover, even when enemy messages were encoded, the general contents could be ascertained according to their communication time, indicator and code form of the message.

Both the 4th and 8th Communications Units intercepted enemy radio communications. However, it was generally untimely and therefore practically valueless in the tactical theater where instant decision was necessary.

In this battle, the Japanese force also communicated frequently in plain language. As these communications included some messages concerning movements, it was quite likely that the enemy intercepted and utilized these messages.

Communications Plan of the Eighth Fleet

As had been mentioned earlier in this chapter, the Eighth Fleet was activated on 14 July 1942, and to it was assigned the CA <u>Chokai</u>, 18th Cruiser Division, 7th Submarine Squadron, 7th Base Force and the 8th Base Force. This fleet took over from the Fourth Fleet the operations in the New Britain, Solomons and the New Guinea area.

The C in C, Eighth Fleet established a communications system with the 8th Communications Unit as the operational communications center. Later, after the Eleventh Air Fleet headquarters moved to Rabaul, an air operations communications system centered around the fleet was organized. However, the communications system centered around the 8th Communications Unit became the mainstay of the operational communications system in this area.

Communications Plan

The Eighth Fleet communications will be in accordance with the Communications Plan of the Second Phase Operations of the Combined Fleet as well as in accordance with the following:

1. Communications within the Fleet:

    a. Ship communications

       (1) Assignment (Chart 61)

Communications Net	Frequency	Ships Assigned to Communications Net	Manning Standard
Common Communications Net	Low freq	Each ship	Continuously
	High freq	All vessels larger than destroyers. Des Div flagship. Ships operating independently beyond the low freq range	By special order or when encountering enemy
Common Radiotelephone Communications Net	Medium freq	All vessels larger than destroyer. Des Div flagship.	Continuously during cruise in formation
Flagship Radiotelephone Communications Net	Very-high freq	Each flagship. Vessels larger than destroyers will receive directly	By special order or when encountering enemy

Chart 61

(2) Except by special orders or when encountering enemy, visual communications will be the standard procedure for communications during cruise in formation.

(3) During cruises, the 8th Communications Unit will be responsible in attending the common communications net and relay broadcasts of the messages used in that net.

(4) When a vessel maneuvers individually, it will, as a rule, attend the ship communications net of the 8th Communications Unit. If necessary, the ship can effect direct communications through the ship common communications net or indirect communications through the 8th Communications Unit.

(5) In case it is possible to conduct communications by means other than radio communications of the 8th Communications Unit, the vessel can disregard manning any of the communication systems mentioned in (1).

b. Aircraft communications

   (1) Communications plan (Chart 62)

Aircraft	Frequency	Control Ship or Station	Manning Standard	Remarks
Search plane	A-type	Base	Continuously	Antisubmarine patrol planes will switch to C-type frequency when homing after completion of mission
Antisubmarine patrol plane	B-type			
Operational aircraft	C-type			

Chart 62

   (2) Classification of the use of low frequencies (Chart 63).

Homing frequency transmitted by base	B-type low frequency
Guiding frequency of contact plane	A-type low frequency
Homing frequency	C-type low frequency

Chart 63

   (3) The fleet flagship will effect control of A-type frequency when necessary.

c. Submarine communications

   (1) The submarine communications will be conducted through the flagship concerned. The 8th Communications Unit will be responsible for relay of these communications. Details will be decided by the submarine force commander.

d. Land-based communications unit (Chart 64).

Communications Net	Frequency	Manning Standard	Broadcast or Relay Station	Assigned Ship or Station	Remarks
1st Local Broadcast Net	In accordance with Navy Communications Regulations				Relaying of broadcast of vital operational communications for the forces in the area concerned will be stressed
2d Local Broadcast Net					
Local Ship Communications Net					
1st Local Communications Net	High frequency	Continuously	8th Comm Unit	8th Base Force	Both administrative and operational communications will use this net
2d Local Communications Net				7th Base Force	
Lookout Communications Net	High frequency	8th Comm Unit (continuously) / Lookout Comm Net (receive on scheduled time)	8th Comm Unit	Lookout Posts and Defense Stations	Both administrative and operational communications will use this chart

Chart 64

2. Communications with forces outside of the Fleet:

   a. It will be conducted through the 8th Communications Unit.

    b. Communications with the land-based air forces.

        (1) Communications with the 25th Air Flotilla will be conducted by wire communications.

        (2) The communications unit will initiate direct reception of aircraft communications and relay broadcast the necessary messages.

3. Radio intelligence:

    a. The main target of the radio intelligence group of the 8th Communications Unit will be the communications of enemy air force and submarines in Australia and New Guinea areas.

    b. The 8th Communications Unit will also be responsible for obtaining enemy communications data as designated by Imperial General Headquarters.

Communications in the Battle of Savo Island

Communications in this battle were conducted according to the communications plan of the Eighth Fleet. Since this fleet had been activated only a short time before the battle, coordinated training among the forces concerned had not been conducted. Therefore, radiotelephone communications for night action could not be entirely relied upon.

Considering that the success or failure of this battle depended greatly upon the movement of the enemy task force, the main target of interception was directed at ship and aircraft communications of the enemy task force. The radio intelligence group conducted intensive interception of enemy communications and contributed valuable information for the Japanese operational forces.

It may be said in general that communications were conducted as planned. There was no instance of any poor communications which might have adversely affected the operation.

Communications in the Battle of Eastern Solomons

<u>Outline of Communications Plan</u> (Plan after Eleventh Air Fleet advanced to Rabaul)

It will be in accordance with the Communications Plan of the Second Phase Operations of the Combined Fleet, and in accordance with the following:

1. Base communications:

    a. Radio communications

    (1) Communications net (See Chart 65).

    (2) Besides the foregoing, each air base will be attached to the local communications net of the 8th Communications Unit and will perform mainly non-operational communications.

    (3) For its own security, each base will directly receive communications of the lookout communications net designated by the Eighth Fleet and will endeavor to obtain antiaircraft warning information as promptly as possible.

    b. Wire communications

    A wire maintenance unit will be organized in each force. The wire repairs between Rabaul and Vunakanau will be conducted by the wire repair team directly assigned to the Eleventh Air Fleet.

2. Aircraft communications:

    a. Communications assignment (Chart 66).

Communications Net Chart 65

Communications Net	Frequency	Broadcast or Communications Center	Assigned Ship or Station
Eleventh Air Fleet Headquarters Broadcast Net	High Frequency / Low Frequency	Eleventh Air Fleet Hq	
Air Base Communications Net No 1	High Frequency	26th Air Flotilla Hq	Rabaul, Buka, Buin, Balalle, Munda
Air Base Communications Net No 2	High Frequency	25th Air Flotilla Hq	Rabaul, Surumi, Lae, Salamaua, Tuluvu, Kavieng
Flagship Communications Net	High Frequency	Eleventh Air Fleet Hq	26th Air Flot Hq, 25th Air Flot Hq, 21st Air Flot Hq, 11th Seaplane Tender Div Hq
Remarks	Important operational communications will be relayed or broadcast		

Assignment	Frequency	Control Station
Search plane Contact plane	A-type high frequency	Eleventh Air Fleet Headquarters
Attack unit		
Fighter unit	A-type high frequency for fighter plane	
Combat Air Patrol	B-type high frequency for fighter plane	Base
Transport plane	Transport's high freq	Base
Local rcn plane	B-type high frequency	Base

Note: After completing the attack, the attack unit will switch to C-type frequency

Chart 66

b. Classification of the use of air low frequency

(1) A plane in contact with the enemy and in guiding friendly planes will use A-type low frequency.

(2) Homing low frequency

Vunakanau Base (Low frequency A, call sign "MU")
Rabaul   Base (Low frequency B, call sign "YO")
Buka   Base (Low frequency C, call sign "RE")
Buin   Base (Low frequency D, call sign "TSU")
Kavieng Base (Low frequency E, call sign "KO")

3. Radio intelligence:

Besides conducting regular friendly communications, radio intelligence work may be undertaken as designated by each commander when capacity permits.

Base Communications

The temporary base installations were equipped chiefly with

mobile equipment while combat operations were in progress. Many difficulties were encountered because suitable mobile equipment had not been manufactured for such operational communications. If the naval technical authorities had foreseen the special requirements inherent in communications of the land-based air force and had improved on it, a greater percentage of the difficulties would have been easily eliminated.

The Problem of Wave Propagation

Owing to the fluctuations of penetration frequencies in short waves and attenuation in long waves which prevailed in the Solomon Islands, there were some periods in a day and some places in which radio communications were impossible. This hindered the operations to a great extent.

The adjustment of medium frequency was very difficult because the basic equipment used was the TM-type mobile high frequency transmitter. There were several instances in which transmission was impossible at the most crucial time during combat operations. What was actually needed was a mobile medium frequency set in this area at the time.

The poor efficiency of communications officers also caused serious setbacks of air operations. Investigations of air bases with poor communications revealed that the chief cause was insufficient effort and guidance on the part of commanders or communications officers in regards to operations, training, maintenance and installations.

Air Combat Communications

Although the land-based air forces in the Solomons were very active and inflicted heavy damages upon the enemy, such operations were not executed without heavy sacrifices. It can be said that most of the well-trained personnel of the land-based air forces were lost during a short period of about half a year. As losses mounted, it became necessary to assign partially trained radio operators with the flight crew. Thorough and complete instructions and training could not be given due to the continuing combat action. Rapid decline in efficiency was observed within these few months.

The decline in the skill of flight radiomen resulted in inefficiency not only in communications alone but also in the very vital aspect of equipment maintenance and its usage. Remedial measures were taken by transferring some ground radiomen and maintenance personnel to aircraft radio maintenance crews. However, replacements for those transferred were numerically unavailable because of the limited number of trainees from the Naval Communications School. For this reason, the Susaki Naval Air Group and the Fujisawa Naval Air Group were established to expedite training in this field.

Another aspect of inefficiency due to inexperienced radio personnel was exemplified in plane-to-base radio communications. The radio operators were prone to overdo this and neglected security precautions. As a result, it had been presumed that the enemy intercepted these communications to a great extent.

As the enemy greatly increased land-based air strength and anti-aircraft positions in the Guadalcanal area, the Japanese resorted to dusk and night air actions. The drawback was that night transmission of high frequency was particularly poor in the Solomons due to the fluctuations in the penetration frequency. (The sunspot which was at its largest about 1937, was at its smallest in 1941 and 1942). Because communications were impossible either with high or low frequencies for certain hours and certain areas, communications had to be conducted with medium frequency. Both the air and ground equipment in use at the time was not within the necessary frequency range and only the large bases with small-type medium frequency transmitters were able to transmit effective radio waves. To cope with this situation, requests were made for the improvement of aircraft radio equipment to permit changes in frequency band. It was after the middle of 1943 that the improved medium frequency equipment arrived at the battle theater to meet the actual need.

For homing communications, the standard procedure was to have the plane use its direction finder on the low frequency transmitted by the base. The low frequencies transmitted from bases at Buin, Vunakanau and Buka proved to be very valuable. However, maintenance of the TELEFUNKEN direction finder (equipped on plane) deteriorated with the decrease in the skill of the maintenance crew. Moreover, some of the radio operators had no conception of the use of the radio direction finder.

In operations in this area, fighter planes rarely used radiotelephones. With the intensification of enemy air raids, the ground command to fighters was advocated. However the fighter unit commanders emphasized the unreliability of radiotelephone equipment and also insisted strongly that the removal of the radio equipment would increase the maneuverability of fighter planes. (Actually the capacities of the Japanese and U.S. fighters were on par with each other at that time). Lengthy discussions were held regarding the feasibility of fighter plane command but the idea was finally abandoned due to equipment shortage.

Communications Unit on Guadalcanal Island

With the increase of enemy air strength on Guadalcanal Island, it became gradually difficult for attack plane units and reconnaissance planes to operate freely in that area. Therefore it was decided to establish an observation post at a suitable spot on Guadalcanal. This observation post was to function as an aid to air operations by reporting to Japanese attack units any information on enemy fighters.

For this purpose, a communications detachment from the 26th Air Flotilla was organized and dispatched to that island. Its organization and equipment were as follows:

```
Commanding officer:
    Naval air force officer ........................ 1
```

Radiomen:
　　Petty officers 2
　　Men 4

Code personnel:
　　Petty officers 2

Non-specialists: 2

Equipment:
　　Portable TM-type high frequency transmitter .. 1
　　Transmitter generators 2

The communications detachment submitted highly important information during this phase of the operation. It can be said that its contribution to the operational command of the air fleet was greater than its contribution to the tactical operation of the flying units. It played an important role until the end of the KE-GO operation (withdrawal operations from Guadalcanal). It must not be overlooked that behind this great service, there were great sacrifices on the part of the radiomen to maintain communications. The decline in physical strength due to malaria, the losses incurred when ships with replacements were sunk as well as those killed in direct combat were heavy tolls which had an adverse effect on the maintenance of communications.

Communications in the Battle of Santa Cruz

Policy

Communications will be conducted in accordance with the Communications Plan of the Second Phase Operations of the Combined Fleet. The Tokyo Communications Unit, 4th Communications Unit and 8th Communications Unit will give over-all cooperation to the communications in this operation. The details for each unit will be formulated by its commander.

Communications Plan of the Support Force

Effort will be exerted to conceal the plan and location by maintaining strict radio silence. For this purpose, visual signals will be used primarily for the communications within the fleet. The communications between the Task Force and the Advance Force during a strategic period will be conducted by written communications via aircraft or destroyer.

Urgent communications within the fleet will be through a general low frequency communications net designated in the Combined Fleet Communications Plan.

All other communications within the force will be conducted in accordance with the Combined Fleet Communications Plan.

Based upon the preceding paragraphs, the communications of the Advance Force will be conducted in accordance with the Communications Plan of the Second Fleet. The communications of the Task Force will be conducted in accordance with the previously mentioned Task Force communications plan. However, in order to operate in concert with the Advance Force, the 2d Task Force will use special A-type aircraft frequency.

Summary of Operations

After leaving Truk Island on 11 October 1942, the Support Force headed south. It maintained complete radio silence according to the communications plan and maneuvered to the north of Guadalcanal keeping a close watch on the enemy fleet. Meanwhile, the Tokyo broadcast announced the following important information obtained by the Special Duty Group (radio intelligence):

> "A strong enemy Task Force sailed from Hawaii and is maintaining strict radio silence. Location and destination unknown."

Consequently the Support Force continued to maintain strict security and alert.

The 1st Combined Communications Unit detected, within the radio direction finder range, the gradual increase in the number of enemy submarines in the waters north of Guadalcanal and transmitted warnings to the fleet on 20 October.

The flagship CVE _Hiyo_ of the 2d Carrier Division returned to Truk on 22 October because of damage by fire and the CVE _Junyo_ was made the flagship. However, there was no noticeable decline whatsoever in the efficiency of flagship communications.

The vanguard of the Task Force was sighted by enemy patrol planes on the 23d. Judging from their communications, it was estimated that the enemy had detected the position of the entire Task Force.

An enemy flying boat contacted the main body of the Task Force on the morning of the 24th. Maintaining an all-out monitoring of radio wave transmission of the enemy patrol plane, it was learned that the enemy flying boat had reported the sighting of the entire Task Force.

At 0050 hours of the 26th, an enemy contact plane dropped bombs near the CV _Zuikaku_. The main body of the Task Force immediately reversed course and proceeded north after transmitting the first warning to the entire force.

Search planes took off at 0215 hours on the 26th and sighted a large enemy force at 0450 hours. The carrier aircraft then took off for attack at the following time intervals:

0710 hours: First attack by 1st Carrier Division

0820 hours: Second attack by 1st Carrier Division

0920 hours: First attack by 2d Carrier Division

1310 hours: Second attack by 2d Carrier Division

1345 hours: Third attack by 1st Carrier Division

1515 hours: Third attack by 2d Carrier Division

Meanwhile, the CVL Zuiho sustained a direct bomb hit at 0540 hours and the flagship Shokaku was hit at 0727 hours. Transmission of communications became impossible on the two ships. The CV Zuikaku, second ship in the formation, immediately conducted flagship communications according to the prearranged plan. However, in the interim, the situation of the Task Force flagship was unknown to the Advance Force and the 2d Task Force during the two hours' climax of action. The Task Force commander had intended to assign the DD Terutsuki as the flagship according to the plan. However, he went aboard DD Arashi at 1730 hours and headed for the CV Zuikaku because the DD Terutsuki was engaged in action along with CV Zuikaku. Meanwhile, he ordered the CV Zuikaku to conduct flagship communications. He took the necessary tactical command aboard the DD Arashi and had this destroyer relay communications. Then on the 27th, he went aboard the CV Zuikaku which became the flagship and at which time communications were restored to normal.

Aircraft Communications

Upon receiving night bombing with flares by an enemy flying boat at 0050 hours of the 26th the Carrier Task Force conducted pincer reconnaissance operation toward the east at 0330 hours in an extensive search for the enemy task force. As expected, the search planes of the first group sighted the enemy and transmitted the first dispatch, "The enemy force sighted at ...."

Upon receipt of the first dispatch that the enemy had been sighted, the first attack unit was immediately launched and the attack course and targets were given by radio to the attack unit.

When the 1st Attack Unit of the 2d Task Force arrived at the combat area, the first and second attacks executed by the 1st Task Force were already over. Two enemy carriers had been destroyed or sunk and there was no trace of them even after search of the battle area. The command plane ordered, "Take attack preparation formation," followed by, "Attack target, cruisers." The flagship intercepted the communications and the 2d Task Force commander immediately advised and ordered the command plane, "There are other carriers. Search the area." The command plane received the order just before launching an attack on the cruiser and conducted the search of the area. It sighted a carrier from which planes were taking off, attacked the carrier and inflicted heavy damages. The 3d Attack Unit located the damaged carrier later and sank her.

As many attack units operated simultaneously in this battle, air communications were extremely congested. However, the 1st and 2d Task Forces used different frequency systems which alleviated much of the congestion.

In the case of the 1st Task Force, the homing device was utilized because communications were impossible on the damaged <u>Shokaku</u>, the flagship. However, in the case of the 2d Task Force the original communications plan was followed.

<u>Radio Intelligence</u>

During this operation, the targets of interception by the operational force were directed mainly at enemy patrol planes, submarine and base communications until actual contact with the enemy. After contact with the enemy, the interception was directed at the enemy attack planes and enemy task force ship communications. Considerable success was attained in the collection of operational information.

The target of interception of the 1st Combined Communications Unit was directed mainly at the movement of the enemy task force and submarines.

<u>Communications in the Battle of Guadalcanal</u>

<u>Advance Force Communications Plan</u>

The plan will be in accordance with the communications plan of the Second Phase Operations of the Combined Fleet as well as in accordance with the following:

1. Ship communications:

    a. Observe very strict radio silence for high frequency and strict radio silence for other frequencies. Strict control will be maintained for radio wave transmission and particular attention will be given to concealing movements of ships and planes.

    b. It will be standard procedure for independent units to use low frequency for communications. In unavoidable cases, communications will be conducted with the Combined Fleet common high frequency.

2. Aircraft communications (Chart 67).

Mission	Frequency	Control Ship
Search plane	A-type high frequency	Fleet and division flagship
Antisubmarine patrol plane	B-type high frequency	Fleet and division flagship
Attack unit	B-type high frequency	Flagship of the 2d Carrier Division
Combat Air Patrol	Fighter A-type high frequency	Flagship of the 2d Carrier Division

Chart 67

3. Radio intelligence:

The targets of radio interception to be selected by the fleet are as follows:

a. Enemy land-based aircraft

b. Submarine communications

c. Ship and aircraft communications of the enemy task force.

Raiding Force Communications Plan

The plan will be in accordance with the Advance Force's plan as well as in accordance with the following:

1. Ship communications:

   a. In order to conceal the plan, radio wave transmission will be kept at the minimum by maximum use of visual communications. However, this should not be strictly adhered to; radiotelephone communications within the force should be fully utilized.

b. Communications assignment (Chart 68).

Communications	Frequency	Center of the Net	Ships assigned to Comm Net	Time
Communications Net	Combined Fleet common high freq	-	Each ship	Continuously
First Radio-telephone Net	Medium freq	Flagship of 11th Battleship Div	Each ship	Continuously
Second Radio-telephone Net	Very-high freq	Flagship of 11th Battleship Div	Each ship & destroyer div flagship	Continuously
Third Radio-telephone Net	Assigned frequencies for destroyer division	Flagships of destroyer division	Each destroyer; however escorted ships in formation will join this net	Continuously

Chart 68

2. Aircraft communications (Chart 69).

Assignment	Frequency	Center of the Net	Note
Spotter plane	C-type high freq	Flagship of the 11th Battleship Division	No special instruction will be given in regards to homing communications when returning to Shortland base
Local rcn plane	A-type high freq		

Chart 69

3. Communications with lookout posts:

   a. Communications net

Frequency for direct communications between Mount Austin lookout post and the flagship of the 11th Battleship Division will be the aircraft frequency of the 3d Battleship Division.

- b. Liaison to be conducted about one hour before commencement of firing.

    Radiomen used in bombardment by the 3d Battleship Division will be assigned to the lookout post.

4. Communications with other forces:

    a. Flagship of the 11th Battleship Division will control the force's communications with other forces.

    b. The force's communications with other forces will be conducted as designated in the communications plan of the Advance Force.

    c. For radio intelligence, the main target will be enemy land-based aircraft.

5. Communications plan of the Southeast Area Force:

    a. It will be in accordance with the previously mentioned communications plan of the Eighth Fleet.

    b. The communications plan of the base air force will be in accordance with the plan mentioned previously.

Operations of the Raiding Force

The bulk of the Raiding Force departed from Truk on 9 October, maintaining strict radio silence, and headed southward. The 4th Destroyer Squadron, assigned as the cover force, left Shortland at 0300 hours on 12 October, joined the Raiding Force at 1330 hours of the same day.

From the morning of the same day, both the 11th Battleship Division and the 4th Destroyer Squadron were contacted by the enemy.

At about 2200 hours they arrived northwest of Savo Island. Encountering a heavy squall, it became impossible to carry on the planned action. Therefore, they decided to reverse the course for the time being. The order to reverse course was transmitted through the second radiotelephone net. But in order to receive acknowledgment from the 4th Destroyer Squadron, the order to initiate reverse course was withheld temporarily, and thus the prearranged turning point was passed. Because of insufficient leeway on course for turning, the order to reverse course was given simultaneously through both the radiotelephone and radio net. At this time, the 4th Destroyer Squadron acknowledged the order to reverse course. However, it interpreted the order for immediate execution and therefore, the formation was deformed with the 11th Battleship Division and the 4th Destroyer Squadron aligned abreast.

Immediately after they had reversed course in the above manner, the squall cleared up and then a report was received from the lookout post on Guadalcanal that visibility was good in the target area. Therefore, they decided to reverse course once more and break through to the island. For the above reasons, the commencement of firing was delayed about 40 minutes.

As visibility was poor, the commanding officer of the 11th Battleship Division concluded that the 4th Destroyer Squadron was at its designated position and firing was commenced. At about 2343 hours, the flagship BB <u>Hiei</u> suddenly encountered the enemy, almost simultaneously with the 4th Destroyer Squadron. The Hiei sustained concentrated fire from the enemy's small and medium caliber guns, receiving considerable damage on the superstructure. Her fore and after radiotelephone rooms were completely damaged, the antenna was also totally destroyed, and for the time being, communications were impossible. Since this situation had not been reported to the officer second in command, the flagship communications could not be carried out, nor was it possible to control communications. Therefore, important tactical command was lost temporarily.

The crippled Hiei retired to the north of Savo Island, but early in the morning of 13 October, she was attacked by enemy aircraft. The commander of 11th Battleship Division boarded the DD Yukikaze at 0615 hours, took command of the 27th Destroyer Division which happened along and screened the BB Hiei. By noon, however, the BB Hiei was almost totally disabled due to continuous attacks by enemy aircraft.

Operations of the Advance Force

The Advance Force was comprised of the following:

    3d Battleship Division
    2d Carrier Division
    4th Cruiser Division
    8th Cruiser Division

    3d Destroyer Squadron:
      Flagship Sendai
      11th Destroyer Division
      19th Destroyer Division

       4th Destroyer Squadron:
         Flagship Asagumo
         2d Destroyer Division

       10th Destroyer Squadron:
         Flagship Nagara
         6th Destroyer Division
         61st Destroyer Division

    The Advance Force left Ruk on 9 October, maintaining strict radio silence, and was maneuvering in support of the Raiding Force in the area north of the Solomons. On the morning of 13 October, the extent of damage to BB <u>Hiei</u> was made quite evident. The commander of the Advance Force immediately ordered the assembly of the whole Advance Force. He then organized the Guadalcanal Island Attack Force which he commanded directly and directed the commander of the 3d Battleship Division to command the remaining strength. The Advance Force commander took charge of the attack force and at 0800 hours of 14 October, advanced southward from the rendezvous point toward the enemy.

    At 1430 hours, the 4th Cruiser Division received torpedo attacks from enemy submarines (no damage). Immediately afterwards, a plain language urgent message dispatched by an enemy submarine was intercepted which revealed evidence of an imminent sea battle. The enemy was sighted at 2010 hours and immediately night action ensued. The communications during the night action were conducted effectively.

CHAPTER X

Communications in Third Phase Operations

General Situation

Since the beginning of 1943, enemy counteroffensives were intensified in various areas. The Northern Force, operating in the Attu and Kiska area in support of the supply operation, encountered and engaged an enemy force centered around two cruisers. It was an unexpected encounter and the Northern Force unfortunately missed the chance of crushing the enemy. Subsequently, enemy pressure in this area increased and by the end of May the enemy had captured Attu. The enemy offensive in the Solomons was also intensified and by the end of June, Rendova Island was attacked. The Japanese counterattacked at a great sacrifice but this island also finally fell into the hands of the enemy. In the meantime, the enemy offensive in eastern New Guinea had increased in intensity and in May, the Japanese and the enemy were fighting along the Salamaua line. From then on the Japanese forces were gradually pushed back as the enemy attacked the Japanese supply lines.

The communications facilities were generally complete in this area with the exception of eastern New Guinea. Many untrained radiomen were assigned to these facilities but they were somewhat compensated for by having as a nucleus, skilled radiomen and code personnel who had been trained since the early phase of the war.

With a view to improving this general situation, a plan was formulated to expedite the completion of communications facilities (including personnel) on the bases established in the Japanese Mandated Islands centered around Saipan, bases in western New Guinea and in the southern Philippines centered around Davao. With the implementation of the plan, improvements were seen in communications facilities which ultimately resulted in furthering communications technique.

As a result of the enemy counteroffensive from the end of 1943 to the beginning of 1944, strategic areas in the Gilbert Islands and the Marshalls fell to the enemy. The Japanese then accelerated the completion of air bases in the Marianas and the entire Philippines. In June 1944, the A-GO Operation ended in failure and the Marianas were lost. Consequently, it became necessary to expedite the defense preparations in the Philippines and to complete as soon as possible the defense preparations on the Japanese Homeland. Actually, communications preparations were commenced quite early, but as the momentum of the enemy counteroffensive increased, transportation difficulties coupled with the presence of many untrained and unskilled radiomen made the situation worse. In fact, the Japanese had to carry on combat operation on one hand and the construction work on the other. In the meantime, considerable anxiety was felt concerning communication security because of the successive loss of strategic areas and the loss of code books and ciphers during their transportation. This tendency became more marked with the intensification of the operations, and the restoration of communications finally became impossible.

First Mobile Fleet Communications Plan

This plan will be in accordance with the Combined Fleet communications plan of the A-TO Operation (Battle of Philippine Sea) as well as in accordance with the following.

1. Ship communications:

    a. Visual communications will be conducted mainly during group movements to conceal plans and movements. If necessary, written communications will be conducted by dispatching an aircraft or a destroyer. When radio communications are unavoidable, the use of long range frequency must be avoided.

    b. Radio communications net will be as follows: (Chart 70).

Communications Net	Frequency	Ship or Station in the Net	Manning
Flagship	High frequency	Each flagship carrier	By special order
Flagship communications (radiotelephone) net	Medium frequency	Each flagship	Continuously
Common communications net	Low frequency	Each ship	Continuously

Chart 70

2. Aircraft communications:

    a. Communications assignment (See Chart 71)

Communications Assignment   Chart 71

Category		Air Communications Assignment No 1	Air Communications Assignment No 2	Air Communications Assignment No 3
Search plane		A-type high frequency A-type low frequency	A-type high frequency A-type low frequency	A-type high frequency A-type low frequency
Attack unit & contact plane	1st Carrier Division	A-type high frequency A-type low frequency	A-type high frequency A-type low frequency	A-type high frequency A-type low frequency
	2d Carrier Division		B-type high frequency B-type low frequency	B-type high frequency B-type low frequency
	3d Carrier Division		A-type high frequency A-type low frequency	B-type high frequency B-type low frequenvy
Fighter unit & combat air patrol	1st Carrier Division	Fighter A-type high frequency	Fighter's A-type high frequency	Fighter's B-type high frequency
	2d Carrier Division		Fighter's B-type high frequency	Fighter's B-type high frequency
	3d Carrier Division			
Antisubmarine patrol plane		First A-type Low frequency	First A-type Low frequency	First A-type Low frequency
Noncombat mission aircraft		C-type high frequency	C-type high frequency	C-type high frequency

b. Changes in air communications assignment will be made through special orders of the C in C, First Mobile Fleet.

c. Broadcast communications will be the standard procedure communications; acknowledgment will be sent by flagships or ships in charge of radio control. The standard classification requiring acknowledgment will entail the following:

   (1) The first dispatch of sighting the enemy.

   (2) The second dispatch concerning enemy carriers.

   (3) The dispatch of any newly discovered targets will be handled in the same manner as (1) and (2).

d. Target identification signs and content indication signs will be attached to important communications as follows: (Chart 72)

		First target sighted	Second target sighted	Third target sighted
Target identification sign		"I"	"RO"	"HA"
Content indication sign	Information concerning force including carriers	"	"	

Remarks:
Target identification and search line number will be placed immediately after the message number and at the end of the text.
Example: "Second target sighted by plane of search line No 19 (19 RO)." Content indication sign will be attached to information on the movement of a force which includes carriers in the indication column.

Chart 72

3. Force's external communications:

   a. The force's external communications will be conducted under the control of the Fleet flagship.

   b. The communications will be conducted through the nearest land-based communications unit. The force will either join the communications net of the nearest land-based communications unit or use aircraft or ship for sending written messages to the communications unit, depending upon the location of operations.

   c. As a standard procedure, aircraft communications of the base air force will be received directly. Efforts must be made to prevent failure to receive the broadcast of the 3d, 5th and the Tokyo Communications Units.

   d. Communications of friendly submarine forces will be handled in the same manner.

4. Radio intelligence

   a. The main targets of interception will be conducted by the fleet as follows:

      (1) Radio waves of communications net of enemy agents in the area of operations (Central and Southern Philippines).

      (2) Radio waves of submarines.

      (3) Radio waves of base air force (patrol planes).

      (4) Aircraft and ship communications of task force.

   b. Special efforts will be made to detect the time of departure and movements of the enemy task force from base in the Marshall area.

   c. Attention will be given to the collection of information to ascertain whether our movement and location has been discovered by the enemy.

   d. No active jamming will be conducted as a rule, except when considered particularly effective.

Summary of First Mobile Fleet Operational Communications

The CV Shokaku was the fleet flagship. When the CV Taiho was assigned to and joined the fleet at Lingga anchorage, studies and discussions were conducted as to whether the flagship should be transferred to the Taiho or whether the Shokaku should remain as the flagship. The advantages and disadvantages were weighed and finally it was decided to change whereby the Taiho became the flagship on 6 May 1944. With the change in the flagship, the Taiho underwent a thorough flagship training.

The possibility of revealing the location and movement of our force during training due to radio wave transmission had to be considered. Along with this incompatible condition, the force rendezvous time and the expected time of operation had to be considered. Therefore, the training was conducted in accordance with the following plan to improve and coordinate communications technique: (1) Until the completion of the rendezvous of the entire fleet, forces were trained in the fundamental communications under the direction of their respective senior commanders. The forces were divided roughly into the force located in the Lingga area and the force in Japanese waters; (2) After the completion of the fleet rendezvous, the training was conducted with the emphasis placed on the coordinated training, including combat training and group training in accordance with the operation plan; (3) In the training, long-range frequencies were avoided. Short-range communications were conducted by selecting proper frequencies in accordance with the location of the fleet to avoid interception by enemy interception stations. In other words, very-high frequencies were used in the daytime and medium and high frequencies during the night.

It was difficult to designate an air communications frequency assignment to be used during training on account of the variety of tactics to be used. As a rule, however, the first air communications frequency assignment was adopted because it was the assignment for basic tactics. According to the plan, communications were to be conducted with one frequency. Therefore, it was favorable to the tactical command, although strict and skillful control of communications was required since the one frequency was used by many planes. As a result of table-top maneuvers held several times, however, it was certain that the communications would be conducted smoothly in simple situations.

The First Mobile Fleet rendezvoused at Tawi Tawi in the middle of May. The following measures were taken to conceal our whereabouts while at anchor there.

In accordance with the plan, the Mobile Fleet used the local communications net. Because of the sudden increase in radio communications in the net, a new communications net was established. Planes and vessels were also used to carry messages to avoid the attention of the enemy. The new setup was as follows:

1. Radiomen were dispatched to the 33d Guard Unit stationed at Tawi Tawi. The 32d Communications Unit, to which the Guard Unit was assigned, handled radio messages of the Mobile Fleet through the local communications net.

2. It was decided to communicate with the Mobile Fleet either through the Tokyo broadcast or the broadcast of the 21st and 31st Communications Units.

3. After consultation with the Second Southern Expeditionary Fleet, a special communications net with low frequency was established between the Mobile Fleet and the Tarakan Detachment, and part of the radio communications of the Mobile Fleet was handled through the 21st Communications Unit using this newly established channel.

4. Aircraft and ships carrying written messages were specially dispatched to Davao, and the 23d Communications Unit stationed there transmitted the messages by radio.

Training was conducted with the emphasis placed on group training and fleet coordinated training as designated in the operations plan. A strict control was maintained on frequency transmission conditions was selected for training. For this reason, aircraft radio communications training was almost suspended and what little training undertaken was limited to theoretical studies.

During the period following the departure from Tawi Tawi to the departure from the Guimaras anchorage, the Mobile Fleet was in the fixed communications net of the Singapore area (Chart 73), and by using false call signs, conducted deceptive communications with land communications stations.

Singapore Area Fixed Communications Net

Central Communications Unit	10th Communications Unit
Assigned Communications Unit	12th, 21st and 31st Communications Unit and Saigon
Communications hours	Continuously

Chart 73

While the Mobile Fleet was at the Guimaras anchorage, CM Yaeyama which was at anchor there and the land communications facility conducted radio transmission for the Mobile Fleet besides the communications mentioned in the preceding paragraph. The radio messages transmitted through these mediums were confirmed by the Tokyo broadcast and broadcasts of the 21st and 31st Communications Units.

During this period, the Mobile Fleet exerted every possible effort to intercept enemy communications and obtained good results in the collection of information. Following were the main targets in the interception of the enemy communications:

1. Information on the movement of the enemy task force.

2. Disposition of the enemy submarines.

3. Communications of enemy land-based air forces.

The radio intelligence group obtained the following information in regard to the enemy's knowledge of the movement of the Mobile Fleet.

1. On the night when the 2d Carrier Division was conducting training on the high seas, the radio intelligence group

intercepted a long communication sent from an enemy submarine a short distance away. The Special Duty Group of Imperial General Headquarters located the submarine by radio direction finders and estimated that the enemy had detected the location of the Mobile Fleet.

2. The radio intelligence group was unable to obtain any information as to whether the enemy land-based air force had actually reconnoitered Tawi Tawi. However, according to the study made jointly by the Special Duty Group and the 1st Combined Communications Unit, there were indications that the enemy force had reconnoitered Tawi Tawi.

When the enemy convoy was sighted in the waters west of Saipan, it became clear that the enemy was planning the capture of Saipan.

On 15 June, Combined Fleet headquarters ordered the activation of the A-GO Decisive Operation. The Mobile Fleet sailed from Guimaras anchorage on the morning of the same day. In the evening of the same day, it passed through the San Bernardino Strait, maintaining strict radio silence.

Since it was vital that the departure time of the Mobile Fleet from San Bernardino Strait be kept secret, the Mobile Fleet requested the Southwest Area Fleet headquarters to jam the communications of enemy agents there as well as their submarine communications. This headquarters, in turn, directed the 3d Combined Communications Unit to plan and conduct jamming.

At 2038 hours, the radio intelligence group intercepted a long message transmitted from an enemy submarine which was presumably transmitting the report that the Mobile Fleet had left the San Bernardino Strait. The 3d Combined Communications Unit jammed communications so effectively that it was delayed about two hours. However, the unit was unable to continue preventing the enemy's communications.

In order to pick up information concerning the movement of the enemy task force, the Mobile Fleet attempted to receive directly the communications of the Japanese base air force. It could receive directly the communications of the air force stationed at Palau but it was impossible to receive the communications of the friendly forces stationed at Iwo Jima and Tinian. However, relay broadcasts were received, chiefly through the Tokyo Communications Unit and the 3d Communications Unit. Through such means, the Mobile Fleet was able to obtain the necessary information regarding the general situation as of 16 June, although delayed as it was. When it was learned that the 5th Communications Unit at Saipan was out of commission, a serious setback resulted in the execution of communications.

On the morning of 17 June, an aircraft was dispatched to Palau to transmit radio messages to Headquarters, Combined Fleet and other components. On 18 June, scouting was commenced in accordance with Daytime Air Tactics No 3 (group disposition). At 0500 hours, the first group of search planes took off. They sighted nothing except enemy patrol planes. At 1140 hours, the second group took off, and between 1425 hours and 1540 hours, they contacted the enemy task force in three groups, each in formation around two aircraft carriers. As the enemy groups were located about 380 miles away from our main force, it was decided to conduct an air strike the next day. On 19 June, the vanguard of the Mobile Fleet was posted at a position 100 miles from the main body, and the 2d Carrier Division was 15 kilometers north of the 1st Carrier Division.

At 0330 hours 19 June, the first group of search planes took off, and at 0415 hours the second, and later a third group was dispatched. At 0635 hours, the first group sighted enemy aircraft carriers. Enemy vessels were sighted successively and, by 0900 hours, information on the entire enemy task force was obtained.

The 1st Attack Unit of the 1st Carrier Division and the 1st Attack Unit of the 3d Carrier Division took off at 0730 hours, and the 1st Attack Unit of the 2d Carrier Division took off at 0830 hours and were ordered to attack the first target. However, when the second target was sighted, the 2d Attack Unit of the 2d Carrier Division was ordered at 0900 hours to the second target and the command plane acknowledged it immediately. At 1000 hours, contact planes for the third target took off and led the 2d Attack Units of the 1st and 2d Carrier Divisions respectively to the objective.

The 1st Attack Unit of the 3d Carrier Division and the 1st Attack Unit of the 1st Carrier Division conducted attacks on the first target at 0945 hours and 1045 hours, respectively. All communications during the preparatory stage for attack functioned in good order. Aircraft communications were conducted according to plan, but after that, no information on the result of the attack could be obtained. The 1st and 2d Attack Units of the 2d Carrier Division and the 2d Attack Unit of the 1st Carrier Division searched respectively for their designated targets over a vast area, but were unable to sight the enemy. The 1st Attack Unit of the 2d Carrier Division and the 2d Attack Unit of the 1st Carrier Division returned to their respective aircraft carriers. The 2d Attack Unit of the 2d Carrier Division headed toward Guam, engaged a large group of enemy fighters over the Guam Base and suffered heavy losses.

Prior to this, at 0810 hours, immediately after the take-off of the 1st Attack Unit, the fleet flagship Taiho was torpedoed by an enemy submarine and a hit was received on the forward starboard side. This damage did not affect the ship's communications. At 1432 hours, however, it was severely damaged by a sudden explosion of gasoline, resulting in total destruction of communications facilities and loss of majority of the personnel concerned. The ship's communications were then solely limited to semaphore signalling.

At the time the air operation was in full swing, it was decided to transfer the flagship immediately to a ship capable of conducting tactical command communications. At 1606 hours, it was transferred to the CA Haguro as previously planned. The emergency communications plan had been formulated under the presumption that tactical command could be carried out by CA Haguro, on the basis that a considerable number (approximately half the number) of radio and code personnel assigned to the fleet headquarters could be utilized on the new flagship. However, because of the sudden explosion on the Taiho, most of the radio and code personnel had been lost. Consequently, the original plan was completely inapplicable. Moreover, since code communications capacity was greatly reduced, acquisition of enemy information decreased considerably and it became impossible to conduct tactical command.

On 20 June, at 1200 hours, the Mobile Fleet flagship was transferred to CV Zuikaku, and the communications of the fleet were finally restored. Because of the disruption of communicatons of the fleet headquarters during this time, it was unable to obtain information that it was being trailed by an enemy task force. Thus, on 20 June it was subject to a one-side attack by the enemy which gravely affected our operations.

Until the sinking of the Taiho, the radio intelligence team had made valuable contributions. Also, the radio intelligence group on the Second Fleet flagship engaged in the interception of enemy communications and greatly aided in the guidance of operations. For example, at 1505 hours, the Second Fleet flagship reported that an enemy flying boat was making contact and was reporting movements of our force in plain language. Therefore, our force abandoned refueling and ordered the immediate withdrawal toward bearing 330 degrees.

At 1615 hours, our search planes sighted an enemy task force formation with two aircraft carriers as its nucleus heading westward. Attack units were launched and torpedo attacks were scheduled at dusk. At 1700 hours, the fourth task disposition was ordered, and night action was to be executed. Our communications net was arranged for night action. The attack units operated under favorable communications condition but were unable to sight the enemy. Consequently, the night action was called off and the entire force withdrew to the northwest. On the same day, the 1st and 2d Carrier Divisions, the Diversion Attack Force and tankers were attacked by enemy fighters for about two hours from 1730 hours. The CV Zuiho sustained a direct hit on the rear part of her bridge. As a result, the antenna was severed and communications were temporarily affected. The CVE Hiyo was sunk and other vessels suffered some damage, but the communications capacity was not affected. During the same night, our force avoided contact with the enemy and withdrew northwest toward Nakagusuku Bay, Okinawa, maintaining radio silence.

At the time of the sinking of the Taiho, the highly secret special code book was lost. Subsequently, orders issued by the Combined Fleet flagship could not be read, and until a report to that effect was made to the Combined Fleet flagship, there resulted a backlog of a considerable number of radio messages which could not be deciphered.

Operational Communications Regulations of the 1st Mobile Base Air Force

Part I. Introduction

Article 1. Operational communications of the Mobile Base Air Force will be conducted in accordance with the Navy Communications Regulations, Navy Communications Procedure Regulations, Combined Fleet Communications Regulations, Communications Plan for the Third Phase Operations of the Combined Fleet, and Aircraft Communications Regulations of the Combined Fleet, and supplemented with the following regulations.

Article 2. By conforming to the regulations presented herein, unit commanders (or base commandants) will be authorized to establish further regulations necessary for their respective units in conducting communications.

Article 3. In these regulations, bases having headquarters of fleet commanders will be referred to as fleet flagship.

Part II. General

Article 4. As a rule, base communications of the 1st Mobile Base Air Force will be conducted by the fleet flagship and the airfield units, and communications with aircraft by fleet flagship.

Article 5. In case both wire and radio communications nets are available, wire communications will be generally used.

Part III. External Communications of the Fleet

Article 6. Communications with other than the 1st Mobile Base Air Force will be conducted via the fleet flagship. However, if necessary, the units (or bases) may join the nearest communications net and conduct communications.

Part IV. Internal Communications of the Fleet

Section 1. General

Article 7. Transmitting and receiving standard of each unit (or base) is as shown in Chart 74 (Charts 74 to 78 follow Article 39).

Article 8. Transmitting and receiving the standard mentioned in the preceding paragraph may be changed in accordance with the communications capacity of the units (or bases), as designated by the senior commander present. However, in such cases, a report will be made to the quarters concerned.

Article 9. All units (or bases) will conduct direct receiving to the utmost and will strive for brief and speedy communications to minimize radio wave transmission.

Article 10. Central unit or station of the communications net concerned will be assigned to relay radio messages to units (or bases) having small communications capacity.

Section 2. Base Communications

Article 11. A-type base communications net will be classified into broadcasting, flagship and general communications nets. See Chart 75 for the radio communications system and assignments.

Article 12. Broadcasts

1. Messages broadcast through the broadcast net will be considered as acknowledged (received) by all units (and bases) of the 1st Mobile Base Air Force, simultaneously with the time of broadcast.

2. Broadcast sign with serial number will be inserted in messages broadcast by the 1st Mobile Base Air Force:

First broadcast sign "MI-KA"
Second broadcast sign "U-RE"

3. Information broadcast

a. Oita, Kanoya, Omura, Matsuyama and other designated bases will broadcast air raid warnings, antiaircraft information and general information by using the designated frequency.

b. Such broadcasts will, as a rule, be made in plain language, and code language will be used, only in cases when utmost secrecy is required.

c. In case of high frequency broadcast, code language (or abbreviation) may be used in broadcasting urgent orders. In such cases, the broadcasting procedure will be the same as that of order broadcast.

4. Order broadcast

a. Orders to be broadcast will be conducted through all assigned communications nets, and, will start with the sign "ME-I-TSU-KE" and end with "ME-I-TE-TSU".

b. This broadcast will be used mainly in broadcasting urgent orders or to broadcast information by code language (or abbreviation).

c. "KIKUSUI Dispatch No. ____" will be placed at the

beginning of this broadcast.

        d. When messages through this broadcast are received, immediate report thereof will be made through the present communications net (including wire and radio telephones). However, in case of radio communications, the radio code "KI-TA-NA____" will be used.

     5. Warning broadcast

        It will be chiefly used to relay radar and lookout reports of the lookout stations in southern Kyushu.

     Article 13. It will be used for communications between fleet flagship, flotilla headquarters and bases with airfield unit headquarters.

     Article 14. General communications

     1. The time of execution will be designated by special order.

     2. If necessary, commanders of all levels will be authorized to utilize this communications net in accordance with agreement or demand.

     Article 15. B-type base communications nets will be classified into eight nets. The radio communications system and assignments are shown in Chart 76.

     Article 16. All bases of this force will assign personnel to more than one of the 1st to 7th Base Communications Nets.

   Section 3. Warning Communications

     Article 17. Warning communications nets will be divided into the 1st to the 5th Warning Communications Nets. The radio communications system and assignments are shown in Chart 77.

     Article 18. This communications net will be used chiefly to report lookout and radar warnings.

   Section 4. Aircraft Communications

     Article 19. A-type aircraft radio communications system and assignment are shown in Chart 78.

Article 20. In accordance with the phase of operation, the following communications control will be carried out without specific order for the purpose of effecting speedy communications of important messages. (Chart 79).

Phase of Operation	Type of Control (Abbreviation)	Ships and Stations Exempted from Control
Until sighting of enemy	First Aircraft Communications Control (1 KO-TSU-SE)	Search planes
After sighting of enemy	Second Aircraft Communications Control (2 KO-TSU-SE)	Contact planes
After sortie of attack units	Third Aircraft Communications Control (3 KO-TSU-SE)	Base and contact planes
30 minutes before the arrival of attack units at the target area until the report of battle result	Fourth Aircraft Communications Control (4 KO-TSU-SE)	Attack planes and contact planes
Homing	Fifth Aircraft Communications Control (5 KO-TSU-SE)	Those unable to home because of trouble, damage or inclement weather etc

Chart 79

Article 21. When necessity arises, aircraft will be authorized to request any base to transmit a homing beam or request bearing of own plane by radio direction finder.

Part V. Wire Communications

Section 1. General

Article 22. Telegrams and telephone messages through a wire communications net will be handled in the same manner as the radio message according to the classification given.

Article 23. The wire communications nets and zones having the Kanoya and Oita Bases as centers are shown in appended sketches (not found in original text).

Section 2. Wire telegraphy

The method of communications by wire telegraphy will conform to radio communications.

Section 3. Wire telephony

Article 25. Wire telephone communications are divided into the following five classes according to their contents and priority:

    a. Telephone communications of antiaircraft defense information.

    b. Operational emergency telephone communications.

    c. Safety precaution and rescue telephone communications.

    d. Urgent telephone communications.

    e. Ordinary telephone communications.

Article 26. The handling of telephone communications and messages will follow the priority given in the preceding article.

Article 27. Telephone communications with higher priority than safety precaution and rescue telephone communications will be authorized if they are designated by the base command.

Article 28. Telephone communications will be controlled by special order when immediate dispatch of important messages is necessary. (Chart 80)

Classification	Control procedure
Emergency telephone communications control	All telephone communications other than those with higher priority than safety precaution and rescue telephone communications will be prohibited.
Urgent telephone communications control	Any telephone communications other than those with higher priority than urgent telephone communications will be prohibited.

Chart 80

Article 29. The telephone communications control will be in effect or rescinded by order of the senior commander of each wire communications zone according to the following:

Effective time: The control for emergency (urgent) telephone communications has been ordered at --- hour.

Rescission: The removal of the control for emergency (urgent) telephone communications has been ordered at --- hour.

Part VI. Emergency Measures

Article 30. An emergency disposition for equipment and men will be made by each base in preparation against possible decrease in communications capacity due to damage or loss or other reasons.

Article 31. Each base will maintain close contact with the nearest communications organ. It will be prepared to utilize it if its communications become inoperable due to damage or loss or other reasons.

Article 32. Whenever the communications capacity of a fleet flagship has declined, some other base may be designated to conduct fleet communications, partly or wholly.

Article 33. The priority of communications assignment will be decided as follows in preparation against possible decrease in communications efficiency at each base;

a. General broadcast net of the mobile base air force.

b. Order broadcast net.

c. One of B-type base communications nets.

Part VII. Communications Commands and General Communications Procedures.

Article 34. Base communications officer will exercise unified command over the communications department personnel of various forces at the base and will establish a definite system for communications command and execution of general communications procedures.

Article 35. In accordance with the conditions of the communications department personnel, equipment, facilities and portable and mobile equipment of the forces, the base communications officer will decide the disposition of communications equipment and personnel (Use classification, personnel assignment and emergency measures), so as to be able to conduct effectively both aircraft and base communications. Thus, the base communications officer will be able to expedite operational communications and fulfil the general communications procedures accurately and promptly. Moreover, he will promote close liaison between the communications department and each force commander to secure prompt and accurate transmission of communications.

Part VIII. Communications Inspection

Article 36. The communications inspection agent of this fleet will be the fleet flagship.

Article 37. The central organ of each communications net will inspect communications of the net. Each base will inspect communications of the B and C-type air communications nets.

Article 38. Each communications inspection agent will inspect radio and wire communications within the 1st Mobile Base Air Force in accordance with the Naval Communications Regulations.

Article 39. Specially important matters resulting from inspection will be reported by telephone (or telegram) each time. Other matters will be reported by written reports at the end of the month.

Chart 74-a

Radio Transmission and Receiving Standard for Each Unit (or Base) of the 1st Mobile Base Air Force

	Communications Net	Fleet Headquarters	Base with Flotilla or Afld Unit HQ	Each Base
	1st Mobile Base Air Force Comm. Net	A	B	B
	Flagship Comm. Net	A	A	
A-Type Base Comm Net	Information Broadcast Net	B	B	B
	Order Broadcast Net	A	B	B
	General Comm. Net	C	C	C
B-Type Base Comm Net	Base Comm. Net No 1			
	Base Comm. Net No 2			
	Base Comm. Net No 3			
	Base Comm. Net No 4	B	A	A
	Base Comm. Net No 5			
	Base Comm. Net No 6			
	Base Comm. Net No 7			
	Base Comm. Net No 8			
	1st Mobile Base Air Force Warning Comm Net or Warning Broadcast Net	B	B	B
	Combined Fleet A-Type Ship Comm. Net	C		
	Combined Fleet A-Type Force Comm. Net	C	C	
	6th Special Communications Net	C		

Radio Transmission and Receiving Standard for Each Unit (or Base) of the 1st Mobile Base Air Force (Cont'd)

Chart 74-b

Communications Net			Fleet Headquarters	Base with Flotilla or Afld Unit HQ	Each Base
Central Fixed Communications Net			C		
Aircraft Communications Net	A-Type		E	E	E
	B-Type		D	D	D
	Air Transport		D	D	D
5th Weather Broadcast Net			D		
Weather Broadcast Net			E	E	E
Local Communications Net			A		
Broadcast Net	Central First Broadcast		B	B	
	Central Second Broadcast		E	E	E
	Local Broadcast		B	B	B
Others by special order			Special order	Special order	Special order

Note:
1. Messages through the broadcast net will be considered to have been acknowledged (received) by each station at the time of broadcast.
2. Personnel for the Combined Fleet A-type ship communications net and Combined Fleet A-type force communications net will be assigned to forces in operation concerned.
3. As a rule, the information receiving set will be used for receiving information and order broadcast.
4. Key to letters:
   A..... Continuous transmission and receiving
   B..... Continuous receiving
   C..... Transmission and receiving by special orders
   D..... Transmission and receiving when necessary
   E..... Receiving when necessary

Chart 75

A-Type Base Radio Communications System and Assignments

Communications Net and Abbreviation	Communications Hours	Frequency (Pro sign)	Central Base	Assigned Base
Flagship Communications Net (KI-TSU-KE)	Continuous	7225 (KE-RI 20) 2612.5 (KE-RI 020)	Fleet Headquarters	Base with flotilla and airfield unit headquarters
General Communications Net (I-TSU-KE)	By special order (request)	6300 (KU-YO 26) 3150 (KU-YO 026)		
1st Broadcast Net (1 HA-TSU-KE)	Continuous	7875 (KE-RI 51) 3937.5 (KE-RI 051)	Headquarters or designated base	Each base of the 1st Mobile Base Air Force
2d Broadcast Net (2 HA-TSU-KE)	By special order	7345 (KE-RI 26) 3672.5 (KE-RI 026)		
Kanoya Information Broadcast Net (KA-YA-HA-KE)		1405 (U-ME 6) 7335 (KE-RI 24)	Kanoya	
Oita Information Broadcast Net (I-TA-HA-KE)	Occasional	1560 (U-ME 15) 8380 (FU-RU 22)	Oita	
Omura Information Broadcast Net (MU-RA-HA-KE)		1440 (U-ME 8)	Omura	Each base of the 1st Mobile Base Air Force
Matsuyama Information Broadcast Net (MA-TSU-HA-KE)		1440 (U-ME 8)	Matsuyama	
Order Communications Net (ME-I-HA-TSU-KE)	By special order	2540 8890 (FU-RU 50)	Fleet Headquarters	
Warning Broadcast Net (KE-I-HA-TSU-KE)	Continuous	271 (A-MA 30)	Kanoya	

Chart 76-a

B-Type Base Radio Communications System and Assignments

Communications Net (Abbreviation)	Frequency (Bro sign)	Communications Hours	Central Base	Assigned Base
1st Base Communications Net (1 KI-CHI-KE)	Primary 6290 (KU-YO 24) 3145 (KU-YO 024) Secondary 271 (A-MA 30) 4690 (KA-YU 15)	Continuous	Kanoya	Each base assigned to the Kyushu Airfield Unit
2d Base Communications Net (2 KI-CHI-KE)	Primary 6105 (KU-YO 7) 3052.5 (KU-YO 07) Secondary 436 (I-MI 59) 4595 (SA-RO 013)		Kanoya	Each base in the Nansei Islands
3d Base Communications Net (3 KI-CHI-KE)	Primary 6765 (KU-YO 57) 3382.5 (KU-YO 957) Secondary 284 (A-MA 34) 4305 (KO-RU 033)		Oita	Each base assigned to the Saikai Airfield Unit
4th Base Communications Net (4 KI-CHI-KE)	Primary 6480 (KU-YO 37) 3240 (KU-YO 037) Secondary 283 (A-MA 33) 4870 (SA-RO 083)		Miho	Each base assigned to the Sanin Airfield Unit
5th Base Communications Net (5 KI-CHI-KE)	Primary 6905 (KU-YO 66) 3452.5 (KU-YO 066) Secondary 267 (A-MA 28) 4595 (SA-RO 013)		Matsuyama	Each base assigned to the Inland Sea Airfield Unit
6th Base Communications Net (6 KI-CHI-KE)	Primary 6070 (KU-YO 6) 3035 (KU-YO 06) Secondary 273 (A-MA 31) 4395 (KO-RU 034)		Geijitsu	Each base assigned to Korea Airfield Unit

Chart 76-b

B-Type Base Radio Communications
System and Assignment (cont'd)

Communications Net (Abbreviation)	Frequency (Bro sign)	Communications Hours	Central Base	Assigned Base
7th Base Communications Net (7 KI-CHI-KE)	6005 (KU-YO 1) 7105 (KE-RI 10) 6195 (KU-YO 13) 273 (A-MA 31) 6260 (KU-YO 20) 3552.5			As designated by the 72d Air Flotilla Headquarters
8th Base Communications Net (8 KI-CHI-KE)	8235 3345 6690 441 4117.5 4690 (KA-YU 15)			As designated by the 12th Air Flotilla Headquarters

Note:
Primary use between seaplane bases is authorized.

Remarks:

1. Medium frequency will be used primarily. In case communications are difficult by medium frequency, high frequency will be switched on or used jointly with medium frequency.

2. In general, day frequency will be used from 0600 hours to 1800 hours, and night frequency from 1800 hours to 0600 hours. However, in case the time is changed depending upon the situation, each central base must make an immediate report to each unit concerned.

3. Although assigned bases of each communications net will be designated by this chart, the designated communications nets may be changed according to strength disposition and operation.

Chart 77

Warning Nets

Communications Net	Assigned Lookout Post	Frequency (Pro sign)	Central Base	Frequency	Comm Hour
1st Warning Communications Net (1 KE-I)	Toisaki Akune	4135 (KO-RU 012)			
2d Warning Communications Net (2 KE-I)	Hisaki Tanegashimaminami	5212.5 (Temporary KE-E 70)			
3d Warning Communications Net (3 KE-I)	Bonomisaki Gohara	3112.5 (KU-YO 017)	Kanoya	5212.5 (Temporary, KI-E 70)	Continuous
4th Warning Communications Net (4 KE-I)	Tanegashimanaka Satamisaki	3522.4 (Temporary name KE-RI 04)			
5th Warning Communications Net (5 KE-I)	Kikai Minamidaito	5512.5 (SA-TA 7)			

Remarks:
1. Broadcast will be the standard procedure for warning communications at each lookout post.
2. Day frequency will be used from 0600 hours to 1800 hours, and night frequency from 1800 hours to 0600 hours. However, it may be changed depending upon the situation.

Aircraft Communications Plan and A-type Aircraft Radio Communications Frequency System of the 1st Mobile Base Air Force

Communications Plan (abbreviation)		A-type High Frequency (Frequency pro sign)		A-type Low Frequency (Frequency pro sign)
1st Air Communications Plan (1 KO-KU-TSU-HA)		7635 (KE-RI 38)	3817.5 (KE-RI 038)	367 (I-MI 27)
2d Air Communications Plan (2 KO-KU-TSU-HA)		6685 (KU-YO 54)	3342.5 (KU-YO 054)	367 (I-MI 27)
3d Air Communications Plan (3 KO-KU-TSU-HA)		6842 (KU-YO 62)	3421 (KU-YO 062)	397 (I-MI 43)
4th Air Communications Plan (4 KO-KU-TSU-HA)		5850 (KI-E 50)	2925 (KI-E 050)	397 (I-MI 43)
6th Air Communications Plan (6 KO-KU-TSU-HA)	A	7635 (KE-RI 38)	3817.5 (KE-RI 038)	367 (I-MI 27)
	B	6685 (KU-YO 54)	3342.5 (KU-YO 054)	397 (I-MI 31)
7th Air Communications Plan (7 KO-KU-TSU-HA)	A	7635 (KE-RI 38)	3817.5 (KE-RI 038)	367 (I-MI 27)
	B	6842 (KU-YO 62)	3341.5 (KU-YO 054)	397 (I-MI 43)
8th Air Communications Plan (8 KO-KU-TSU-HA)	A	6685 (KU-YO 54)	3341.5 (KU-YO 054)	367 (I-MI 27)
	B	6842 (KU-YO 62)	3421 (KU-YO 062)	397 (I-MI 43)
11th Air Communications Plan (11 KO-KU-TSU-HA)		6650 (KU-YO 52)	5895 (KI-E 55)	To be used by fighter plane unit. Details will be designated by the 72d Air Flotilla.

Chart 78-a

Remarks:

1. Use of B or C-type frequencies will be designated by each unit commander. In this case, appropriate reports on the working frequency must be made immediately.

2. Day frequency will be used from 0600 hours to 1800 hours, and night frequency from 1800 hours to 0600 hours, unless special orders are issued.

3. In case communications between the fighter plane units and attack units (contact planes and search planes) are necessary, the A-type frequency of the fighter plane unit concerned will be used. However, depending upon the situation, B or C-type frequency of the fighter plane units concerned may be used by agreement.

4. A-type high frequencies will be used by planes of patrol, search, contact and attack missions except in the case of 11th Air Communications Plan.

5. Headquarters, 1st Mobile Base Air Force will be responsible for the control of the A-type high frequencies except in the case of 11th Air Communications Plan.

6. A-type low frequencies will be used by each unit and base after combat operations. In this case, the base to which each air unit belongs, will be responsible for the communication control.

CHAPTER XI

Communications Plan for KETSU-GO Operation

In the general planning for communications as required for the KETSU-GO Operation, there were two predominant factors which had to be considered.

The first factor was the deficiency in the communications personnel. It was difficult to immediately replace the many excellent aircraft radiomen and ground radiomen lost in combat. Furthermore, the increase in newly-created units increased the need for communications facilities and personnel.

The second factor was the question of a communications agreement with the Army. In the past, the Army had not utilized radio communications as much as the Navy, and, had used only restricted radio power and few radio waves. Therefore, the Navy, which depended largely upon radio communications in operations, was not met with any serious obstructions. It was not until the Army started expanding its radio communications that it was realized an agreement concerning radio waves transmission was necessary. Moreover, as the theater of war converged on the Homeland and necessitated the Army and Navy to operate in the same battle area, such an agreement became imperative. With the units of each service destined to operate under the command of the other, direct liaison between the two services became necessary. Difficulties were inevitable as the Army and Navy had different communications methods (this being the main problem) as well as different communications equipment. Therefore, except in special cases, each service was to dispatch its own communications team to the other service to maintain liaison between the two services.

In formulating communications plans, the major points taken into consideration relative to the foregoing problems were the following:

1. Since the main strength used in the air operations was the air special attack forces with limited communications capacity, they were deployed virtually throughout Japan Proper because of their combat range and air base accommodations. Thus, it was the policy to enable these forces, in the event of enemy invasion, to move to the main areas of invasion within a short time and concentrate attack there.

2. The surface and underwater special attack forces' range of action was so restricted that they could operate only locally and thereby required close coordination with the air forces for effective operations.

3. As for the chain of command, the combat aircraft of the air forces were commanded (unified command) by the commanders of the Third and the Fifth Air Fleets, and the special attack units composed of training planes were commanded by the C in C of the Tenth Air Fleet. Both categories were under the unified command of the C in C, Navy General Command. The surface and underwater special attack

units were under the command of the commandants of the various naval districts and guard districts according to the areas of deployment. The Koryu submarines (with crew of 5 men), which had a relatively longer cruising range and better maneuverability than the other special attack submarines, were under the unified command of the commander of the 10th Special Attack Squadron and under the direct control of the C in C, Navy General Command.

4. The communications capacity of all the above-mentioned forces of various types was so limited that it was almost impossible to command and direct these forces after their departure from the bases except in the case of combat planes. It was, therefore, very important to obtain full information at the various bases as the success or failure of operations depended on this.

5. In the event of a decisive battle in the Homeland, it was anticipated that the enemy would carry out full-scale air raids against potential landing points, operational bases and rear bases. As such, since it was hardly feasible to depend on wire communications within the bases, the only alternative was to depend entirely on radio communication.

6. In view of the limited strength of air forces to be employed for reconnaissance and interception, very little could be expected from the reconnaissance planes to gain information on the enemy situation. Therefore, it was necessary to attach particular importance to the strengthening of lookout post facilities. Also, the gathering

of information and its prompt transmission were absolutely necessary.

7. The close cooperation and the exchange of information between the air forces and the surface-underwater special attack units were particularly important.

8. It was absolutely necessary to obtain flight weather information in order to concentrate forces and conduct large-scale movements. At the same time, it became necessary to transmit forecasts on local weather conditions to surface and underwater special attack units since their activities depended largely on weather and sea conditions.

9. The following aspects aggravated the communications problem: The acute shortage of communications officers and the deterioration of efficiency; the inferior technical skill of radiomen and especially the difficulty of recruiting skilled radiomen; the sharp increase in newly-created units (the rapid increase in air bases, new surface and underwater special attack units, new observation units et cetera); and the inadequacy of communications equipment.

Establishment of Communications Centers and Nets

After the communications center for air operations and surface and underwater special attack operations were established, communications equipment and skilled radiomen were assigned and communications systems established along this line: (Chart 81).

Main Center	Main Reserve Center	Main Operational Front	Auxiliary Center
Kanoya	Oita	Kyushu, Shikoku Area	Matsuyama, Omura
Yamato			
Kisarazu (Yokosuka)	Vicinity of Takasaki (tentative)	Central Kanto Area	Meiji, Yokosuka, Jimmachi

Chart 81

It was decided to strengthen communications units as communications centers for surface and underwater special attack operations. Communications units had already been organized as operational units and additional staffs were assigned for the purpose of effecting active functions in regard to operations, which superseded former administrative functions.

Close contact was established between the air operation communications nets which were mainly concerned with air operations, and the communications unit nets which were mainly concerned with surface and underwater special attack operations. At the same time, the operational communications nets were separated from the administrative communications nets in an effort to conduct efficient communications in combat operations.

Each unit endeavored, within the limits of its communications capacity, to obtain information by monitoring communications (mainly, broadcast communications) of the other units located in the area.

Moreover, each center established close and direct contact by entering the local communications net of the nearest communications unit, and the administrative communications of air units were handled by these units which were more powerful in their capacity than air units. Radiotelephone communications were generally employed and utilized as much as possible.

Since air operation communications centers were to be provided with communications capacities equivalent to those of communications units, the equipment was installed to effect broadcast communications. At the same time, a fixed broadcast system was added to the projects of the communications plan. This broadcast system was generally aimed to accomplish transmittal within the operational area of the unit and to the communications centers in the adjacent areas. The broadcast consisted mainly of operational communications and the objective was to enable most of the units' operational communications to be picked up through this broadcast.

Small-type radiotelephone equipment was used for liaison purposes and for the transmission of intelligence reports and orders within bases. This means was set up in order to connect the various departments dispersed within the bases and to alleviate any confusion in the event of destruction of wire communications due to heavy bombings.

In view of the prevailing conditions of communications equipment, conversation broadcast by small-type radiotelephone sets was mainly adopted and the multiple duplex system was employed. This system was used particularly by air units in transmitting or receiving communications concerning air raid intelligence reports, necessary orders and other various reports with bases where air supremacy had been lost.

Establishment of Lookout Posts

As the situation became grave with the imminent possibility of the enemy invading the Homeland, special lookout posts were deployed at anticipated landing fronts. Lookout communication nets were formed, and these, together with intelligence collating bodies, were used as the means to seek information on the enemy situation.

A special lookout posts was comprised of 10 observers, 3 radiomen and a TM-type portable telegraph set with hand generator. Approximately 10 of these lookout posts were attached to each special attack unit (surface and underwater suicide attack). The reason for the above assignment was that since the bases of these special attack units were located on the coastline, it was more advantageous to assign the nearest group of lookout posts to these bases, insofar as administration and logistics were concerned.

In the establishment of these lookout posts, certain precautionary measures were advocated for the maintenance of assigned functions. For one, total concealment was fundamental to prevent communications equipment from being a target for artillery bombardment and aerial bombing. Secondly, it was necessary for the lookout posts to select such positions as would enable them to survive and continue to function even within enemy landing areas.

Establishment of Weather Communications Nets

Weather reports were conducted through the wire communications of the Communications Ministry. By the beginning of 1945 however, such communications means were paralyzed owing to destruction by successive aerial bombings and it was necessary to resort to radio communications. The function of weather communications was then conducted by a committee of the three ministries (Army, Navy and Communications Ministry Joint Committee).

The Navy decided to broadcast overall weather conditions as reported in from its various central base (mainly from air bases). Consequently, a flight weather communications net was established (Chart 82) in order to facilitate air operations as well as any large-scale movement of forces after the start of operations.

Communications Among the Principal Operational Command Centers

A special communications net was set up for the purpose of establishing close contact among the commanders of the Fifth Air Fleet, the Third Air Fleet and the C in C's of the Navy General Command and the Navy General Staff, or in other words, the air operational command centers. For this communications net, it was decided to utilize the 6th Special Communications Net prescribed by the Navy Communications Regulations. The 6th Special Communications Net was reorganized to accommodate the requirements of the command centers.

Chart 82-a

Frequencies of Flight-Weather Communication Net

Communications Net		Key	1st Flight-Weather Communications Net		
Broadcasting Base		1	Chitose (5th Weather Unit Headquarters)		
Code		2	MI-HA		
Broadcasting Base		3	From 10 minutes past every hour		
Broadcasting Frequency	Normal	4	3,430 KC and joint use of second and third harmonic frequencies		
	Auxiliary and Evading	5	3,647.6 KC and joint use of second and third harmonic frequencies		
Central Base (Communications Unit)		6	Chitose		
Stations of the Communications Net		7	Bihoro Nemuro Akeshi	Odomari Motodomari Wakkanai	Ominato Yamada Misawa Kabayama
Communication Time		8	Regular		
Telegraphic Frequency	Normal (Auxiliary and Evading)	9	Harmonic	Harmonic	Harmonic
		10	2.867.5 KC	2,610 KC	2,362.5 KC

350

Frequencies of Flight-Weather Communication Net (Cont'd)   Chart 82-b

Key	2d Flight-Weather Communications Net		3d Flight-Weather Communications Net
1	Kisarazu		Yokosuka
2	TA-CHI		
3	From 10 minutes past every hour		From 10 minutes past every hour
4	2,887.5 KC and joint use of second and third harmonic frequencies		
5	3,212.5 KC and joint use of second and third harmonic frequencies		
6	Kisarazu		Yokosuka
7	Katori Koriyama Matsushima Jimmachi Tateyama	Fujieda Meiji Hachijojima	Minamitorijima Chichijima Hahajima Torijima
8	Regular		Regular
9	Harmonic	Harmonic	Harmonic
10	2,430 KC	2,670 KC	4,002.5 KC

Frequencies of Flight-Weather Communication Net (Cont'd)   Chart 82-c

Key	4th Flight-Weather Communications Net		5th Flight-Weather Communications Net		
1	Suzuya (Yamato)		Kanoya		
2	SA-YO		KA-RA		
3	From 10 minutes past every hour		From 10 minutes past every hour		
4	2,922.5 KC and joint use of second and third harmonic frequencies		3,567.5 KC and joint use of second and third harmonic frequencies		
5	3,132.5 KC and joint use of second and third harmonic frequencies		3,910 KC and joint use of second and third harmonic frequencies		
6	Suzuya (Yamato)		Kanoya		
7	Komatsu Maizuru (Mineyama) Kushimoto Miho	Matsuyama Tokuyama Iwakuni Kannonji	Oita Saeki Miyazaki	Hakata Omura Goto	Minamidaito Okidaito Kikaigashima Koroku
8	Regular		Regular		
9	Harmonic	Harmonic	Harmonic	Harmonic	Harmonic
10	2,337.5 KC	2,397.5 KC	2,307.5 KC	2,437.5 KC	2,962.5 KC

Frequencies of Flight-Weather Communication Net (Cont'd)　　　Chart 82-d

6th	7th	8th	9th	10th	11th	12th	13th	14th
Shanghai	Takao	Samah	Philippine Area Base, determined by C in C, SW Area Fleet	Singapore	Soerabaja	Amboina	Rabaul	Truk
Determined by respective Commander in Chief									
Omitted									

Frequencies of Flight-Weather
Communication Net (Cont'd)

Chart 82-e

Notes

1. Attention will be paid particularly to maintenance of regular transmission of weather reports.

2. Weather reports will be transmitted to central base from stations of the communication nets by means of series of communications (in the order listed herein) so as to start two minutes after the scheduled observation time and finish within ten minutes after the said time.

3. Matters concerning weather reports at other than regular time will be determined by the C in C.

4. Communications of the 3d Flight-Weather Communication Net between the Yokosuka Communications Unit and stations thereof will be received at Kisarazu and will be broadcast by the 2d Flight-Weather Communication Net.

5. As a rule, three broadcasting frequencies will be used simultaneously in the daytime and at night.

6. Broadcasting bases will send operator's signals, sometimes with broadcast classification signals, for three minutes immediately before starting regular weather broadcasting; however, broadcast classification signals may be omitted, depending on the situation.

7. As a rule, broadcast messages will be transmitted twice.

8. The C in C of the central base may increase or decrease the number of stations of the communication net as may be necessary; in such instance, he will report to or notify beforehand the quarters concerned.

For operational liaison among the operational command centers of surface and underwater special attack units, it was decided to use mainly the 1st Special Communications Net and this net was reorganized as shown in Chart 83.

Air Fleet Headquarters Broadcast Communications Net

A broadcast communications net was established with the base headquarters of each air fleet. Since each air fleet had been assigned a definite area of operations, continuous communications for the overall area was unnecessary; therefore, one radio wave was used during the day and another was designated for night. Also, it was decided that the broadcast communications nets of the reserve bases would use one radio wave. In anticipation of a sharp increase in communications traffic, each net was permitted to establish a second broadcast, the details of which were left to the discretion of the headquarters of the Combined Fleet, and the headquarters of each air fleet.

Air Base Telecommunications

The following communications nets and functions came under the category for telecommunications:

1. Order broadcast communications net:

    This was used mainly for the transmission of important orders and operational intelligence. It was designed to transmit necessary orders and intelligence reports directly

Operational Command Centers

Chart 83

Communications Net	Communications Center	Assigned to Communications Net	Frequency (KC)		
			Primary	Secondary	Reserve
6th Special Communications Net	Commander, Fifth Air Fleet	Tokyo Commander, First Air Fleet	4742.5 (TO 7108)	9485 (TOKU 208)	4420 (TOKU 106)
		C in C, Navy General Command (To join when necessary)	10265 (TO 7210)	5132.5 (TOKU 110)	8840 (TOKU 206)
		Commander, Third Air Fleet (To join when necessary)			13260 (TOKU 306)
		Commander, Tenth Air Fleet (To join when necessary)			17680 (TOKU 680)
1st Special Communications Net	Tokyo	Yokosuka Kure Sasebo	4045 (TO 7104)	3752.5 (TOKU 102)	
		Various Special attack squadrons (To join when necessary)	7505 (TO 7202)	11257.5 (TOKU 302)	
		Osaka (To join when necessary)		15010 (TOKU 402)	
		C in C, Navy General Command (To join when necessary)		8090 (TOKU 204)	

Note: "To join when necessary" was ordered in an attempt to curtail traffic and insure rapid communications by having units in the areas where operations occurred to join the communications nets only when necessary. It was decided that as a principle, the commanders of the various units would effect participation in the nets at their own discretion.

to commanding officers or to pertinent agencies by means of small medium wave transmitters. Receiving was by telephone receivers (radio receivers) installed at each revetment group, maintenance command post, air defense command post, flight personnel alert station and at other important installations.

2. Combat duty communications net:

Small transmitters were installed at each revetment group, maintenance command post, combat command post and other installations, and they were used to convey assignment of combat duties within the base.

3. Intelligence broadcast communications net:

This was used mainly for the transmission of air defense intelligence. The central base of each base group was equipped with a transmitter, and consolidated intelligence reports were transmitted directly to the installations mentioned in the previous paragraph.

In a situation involving a large-scale movement of air forces, the radio waves of both aircraft and base communications nets were established according to movement plans. In case the weather conditions necessitated changes in frequency band for that day, the aircraft radio waves could be changed as well as in other unavoidable cases wherein radio waves could be changed partially.

The emergency assignment for the central fixed communications net was prescribed in preparation for the suspension or curtailment of the functions of the Tokyo Communications Unit. The outline of the above communications net is shown in Chart 84. This was to start functioning through the directive or order of the Chief of Naval General Staff or the Navy Minister.

Communications Plan for Surface and Underwater Special Attack Units

The communication capacity of a special attack craft was so limited that it was almost impossible to direct or conduct it from its base in accordance with the change in the situation after its departure from the base. Therefore, primary importance was attached to base communications with the object of enabling base commanders and division commanders to make necessary estimates of the situation and obtain all the necessary information before sailing from the base.

The radiotelephone was to be utilized mainly because of its simplicity and reliability of communications. In particular, speed was an important factor for special attack craft which, in view of their range of action and their tactics, were to operate on the enemy's landing fronts where the most intensive aerial bombings and naval bombardment were anticipated.

Considering the anticipated time of the enemy invasion and the time required for the deployment of forces as estimated from the general situation, it was necessary that the equipment be complete and the personnel concerned attain and maintain the desired level of

Emergency Central Communications Net

Chart 84

Emergency Central Communications Unit	1st Assigned Stations (O-HA No 1)	Kure (Maizuru)			Ominato				Sasebo	
	2d Assigned Stations (O-HA No 2)	Sasebo	Ominato							Sasebo
	3d Assigned Stations (O-HA No 3)	Kure (Maizuru)							Ominato	
Stations of the Communications Net		Takao	Shokosan	10th Comm. Unit	4th Comm. Unit	8th Comm. Unit	3d Comm. Unit	32d Comm. Unit	31st Comm. Unit	21st Comm. Unit	24th Comm. Unit
Communications Time		Continuously									
Communications Frequency (Kilocycle)	Normal	4,705 (TO 125) 13,520 (TO 150)	5,085 (TO 130) 10,170 (TO 230)	6,235 (TO 141) 17,590 (TO 153)		5,125 (TO 131) 17,630 (TO 154)	7,282.5 (TO 145) 17,925 (TO 147)		4,270 (TO 119) 12,810 (TO 319)	6,122.5 (TO 140) 18,367.5 (TO 340)	
	Simultaneous Transmission and Reception and Evading	4,980- (TO 128) 9,960 (TO 228)		5,545 (TO 135) 16,535 (TO 335)		5,047.5 (TO 129) 17,235 (TO 151)	7,305 (TO 146) 16,440 (TO 334)			5,905 (TO 139) 19,335 (TO 249)	

Notes:
1. The central communications unit and the stations thereof will use the same frequencies, and the frequencies for simultaneous transmission and reception will be used, when necessary, by the Central Communications Unit.
2. Request for simultaneous transmission and reception will be made by the central communications unit to any station it desires to communicate with, and "HO-NI" will be the abbreviation for the request.
3. Communications between the Tokyo Naval Communications Unit and the emergency Central Communications Unit will be maintained through a convenient communication net, depending on the situation.
4. "O-HA" will be the abbreviation for the assigned station and the number of the assigned station will be indicated by placing the necessary figure(s) before the abbreviation.

skill by mid-August at the latest. However, since electrical installation work had grown to vast proportions in the midst of preparations for the all-out decisive Homeland battle, the Navy depot technicians available for the execution of this plan were more or less limited to those on the instructor-worker level. This limitation required that portable equipment was necessarily of low-power output, it was an important factor which had to be considered in the formulation of the communications plan.

A-Type Communications Net

This was the communications net used exclusively for operational liaison among important commanders, and the 1st Special Communications Net prescribed by the Navy Communications Net was modified to meet this demand (Chart 85).

Communications Net	Central Communications Unit	Assigned to Communications Net	Frequency (KC) Primary	Frequency (KC) Secondary	Remarks
1st Special Communications Net	Tokyo	Yokosuka			Headquarters of various special attack units on combat fronts will hook up with this communications net through special order.
		Kure			
		Sasebo		3752.5	
		Commanders of special attack squadrons (To join when necessary)	4045	11257.5	
		Osaka (To join when necessary)	7505	15010	
		C in C, Navy General Command (To join when necessary		8090	
		Commander each air fleet (To join when necessary)			

Chart 85

B-Type Communications Net

This was used mainly for operational liaison between the headquarters of a special attack squadron and the headquarters of various special attack units and detachments under its command. This was a radio communications net wherein either medium or high frequency was used, depending on the distance and installations.

C-Type Communications Net

This was a radio communications net used mainly for liaison communications (including administrative functions) among the various bases within each special attack unit and had its center at the headquarters of the special attack unit. Ordinarily, communications by scheduled time were in effect, but continuous communications were effected by special order, depending on the operational situation.

Lookout Communications Net

This was used mainly for lookout report communications from the lookout posts within the area under charge of each special attack unit and the various bases. These communications were conducted in addition to administrative communications.

Broadcast Communications Nets

Squadron broadcast communications net: This was a radio communications net used mainly for the transmission of operational intelligence and operational orders to the various subordinate units. Low or medium frequency was used and the standard range of reception covered the headquarters of the various subordinate special attack units and their detachments.

Second broadcast communications net: This was used by the headquarters of the 10th Special Attack Squadron for directing operations when necessary. The principles for this broadcast were the same as those for the squadron flagship broadcast.

Base broadcast radiotelephone net: This was mainly used by each special attack unit to transmit intelligence, orders, et cetera to all its subordinate units and the messages were broadcast in plain or coded language. It was conducted on medium frequency (1200 KC to 1500 KC) telephone.

Special Attack Craft Communications

Each craft was to execute communications with the headquarters of its special attack unit as the communications center, but since the communications power differed in each craft, the headquarters of the special attack unit located nearest to the position of a craft as it moved was to assume charge of communication at an appropriate time according to the situation in the sea area of action and the conditions of communications. (See Chart 86 for Special Attack Craft Communications)

External Communications

The local communications net of the nearest communications unit

Special Attack Craft Communications

Craft	Factors for Communications	Standard Transmission Distance & Equipment
Koryu (Midget Submarine)	The object is to enable each craft to communicate with the base charged with the communications of that boat.	Base to craft: 200 miles (desired) Craft to base: 100 to 150 miles
Kairyu (Midget Submarine)	1. The object is to enable each boat to communicate with the base charged with the communications of that boat. 2. The Kairyu will transmit messages by telegraph and receive messages from the base by telephone.	Base to craft: 70 to 80 miles (desired) Craft to base: approx 30 miles
Shinyo (Suicide Boat)	1. Communications will be conducted within units only. The equipment and the communications methods are as follows: a. Type-5 Unit (24 craft in one unit): The command craft and a reserve command craft will be capable of both transmission and reception, while the other craft will be capable of reception only. b. Type-1 Unit (48 craft, including four Type-5 boats in one unit): One unit will be divided into four sections. Each section will have one Type-5 craft, which, as the section commander's craft, will be capable of both transmission and reception. Other craft, being Type-5 craft, will have one radio equipment and will communicate by visual means. 2. When motor torpedo boats are attached as the lead craft, communications similar to those of motor torpedo boat divisions will be conducted.	1. Standard transmission distances: Craft to base: approx 20 miles Craft to craft: approx 5 km 2. Equipment: Radio set type: "KU" No 1. (Diverted from its normal use on fighter planes).
Motor Torpedo Boats	The object is to enable the lead boat to communicate with the boat and enable other boats to conduct only intra-division communications.	Equipment: TM portable telegraph

Chart 86

was used for liaison between the naval district or guard district headquarters and the headquarters of the special attack squadrons attached thereto. This net was used mainly for administrative communications, and, for operational communications, the broadcast net of the communications unit and the broadcast net within the special attack squadron were used principally.

Weather Communications

Because of the poor seaworthiness of special attack craft, it was found necessary to arrange special weather communications to report oceanographic data. To meet this requirement, the D-type broadcast was initiated. The receiving of this type of broadcast was limited to the special attack unit headquarters, detachment and higher echelons in consideration of equipment, personnel et cetera, and the special attack unit headquarters reported extracts of necessary matters (mainly by broadcast) to lower echelons.

Frequency System

When the national wire nets and assignment of the land defense forces were disrupted due to enemy bombings, there was an increasing demand for radio communications channels, and the need for effecting agreement on radio channels between the Army and the Navy was very acute. But the situation was such that the realization thereof was not simple by any means. Moreover, the calibre of the telegraph crew dropped and an efficient functioning of communications was impossible without the use of crystals.

Since comparatively low-powered sets were selected for distribution, it was presumed that the assignment of different frequencies to adjacent areas alone would not create radio interference when similar frequencies were used between non-adjacent areas. For this reason, two or three sets of frequency systems were prescribed for each communications net and assigned in such a manner that neighboring special attack squadrons operated on different frequencies. Such measures tended to alleviate problems of crystal production and supply, and moreover, the special attack forces were able to hasten the completion of war preparations as well as to promote and simplify training.

With the special attack squadron as one unit, two sets of a series of frequency systems were composed and assigned so that adjacent special attack squadrons used different frequency systems (Chart 87 incomplete.) However, separate frequencies were assigned to the 2d Surface Special Attack Squadron (training unit) and the 10th Special Attack Squadron. The details are as follows:

1. B-type communications net:

    Two sets of frequency series comprising one medium frequency and one high frequency (one for day and the other for night) were prescribed and assigned so as to avoid the use of the same frequencies by adjacent special attack squadrons.

2. C-type communications net:

    Different frequencies were assigned to each special attack

Special Attack Squadron Frequency System (Incomplete)

Special Attack Squadrons	7th	1st	4th	6th	8th	5th	3d	10th	2d
Type B Communications Net	A	B	A	B	A	B	A	D	R
Type C Communications Net	M (cadb)	N (genf)	M	N	M	N	M		S T
Special Attack Squadron Broadcast	Y	Z	Y	Z	Y	Z	Y	X	
Special Attack Unit Broadcast	P (kilj)	Q (ompn)	P	Q	P	Q	P		U V W
Communications to Special Craft — Koryu Midget Submarine	E F	E F	E F	E F	E F	E F	E F	E F	
Communications to Special Craft — Kairyu Midget Submarine	G H	G H	G H	G H	G H	G H	G H		
Communications to Special Craft — Shinyo Suicide Boat	J (sptr)	J	J	J	J	J	J		
Lookout Communications Net	K (ywzx)	K	K	K	K	K	K		

Description:
1. Certain special frequencies will be assigned to the 1st Special Attack Squadron for Kairyu midget submarine training as well as to the 3d Special Attack Squadron for suicide boat training.
2. Special frequencies for exclusive use of midget submarines will be assigned to the 2d Special Attack Squadron as the training unit of midget submarines.

Chart 87

unit, and two sets of frequency series were prescribed for each special attack squadron and were assigned so as to avoid the use of the same frequencies by adjacent special attack squadrons.

3. Squadron broadcast net:

   Two sets of frequency series comprising one low frequency, one medium, and one high frequency were prescribed and assigned so as to avoid the use of the same frequencies by adjacent special attack squadrons. Each special attack squadron headquarters selected a low, medium or high frequency depending upon geographical and other conditions. One frequency was separately prescribed for the 10th Special Attack Squadron and provisions were made to enable it to use this channel as the second broadcast net, solely for command communications when necessary in mobile operations.

4. The base broadcast net:

   Frequencies from 1,200 to 1,500 KC were selected and assigned on the same principle as the C-type communications net.

5. Craft communications:

   Both the Koryu and Kairyu midget submarines had one primary frequency and one auxiliary frequency, and all these midget submarines used one and the same frequency. One frequency for each Shinyo (suicide boat) assault unit was the standard and each special attack squadron used one and the same frequency.

6. The lookout communications net:

   One frequency for each special attack unit was the standard and each special attack squadron used one and the same frequency.

7. Frequency for training purposes:

   For training purposes of the craft, the frequencies for the Koryu and the Kairyu were assigned respectively to the 2d Special Attack Squadron and the 1st Special Attack Squadron, and some of the waves for the Shinyo suicide boats and some for security communications were assigned to the 2d Special Attack Squadron.

Communications Equipment for Secret Bases of Special Attack Planes

In April 1945, the construction of scores of secret airfields (provisionally called "pastures") was undertaken in the Homeland to conceal special attack planes and to launch suicide air attacks in the event of enemy landings on Japan Proper.

The communications personnel and facilities for these airfields were limited to a bare minimum in view of the acute shortage of materials, construction capacity and radio personnel at the time. Therefore, the objective was to establish one circuit of liaison communications net between one airfield and its nearest central base and thereby obtain adequate operational information to facilitate operations of the special attack plane unit. Each "pasture" was equipped with one aircraft radiotelephone and one radio receiver to effect radiotelephone liaison with the central base as well as pick up the intelligence broadcast of the central base. The installation of this equipment was to be carried out by the unit assigned to the base and the supply of equipment was started early in July, but due to transportation difficulties caused by air raids, this work was not completed before the end of the war.

Since base radiotelephones were required to be installed inside air raid shelters in accordance with the communications plan (wire telephone was susceptible to damage by air raids), an experiment for its installation and transmission was conducted at Atsugi Airfield.

Favorable results were obtained so preparations were made to install the equipment at each base.

Since it was urgent that installations be expedited for these special attack unit bases, a policy was adopted wherein the unit members themselves conducted the installation work. Accordingly, it was planned to install mostly the small portable type. However, since this equipment was to be installed in cave-type air raid shelters, skill was required for installation as it had a great bearing on the transmission capacity. Preparatory experiments were conducted at the Communications School and the Yokosuka Branch of the Technical Research Laboratory, and technical instructor groups from the Communications School and Navy Yard were dispatched to each unit to render instructions. Despite such efforts, favorable results were not obtained owing to the lack of knowledge of the staff and the incompetency of the radio crew concerned.

Radio Equipment for the Surface Special Attack Unit Bases

The construction of the special attack unit bases was hurriedly started in April 1945 for the purpose of sheltering and keeping one or all types of sea-borne special attack craft, such as Shinyo, Koryu and Kairyu, in readiness for action. However, the actual start of construction was delayed considerably because the sites of the bases were not specified for some time.

As the decisive battle of the Homeland became imminent, all the authorities concerned renewed their efforts to overcome the diffuculty of transportation and the shortage of materials. By mobilizing the total strength of the forces as well as those concerned with the Construction Board, these bases were generally completed in Kyushu, Shikoku, Izu and Boso areas by the end of July.

Radio receivers mainly for the reception of broadcasts and the TM-type portable radio sets as auxiliary apparatuses were distributed to the dispersed detachments, but there was considerable difficulty in obtaining power supply.

Problem of Communications Personnel

As the war situation became critical, it was necessary to make revisions in the communications plan as well as readjustments in personnel assignment. The personnel situation at that time is shown in Chart 88. The figures show that the total number of personnel was more than adequate (ordinary communications personnel), but an overall enforcement of assignment was impossible as the available number of advance personnel was entirely inadequate, aggravated by the fact that even such personnel that were available could not be assigned due to disrupted transportation.

It was decided out of sheer necessity to effect assignment to important positions, and the assignments were made in the following priority:

First: Base air force

Chart 88

A Comparative Table of Authorized, Required and Available Communications Personnel
(As of 1 March 1945)

Classification		Authorized Strength	Personnel Required for Assignment	Personnel Available for Assignment	Difference between Personnel Required and Personnel Available
Radiomen	Advance	6,398	12,879	4,126	-8,753
	Ordinary	9,067	18,436	22,147	+3,711
	Total	15,465	31,315	26,273	-5,042
Codemen	Advance	1,786	3,770	907	-2,863
	Ordinary	636	4,924	6,572	+1,648
	Total	2,422	8,694	7,479	-1,215
Signalmen	Advance	2,714	4,892	1,876	-2,016
	Ordinary	6,384	11,148	14,459	+3,311
	Total	9,098	16,040	16,335	+ 295

Second: Communications units in the Homeland

Third: Special attack units

However, despite priority assignments it was impossible to fulfill the great need for communications department officers and specialists of advanced skill and an improvement of over-all communications skill which the Central Agency desired could never be expected if the status quo were maintained. As a replenishment source, there were only crews of surface vessels and senior and junior instructors of the communications schools; advanced course enlisted trainees were not available due to the several advance graduations of trainees. It was finally decided that there was no alternative but to close the naval communications schools in view of the prevailing crisis of the war.

When the decision for closing the communications schools was made, an announcement was made to that effect (See Chart 89 for schedule). The Yokosuka Communications School (including the Toyokawa Annex School) was closed temporarily on 15 July 1945. The Bofu Communications School suspended technical education and operated only as an educational institute for class-A and class-B primary flight enlisted trainees.

Following the closing of communications schools, the research work and instructive matters which had been conducted by the Research Department was a matter of grave concern. The duties thereof were transferred to the 1st Combined Communications Unit headquarters

Chart 89-a

Advance Graduation of Officers and Enlisted Trainees and Discontinuance of Enrollment

School	Trainee Course	Graduating Class	Steps Taken	Notes
	Specialist Officer Trainee	53d	Advance graduation on 10 July	
	Special Duty Officer and Warrant Officer Cryptology Short-term Course Trainee		No admission	
	Reserve Officer Cryptology Short-term Course Trainee	First	Advance graduation on 20 June	The scheduled date of admission was advanced to 20 June.
		Second	Advance graduation on 10 July	
	Ordinary Course Radio Enlisted Trainee (Exchange of Communications)	73d	Advance graduation on 10 July	
		74th	Training discontinued on 10 July	
Yokosuka Naval Communications School	A-Class Primary Flight Enlisted Trainee	2d	Advance graduation on 8 July	
	Reserve Enlisted Trainee	A-Class) 3d B-Class)	Advance graduation on 10 July	
		A-Class) 4th B-Class)	No admission	
	Reserve Cadet Trainee	2d	Advance graduation on 10 July	
		3d	No admission	
	Communications Staff Trainee		Training discontinued as of 1 July	
	Ordinary Course Cryptology Enlisted Trainee	10th	Advance graduation on 10 July	

Chart 89-b

Advance Graduation of Officers and Enlisted Trainees and Discontinuance of Enrollment (Cont'd)

School	Trainee Course	Graduating Class	Steps Taken	Notes
	Special Communications Staff Trainee	2d	Trained at the Yokosuka and Maizuru Communications Units	The scheduled date of admission was advanced to 20 June.
	B-Class Primary Flight Enlisted Trainee	1st	No admission	
	Ordinary Course Radio Enlisted Trainee A & B	73d	Advance graduation on 30 June Advance graduation on 10 July	
	Special Communications Staff Trainee		No admission, but trained at the Kure and Sasebo Communications Units	
Bofu Naval Communications School	A-Class Primary Flight Enlisted Trainee	2d	Advance graduation on 10 July	The date of admitting A-Class and B-Class primary flight enlisted trainees originally scheduled to be admitted after June was changed to some extent; also only basic training was given.
		3d	Advance graduation after the middle of June	
	B-Class Primary Flight Enlisted Trainee	2d	Training discontinued prior to and as of 10 July	
		3d	Same as above	
	Ordinary Course Radio Enlisted Trainee	74th		
		1st, B-Class Flight	Advance graduation on 10 July	
	Emergency Radio (Exchange of Communications) Short Course Trainee	73d, Ordinary Course Radio	No admission	

which was then the guidance institute for communications of the Combined Fleet, and the work was scheduled to be continued there. Most of the personnel concerned were transferred to the said headquarters without any change of status.

Communications Preparations Relative to the Moving of Imperial General Headquarters

As the preparation of the operational plan for the KETSU-GO decisive battle was being made, it became evident that auxiliary installations for the Tokyo Communications Unit (which was the communications center for naval operations) would be required. It was realized that such a project would require six months even with hasty construction. Moreover, since the Army was in the midst of constructing a big air raid shelter at Matsushiro in Nagano Prefecture to accommodate Imperial General Headquarters, the Navy arranged necessary equipment to be sent to Nagano and to Maizuru Naval District in accordance with the following policies:

1. The Ominato Communications Unit (Sasebo or Kure as its reserves) will take charge of the fixed communications net with isolated areas overseas (Refer to: Emergency Communications Assignment and the Revised Communications Regulations); the communications installations required for other communications nets being carried out by the Tokyo Communications Unit and others required for Owada Communication Unit's counterintelligence operations against the United States and Great Britain are to be prepared at the new shelter at Matsushiro.

2. Similar equipment will be installed in the Maizuru Naval Station as the second reserve installation.

In order to expedite the foregoing, a detachment of the Tokyo Communications Unit was sent to the localities concerned late in July 1945 and various projects were begun, but the war came to an end before they were completed.

Operational (Communications) Preparations of the Navy General Command

The communications plan of the Navy General Command in the KETSU-GO Operation was drafted early in June and a suitable plan was completed early in July. However, as there was much to be desired concerning communications equipment and personnel in the various units under the command, the headquarters maintained close contact with the Central Agency, discussed and studied various problems and endeavored to hasten technical preparations and replenish the personnel. Also, it endeavored to promote intensive training so as to effect efficient operation of communications and meet the requirements of the operation. All such efforts were aimed to attain full efficiency by the middle of August.

Communications Plan

The communications of the Navy General Command for the KETSU-GO decisive battle operation will be carried out in accordance with the Naval Communications Regulations and the Combined Fleet Operational Communications Regulations and supplemented with the following principles. Wire communications will be utilized to the fullest extent:

1. The communications of the ground forces:

    This will be based on the decision of the commanders of

the naval district and guard district units in accordance with the newly revised naval communications regulations.

2. Communication of air units:

   a. Base communications: Telephone communications (intelligence broadcast) will be used in addition to the existing base communications (Chart 90). In particular, the base communications of the combat planes and special attack planes will mainly utilize the telephone to effect rapid communications. The prerequisites for communications will be speed and accuracy, and mutual intelligence exchange will be conducted. The principal bases will monitor and utilize the intelligence broadcast of the surface and underwater special attack units.

   b. Aircraft communications: The communications of combat planes will be based upon the directives of commanders of the respective air force in accordance with the Combined Fleet Operational Communications Regulations. Special attack planes will use the designated frequency according to the following areas and the crystals on hand in the advance bases will be used for transmission only: South Kyushu; North Kyushu and Korea; Shikoku and Chukoku; Kinki, Hokuriku and Tokai areas. However, while the special attack planes are in flight from one base to another for transfer, every unit will use the frequency for common communications or fixed B-type frequency.

3. The communications of the surface and underwater special attack units:

   a. Base communications: This will be classified as in Chart 91. Communications of the 10th Special Attack Squadron will be the responsibility of the base to which the units of the squadron are located, and the communications net of the surface and underwater special attack squadron concerned will be utilized as much as possible. However, an intelligence boradcast channel of the 10th Special Attack Squadron will be provided separately. Moreover, the bases will receive and utilize the intelligence broadcast of the air forces as much as possible.

   b. Special attack craft communications:

   (1) <u>Koryu</u> communications: Communications by the time-schedule method with the base to which the

Chart 90

Base Telephone Communications

Communications Net		Assigned Bases and Purpose	Equipment
Telephone Communications	Type A	Telephone communications between central bases (Kisarazu, Kanoya, Oita, Yamato)	High frequency radio set No 4
	Type B	Telephone communications between central base and bases, and between bases	Aircraft radio set No 5
	Type C	Telephone communications between a base and secret base or section within the base.	Aircraft radio set No 5 Telephone set No 2
Intelligence Broadcast	Type A	Intelligence from central base	High frequency radio set No 3
	Type B	Intelligence and directives from base	Aircraft radio set No 5 Telephone set No 2
	Type C	Intelligence and directives within base	Aircraft radio set No 3 Telephone set No 2

Remarks: Part of the above may be omitted or combined with another, depending on the equipment, installation, personnel and other factors.

Special Attack Squadron Base Communications — Chart 91

Communications Net		Assigned Bases and Purpose	Frequency
Communications Net	Type A	For communications between naval district or guard district: Navy General Command and special attack squadron commander join when necessary.	1st Special Attack Communications net
	Type B	Communications between naval district or guard district and commander of special attack group and higher units under command.	Local net of naval district or guard district (Assigned to each special attack group)
	Type C	Telephone communications between special attack group commander and deployment base.	Assigned to each special attack group
Intelligence Broadcast	Type A	Intelligence from naval districts and guard districts (combined with air defense intelligence broadcast)	Intelligence broadcast nets of naval district and guard district
	Type B	Intelligence and directive of special attack squadron commander	Assigned to each special attack squadron
	Type C	Intelligence and directive of special attack group commander	Assigned to each special attack group
Lookout Communications		Communications between special attack group lookout base and lookout post	Same as above

craft is attached will be conducted in accordance with the submarine communications principles. The seas around the Homeland will be divided into four sections and each section will use different frequencies. However, the Koryu's attached to the 10th Special Attack Squadron will be assigned a specific channel and this will be used when necessary. The Koryu bases will monitor the above continuously while the Koryu's are at sea.

(2) The communications of the Shinyo suicide boats, Kairyu submarines and torpedo motor boats: These craft will maintain constant liaison with their bases while at sea and the radio waves will be assigned to the bases separately.

(3) Communications procedure: Abbreviated method using conventional call signs for aircraft communications will be carried out.

4. Communications of the surface forces:

    a. Ship communications: Type-A general communications net for vessels of the Combined Fleet and the nets for the vessels in the naval district and guard district sectors in the operational front will be utilized.

    b. Submarine communications: This will be based upon the communications plan prescribed by the Sixth Fleet (submarine fleet).

At the Navy General Command headquarters in Hiyoshi, the following measures were taken in order to strengthen its communication facilities:

1. In order to increase the control circuit with the Tokyo Communications Unit, a part of the control circuit of the Umegaya Detachment was taken over.

2. Three sets of radio control apparatus were installed for the transmitter control of the Totsuka Detachment.

3. Two portable high frequency transmitters were installed for the purpose of liaison with Headquarters, Tokyo Communications Unit.

4. The reserve transmitting station was hastened to completion.

5. The visual communications system with the Naval Ministry was installed.

6. Effort was directed to maintenance of the telephone lines with each important air base and the connecting circuits were increased.

7. Bombproof installations were strengthened and preparations were made to ensure handling of communications of the Central Agency in the event of destruction of the Tokyo Communications Unit.

Maintenance of Command Posts

The 2d Command Post (Kanoya) had been completed and used in the Okinawa and other operations with satisfactory results, but with the movement of the Fifth Air Fleet headquarters to Oita Base, it was planned to effect combat command of the Navy General Command by moving part of the equipment to Oita.

The preparation of the 3d Command Post (Yamato) was hastened insofar as possible by the Third Air Fleet headquarters after the headquarters had moved there, and it was expected to be used by the scheduled date (middle of August). However, there were many defects in the wire communications system centered around that base.

The Technical Advisory Staff

Up to this time, each fleet had been rendering instructions by dispatching its own advisory staff, but as the war situation became increasingly adverse, it was decided that the Navy General Command headquarters conduct instructions on a uniform basis from the standpoint of unifying technical instruction, economizing on personnel and meeting the requirements of the current operation. As the guiding organ for that purpose, the Technical Advisory Staff of the Navy General Command was organized at the end of July. Captain Sakura, Yoshio of the Headquarters was appointed chief, and the instructors were selected from the Communications School, Radar School, 2d Naval Air Depot, Yokosuka Air Group and the 1st Combined Communications Unit. The staff was divided into the Air Section, Ground Section, Radar Section, Equipment Maintenance Section, Code Section, Wire Section et cetera, and the personnel were dispatched to various areas to render instructions concerning the technical aspects of communications with priority fixed by the Navy General Command headquarters in accordance with the objective of the current operation.

Training and Guidance

Because of the severe drop in the standard of communications technical skill in addition to the shortage of equipment and personnel, there was an immediate need for the improvement of training. As such the following educational training and guidance were carried out.

    1. Aviation communications:

        The personnel detached from the Yokosuka Air Group and who had been responsible for instruction in the past were incorporated into the Technical Advisory Staff of the Navy General Command and charged with training instructions in aviation communications and equipment maintenance. Prior to the creation of the Advisory Staff, requests had come in at every opportunity for the dispatching of instructors, but the effective results could not be attained because of the large number of air bases and the lack of time for training due to intense air operations.

2. Air base communications:

This is similar to what had been mentioned in the preceding paragraph, and includes the personnel detached from the 1st Combined Communications Unit who took charge of maintenance of installations as well as training and guidance.

3. Communications of the surface and underwater special attack units:

This was relatively a new set-up of communications with little or no past experiences, and there was much to be desired in the way of equipment installations and personnel. Therefore, with a view to improving maintenance and training, the Sasebo and Kure Naval Districts carried out joint training early in June and in the middle of July (Fifth Air Fleet participated in the second training). In addition, training was held as often as possible in each Naval District.

The results were fair, but many unsatisfactory matters still existed, especially those attributable to incomplete installations and shortage of personnel. Requests were made to the Central Agency for strengthening the organization of each Naval District communications unit. Representatives of each communications unit were summoned to the Navy General Command headquarters late in June in an attempt to unify the conception of "operational-communications-first" principle. Moreover, arrangements were made for accelerating the work on installations and at the same time conduct intensive training. In addition, personnel were dispatched from the 1st Combined Communications Unit to be responsible for the supervision of the foregoing.

General Communications Training Maneuver

In order to analyze the potential capacity of communications of each unit for the decisive battle operation, a general communications maneuver was scheduled to be carried out in mid-August with all the units under the command of the Navy General Command participating. The Technical Advisory Staff of the Navy General Command and 1st Combined Communications Unit were to dispatch personnel for guidance and investigation of the results. (This was suspended, however, due to the termination of war.)

On 1 August, a report came in of an enemy invasion in the Sagami Bay area (this report later proved to be a false alarm). The "decisive battle alert" was sounded and other pertinent radio messages were dispatched. In this incident, an investigation was made on the efficiency of the communications procedure. Except for the air force communications, numerous shortcomings were depicted in the receiving and handling of communications.

Training of Apprentice Radiomen

Following the reduction and closing of communications schools, each communications unit was charged with the training of apprentice radiomen. Principal air bases carried out the education and training of apprentice radiomen under the direction of the respective air fleet headquarters. The Combined Fleet headquarters carried out the training of 50 trainees on two occasions and they were assigned to the units after about two months of training.

Survey of Reserve Equipment

The demand for crystal pieces increased tremendously with the assignment of more radio frequencies to the Combined Fleet. The crystal reserve stock was insufficient, particularly for aviation insofar as the radio frequency assignment plan was concerned. Accordingly, all crystal pieces possessed by the naval air depots, ships and craft were collected at the Navy General Command headquarters to expedite their availability as well as to facilitate transportation. Moreover personnel from the Technical Advisory Staff were dispatched to air bases and air depots to conduct a survey for the purpose of utilizing idle equipment, expediting transportation and inspecting the status of preparation of equipment.

Communications Preparations of Fifth Air Fleet

The Kanoya and Oita Bases were thoroughly equipped as the Central and auxiliary communications bases respectively in case air operations were launched from the western part of Honshu and Kyushu. Operational zones were divided as follows and each zone had its communication center as indicated in parentheses; Nansei Islands (Koroku), Southern Kyushu (Kanoya), Northern Kyushu (Oita), Shikoku (Matsuyama), Chugoku (Shinkawa) and South Korea (Yonil).

In addition to the above, individual communications nets were established where close liaison for operations was especially required. They were the 71st Air Flotilla Communications Net for interception operations of the fighter plane units (Kanoya was designated the relay point but was changed to Oita Base later); the 12th Air Flotilla Communications Net for the 12th Air Flotilla special attack operation (Hakata Base was designated the relay point, but was changed to Oita Base later); the 634th Air Group Communications Net for seaplane unit operations (Genkai Base as the relay point).

Regarding the installation of radio communications equipment at Kanoya Base, efforts had been made since the middle of 1944 to complete the underground installations. However, in consideration of battle experiences, it became necessary to move the headquarters facilities underground. With a partial change made thereto shortly after the end of 1944, the work was generally completed by middle of 1945. The receiving room in the air defense tunnel was ready (equipped with approximately 60 Type-92 special receivers) early in February 1945. The moving was completed, and all communications were conducted in the air defense radioroom within this tunnel.

The 1st, 2d and 3d bombproof transmitting stations at Kanoya were completed in October 1944 and were equipped respectively with one each of Nos 3 and 4 high frequency transmitters, one TM-type portable high frequency transmitter and one low frequency transmitter. The 4th transmitting station was completed in mid-March 1945, and was equipped with four No 2 high frequency, two No 4 high frequency, two No 3 high frequency, four No 5 medium frequency and one low frequency sets.

The 1st generator room was constructed close to the 1st, 2d and 3d transmitting stations, the 2d generator room constructed close to the 4th Transmitting station. All were of the bombproof tunnel type and each was equipped with one 150-KW diesel generator; thus transmission of power to all the transmitting rooms and the receiving station was made possible. These were kept as reserve power sources, as normally, city electric power was used.

The Oita Base was originally planned and equipped as the auxiliary for the Kanoya Base. However, since the headquarters of Fifth Air Fleet, 27th Air Flotilla and 12th Air Flotilla were concentrated here in June 1945, installation of communications equipment similar to that of the Kanoya Base became necessary. The underground radio-room at Oita was completed late in July 1945 and it was equipped with approximately seventy Type-92 special receivers. In addition, a radio-room for the Fifth Air Fleet headquarters was under construction in the tunnel at Oita but it had not been completed. The 1st and 2d bombproof transmitting stations at Oita were nearly complete late in July 1945 and the 3d transmitting station was under construction when the war ended.

In all bases other than those in South Korea, transmitting and receiving stations set up in tunnels were quite complete and communication could be effected as provided for in the operational communications plan. In the South Korea sectors, construction was at a stalemate due to the loss of materials during the sea transportation.

With Kanoya Base as the relay point, the wire communications system connecting various bases in the Kyushu area was established. The long distance line to Tokyo was established about June 1945 with two circuits although only one circuit was in use most of the time as the other circuit was out of order. Also, a device for conducting secret conversations was completed.

The establishment of the communications net of the same scale as the Kanoya Base was planned with the Oita Base as the relay point. After the Air Fleet headquarters moved there, one of the Kanoya – Tokyo circuits was connected to the Oita Base, thus establishing two direct circuits. However, only one circuit was in actual operation as in the case of Kanoya.

Regarding communications personnel, approximately 700 apprentice seamen from the Kure, Maizuru and Sasebo Naval Districts were sent to the bases as reinforcements. In addition, the bases were strengthened with a crew of women communications personnel from the Women Volunteer Emergency Service. (120 women for Kanoya and Oita respectively).

In radio intelligence, efforts were made to obtain intelligence on the situation through interception of enemy radiotelephone communications in the Fifth Air Fleet area of operation. For this objective, about 70 radiomen and 20 radiotelephone men of the Special

Duty Group were assigned to Fifth Air Fleet headquarters. Twenty-five Type-92 special receivers and five all-wave radio receivers were supplied for use in this connection.

Communications Preparations of Third Air Fleet

The transfer of the Third Air Fleet headquarters to Yamato Base was definitely decided in May during the middle phase of the Okinawa Operation. Therefore, preparations for the KETSU-GO Operation were made with Yamato as the central base and efforts were exerted to equip the said base as early as possible.

The Yamato Base as Fleet headquarters (also Combined Air Fleet headquarters), was designated to install facilities necessary for friendly communications, radio direction finding control communications, weather reports, air defense intelligence and for the special intelligence section. The headquarters started construction of bombproof air defense shelters with the following equipment to be installed:

Receiving sets:	80
Telephone receivers (all-wave):	15
Telephone receivers (medium frequency):	20
Medium-size transmitters:	15
Small-size transmitters:	15
Generators (250 KVA)	2

As far as receiving sets were concerned, air raid shelters for them were nearly complete when the war ended. Installation of the transmitters was delayed as compared to that of the receiving equipment due to the delay in construction of bombproof shelters. However, when necessary, communications could be readily conducted without any trouble by placing in two places the transmitters which were originally to be installed in three places.

For radiotelephone communications, one of the basic factors which had to be considered was the range as far as communications plans were concerned. Experiments had been conducted in the Kanto area and on the basis of 80 percent of the results obtained thereof, concrete steps were taken for planning. Transmission to the west of Yamato was very satisfactory due to the topography and position of the transmitting station, but transmission to the eastern bases did not come up to expectation.

Communications Plan

The plan will be formulated in accordance with the Communications Plan for the KETSU-GO Operations of the Combined Fleet and its main points are as follows:

1. Radio Communications:

Strategical communications will be carried out mainly by radiotelegraph, and the tactical and the air defense information communications by radiotelephone. Emphasis will be placed on the efficient use of the command telephones within the base. In particular, the duties connected with antiaircraft control currently performed by the Osaka Naval Guard District will be transferred to Yamato Air Base and the pertinent communication facilities will be concentrated in the latter base.

   a. Communications Nets:

      (1) Broadcast net (use medium and high frequencies): The 1st Broadcast Net of the Third Air Fleet -- Yamato will be the center. The 2d Broadcast Net of Third Air Fleet -- Kisarazu will be the center.

      (2) The 6th Special Communications Net: The communications net prescribed by the Naval Communications Regulations will be adopted and used in communications among Yamato (Third Air Fleet headquarters), Oita (Fifth Air Fleet headquarters) and Tokyo Communications Unit (Imperial Headquarters), all being the principal operational command centers.

      (3) Telephone nets for air defense intelligence: These will be used mainly for the exchange of air defense intelligence between the headquarters of all fleets and those of naval districts. They will be consolidated into two telephone nets (For eastern and the Western Districts), with Yamato as their center.

      (4) Weather communications net: Until the flight weather report net prescribed by the Naval Communications Regulations is established, communications will be conducted to facilitate operations of the Third Air Fleet. The communications to be effected are as follows: Weather reports will be broadcast by such air bases as Matsushima, Kisarazu, Fujieda, Suzuka, Yamato, Matsuyama, Kochi, Omura, Oita, Tomitaka and Kanoya, where the actual weather conditions will be broadcast and exchanged at the beginning of every hour from 0400 to 1800 hours and every even numbered hour from 1800 to 0400 hours.

      (5) Flagship communications net (mainly by means of radiotelegraph): The following stations will be assigned to the net: Yamato (Third Air Fleet headquarters), Oita (Fifth Air Fleet headquarters), Meiji (Tokai Air Group headquarters), Kisarazu (Kanto Air Group headquarters), Matsushima

(to be included depending on the situation) and Yokosuka Naval District (to be included depending on the situation).

(6) Local communications net (mainly by means on the situation).

    (a) Tokai Local Communications Net:

        With Meiji as its central station, the net will include Nagoya, Fujieda and Toyohashi Air Bases.

    (b) Kanto Local Communications Net:

        With Kisarazu as its central station, the net will include Naruo, Himeji, Shiga (depending on the situation), Fukuchiyama, Iga-Ueno and Komatsu Air Bases.

(7) 12th Air Flotilla Communications Net (Radiotelegraph): With Yamato as its central station, the net will include the bases connected with the 13th Air Flotilla such as Oi, Okazaki, Suzuka, No 2 Kowa and Mineyama.

(8) Communications nets for air defense intelligence:

    (a) Air defense intelligence broadcast net (medium and high frequencies used jointly):

        Broadcasting base -- Yamato. It will be used exclusively for broadcasting the consolidated air defense intelligence.

    (b) Fighter-plane command communications net (medium frequency):

        This will be used mainly for fighter-plane command communications between Yamato and the bases where fighter-plane units are stationed, which included Naruo, Himeji, Fukuchiyama, Suzuka, Meiji and Nagoya, with Yamato as the center.

(c) Lookout communications net (medium frequency):

This is composed of antiaircraft lookout stations of Daiozaki, Shionomisaki, Tanabe and Muroto, with Yamato as the center and they will be used exclusively for reporting and transmitting directives. This communications net will be provisionally established with the personnel and equipment of the Third Air Fleet in addition to the Homeland Air Defense Communications Net mentioned in another section and used exclusively to direct the air defense operations of the Third Air Fleet.

(9) Type-C communications net: This will be used to transmit orders and information from the main operational base to the secondary bases attached thereto and includes the following communications nets: Yamato -- No 2 Yamato, No 3 Okazaki -- Shin-Okazaki, Oi -- No 2 Oi, Suzuka -- No 3 Suzuka and Mineyama -- Sasabe.

(10) Combat directive broadcast net: This will be used mainly to transmit the orders of commanding officers to control stations and standby rooms within the base by the small-type medium frequency transmitter.

2. Wire Telephone Communications:

    a. The communications net with Yamato as the center is shown on Chart 92.

    b. Radio direction finder control communications: For the purpose of determining the positions of friendly contact and attack planes as a means of insuring accurate information on enemy positions (which was difficult to obtain due to the lack of trained flight personnel and loss of air superiority),

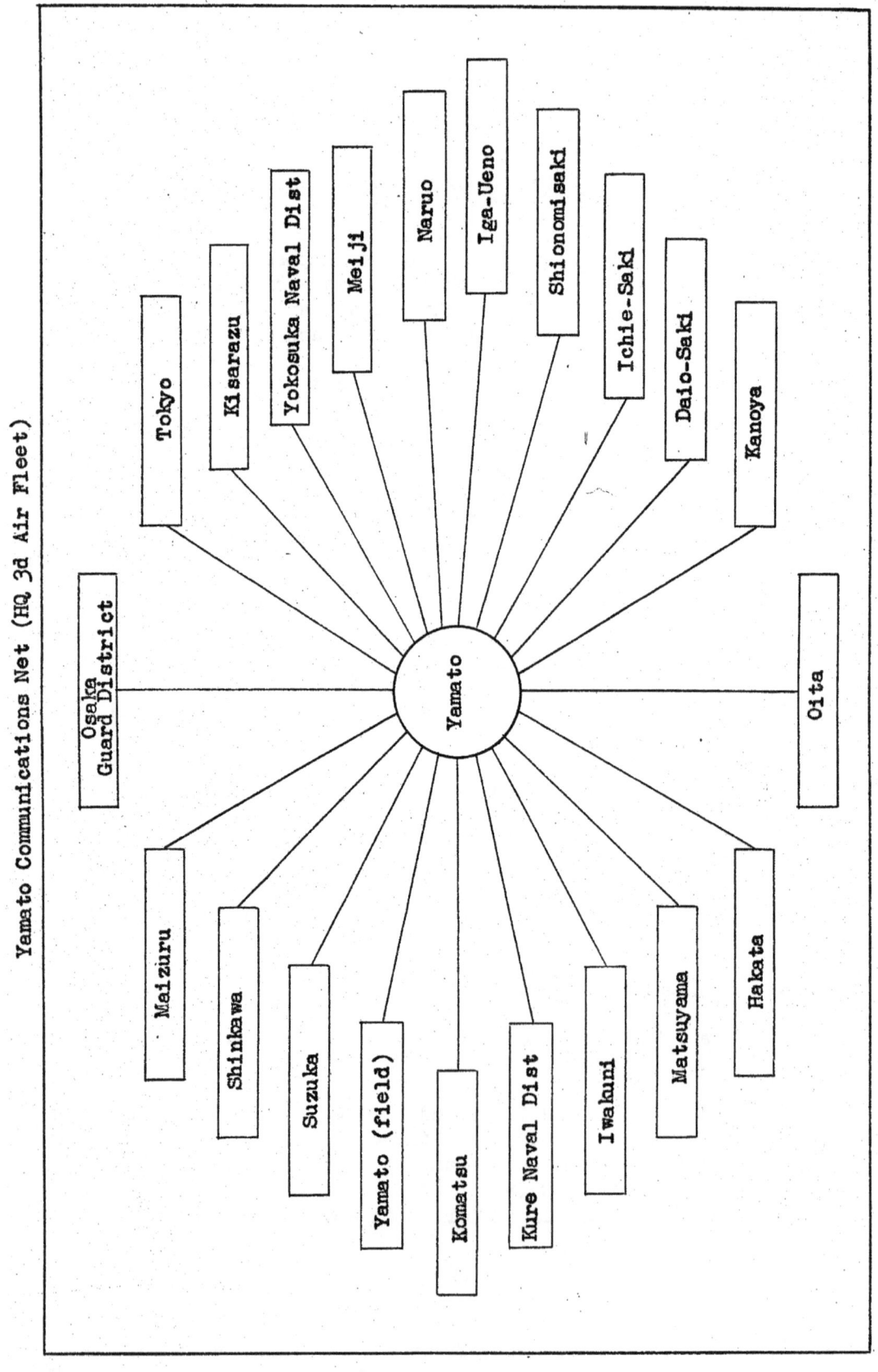

the following radio direction finding system will be planned separately from that used mainly by the communications unit:

Control communications center: Yamato:

Radio direction finding stations: Kisarazu, Kochi, Oita, Kanoya, Meiji.

   c. Aircraft communications

      (1) Frequency to be used:

      No 1 Type-A high frequency

         Land attack planes (BETTY)
         SAIUN (type of reconnaissance plane) (MYRT)
         GINGA (type of land bomber) (FRANCIS)
         TENZAN (type of carrier torpedo planes) (JILL)

      No 2 Type-A high frequency

         SUISEI (type of carrier dive bomber) (JUDY)
         Zero special attack plane (ZEKE)

      Special attack unit of 13th Air Flotilla:

         The frequencies for this unit to be prescribed according to the area.

      Type-C frequency

         Interceptor fighters

      (2) Low frequency communications for homing device: The Combined Fleet headquarters will consolidate and regulate the operating frequency.

Situation of the Various Air Fields

During the final planning stage of the KETSU-GO decisive battle for the Homeland, the majority of the air bases of the Third Air Fleet were completed insofar as construction and equipment were concerned. The following bases were completed except where otherwise noted:

    Fujieda, Toyohashi, Oi, No 3 Okazaki, No 2 Kowa and Nauro Air Bases were completed; Suzuka and No 2 Suzuka Air Bases were nearly completed.

    Meiji Air Base:
        Completed as the Tokai Airfield Unit headquarters.

    Nagoya Air Base:
        A carrier dive bomber unit and a fighter unit were assigned and the transmitters and receivers were transferred over from the Meiji Base. In addition, the mobile equipment of the 601st Air Group was installed.

    Shiga Air Base:
        No plans were made for this base as there was no assignment of personnel.

    Fukuchiyama Air Base:
        Approximately 50 percent of the scheduled installation was completed.

    Himeji Air Base:
        Equipment was being moved and installed.

Of the base equipment, the transmitting power of the Type-B3 intelligence receiver was weak, and moreover, the distribution thereof was delayed so scheduled transmission tests could not be carried out. Communications with the branch bases such as No 2 Yamato, No 2 Oi, Shin-Okazaki and Sasebo were nearly complete.

The bottle-neck in the construction work of the cable network described in the communications plan was the laying of 16 kilometers of cable between the Nara Construction Bureau and the Yamato Base. The work took considerable time due to difficulty in transporting the 108-circuit cable from the abandoned line between Hiroshima and Ogori. In addition, the project was undertaken entirely by Navy personnel and student volunteers which did not expedite matters. The heavy rainfall and frequent air raids further retarded the progress. The cable was eventually brought close to the entrance of the air raid shelter but the work was not completed as the war ended. Meanwhile, liaison with Tokyo and four Iga-Ueno posts had been generally established by means of temporary lines.

The delivery of relay amplifiers to the relay stations were delayed but liaison with the Osaka Naval Guard District had been secured by the existing lines. Because of the few circuits in the channel to the Oita lines and Kanoya lines, considerable difficulty was encountered. The advantage of the wire communications of the Yamato Base over these lines was that the Third Air Fleet headquarters was able to select the best circuits to various points. This was possible because the base was able to utilize a nearby government-owned facility, the Nara International Communications. Liaison was admittedly more easy when civil lines were utilized.

Personnel Problems

The Yamato Base had a great number of communications department personnel, including the personnel of the headquarters of Third Air Fleet, 13th and 15th Air Flotillas, the Kinki Airfield Unit and the Yamato Base, and the work was generally carried out expeditiously. However, it had like other bases, a number of apprentice and inexperienced men who needed considerable training.

Because of the enforcement of the air-ground separation system, the bases suffered from a shortage of officers. Though the bases were staffed with a sufficient number of reserve code officers, there was a considerable shortage of officers in both the communications officer class and special duty officer or warrant officer class. Therefore, it was decided to face the KETSU-GO Operation with the assignment of 80 percent of the officers of the communications officer class and 70 percent of the special duty officer or warrant officer class. As such, there followed a sharp deterioration in communications efficiency.

The shortage of petty officers was very acute and all the bases and headquarters were seriously affected. The approximate assignment proportion (in percent of T/O) was: Fleet headquarters, 90 percent; flotilla headquarters, 50 percent; and the unit bases 20-30 percent.

Most of the leading seaman class personnel had been primary enlisted trainees. The majority of those assigned to the Air Fleet headquarters were qualified to carry out operations as the headquarters had enforced rigorous training. However, as for the unit bases, there was hardly any opportunity for training and most of the personnel were incapable of performing their duties.

Communications Preparations of Tenth Air Fleet

On 1 March 1945, the Combined Naval Air Training Command was dissolved and the units within that command were reorganized as the

Tenth Air Fleet. In line with this change, the air groups stationed in Korea and Kyushu areas were assigned to the Fifth Air Fleet, and those stationed in Chubu and Kinki Districts to the Third Air Fleet. (By the end of the war, the Tenth Air Fleet was composed mainly of the remaining air groups stationed in Kanto, Tohoku, Hokkaido and including the Ou air-field Unit.)

Since the Tenth Air Fleet was organized from the Combined Air Training Command, there was an extreme shortage of equipment and facilities and some of the bases had none whatsoever. Shortage of communications personnel also existed and most of the bases had no communications officers and a great many were even without communications warrant officers. In most cases only four to six radiomen and one or two code personnel were assigned; consequently, even simple base-to-base communications were impossible.

Urgent requests were made to the Central Agency and the Navy General Command (established 25 April 1945) for equipment, construction of necessary installations and reinforcement of personnel. Although these demands were partly realized, efficient operational communications could not be conducted and this was the situation when the war ended.

The headquarters was established in the Kasumigaura Base which, at the time of the organization of the Tenth Air Fleet, had the greatest communications power among the air groups under its control. It was also very conveniently located for liaison with the Central Agency, the Navy General Command and Third Air Fleet. However, there was dire lack of equipment and facilities at the Kasumigaura Base to maintain communications of an air fleet. Therefore, as a temporary measure, the personnel of the base constructed a simple air raid shelter in which a code room and a temporary radio receiving room was set up. The receiving sets used were those which had been used for training purpose.

The construction of bombproof communications installations of the fleet headquarters was planned and immediately undertaken. A radio receiving room (with 30 receiving sets) and a power station (with one 6-KVA generator) were completed by the end of June.

As the transmitting stations were concentrated in a single area, construction work was carried out to disperse the 1st, 2d and 3d underground transmitting stations and attached power stations. The 1st transmitting station (with the most number of transmitters and a power station with one 60-KVA generator) was completed by the beginning of July. The 2d transmitting station ((with the least number of transmitters and a power station with one 6-KVA generator) was completed in the latter part of July; but the work on the 3d transmitting station and its power station (one 25-KVA generator) had not started when the war ended.

Communications Plan

This plan will be based on the communications plan of the Combined Fleet in the KETSU-GO Operations and will be generally in accordance with the following principles:

1. Radio Communications:

    Radiotelegraph will be used mainly for strategic communications and telephone for tactical communications and air intelligence. Wire and radiotelephone nets of each air base will be fully utilized.

    1. Communications system:

        a. Broadcast net (joint use of high and medium frequencies):

            Tenth Air Fleet radiotelegraph net and Tenth Air Fleet radiotelephone net. (The frequencies of the radiotelegraph net will be used; in case of emergency, radiotelephone will be used).

        b. The 6th Special Communications Net:

            This will use the communications net prescribed in the Naval Communications Regulations and will handle the liaison of the Central Agency, the Navy General Command and the flagship of each air fleet.

        c. Flagship communications net (radiotelegraph used mainly):

            This is the communications net between Tenth Air Fleet headquarters and the Ou Airfield Unit headquarters (Jimmachi Air Base), and the line will be used by special order.

        d. Ou Base Communications Net (radiotelegraph used mainly):

            The central base will be Kasumigaura and will include Yatabe, Hyakurihara, Tsukuba, No 2 Koriyama, Matsushima, Jimmachi and Chitose, all of which are under the control of the Ou Airfield Unit.

 e. The operational radiotelephone net within the base:

  This is the telephone net between the base and the emergency landing fields assigned to the base, and will be classified as follows:

  (1) Radiotelegraph broadcast net for combat liaison:

  This will be used for transmitting important orders as well as operational and air defense intelligence. Medium frequency small transmitters will be used and the receivers will be installed in assigned emergency landing fields, revetment groups, maintenance command post, air defense command post, flight personnel standby rooms and other important places of the base, to insure prompt and positive transmittal of necessary orders and intelligence directly to the commanding officers or quarters concerned.

  (2) The combat duty telephone net:

  Small transmitters will be installed at the attached emergency landing fields, revetment groups, maintenance command post, and combat command post et cetera, for communications of combat duty within the base.

 f. Yokosuka Communications Unit Local Communications Net:

  This will be used for communications between the Tenth Air Fleet headquarters and the Yokosuka Naval District headquarters.

2. Wire Communications:

The telephone system between Tenth Air Fleet headquarters

command post and the bases is shown in Chart 93.

3. Aircraft Communications:

   a. Frequency to be used:

   Type-A high Frequency.
   For land attack planes and carrier attack planes.

   Type-C fighter plane frequency.
   For fighter planes.

   Frequencies prescribed by the Navy General Command alotted for various areas:
   Various special attack planes.

   b. Low frequency for homing device.

   Low frequency for the homing device of the various bases as prescribed by the Navy General Command.

Situation of the Bases at the End of War

The following bases were completed:

Kasumigaura, Tsukuba and Matsushima.

Other bases:

Yatabe:	Generally completed but the construction of facilities for SHUSUI (rocket interceptor plane) was not started.
Hyakurihara:	Generally completed but 2d receiving station and 2d transmitting station were only temporarily equipped.
Ishioka:	Work was not started.
Koriyama:	30 percent of the main installation was completed, while temporary installations were in use.
No 3 Koriyama:	Work was not started.

Tenth Air Fleet Headquarters Telephone System

Chart 93

- Navy General Command
  - Tokyo Comm Unit
  - Yokosuka Naval District
    - No 2 Koriyama
    - Matsushima
    - Other units in Yokosuka area
  - Tenth Air Fleet Hq
    - Kasumigaura
      - Katori
    - Hyakurihara
      - Yatobe
    - Kitaura
      - Kisarazu
    - Tsukuba
      - Other units in Kasumigaura area
    - Fifty-first Army Hq

Jimmachi: Construction of installations for the headquarters of the Ou Airfield Unit was not started; temporary installations were in use.

"Pastures" (Secret bases): Only part of the equipment was delivered and work was generally incomplete.

The radiotelephone facilities of the Kasumigaura, Yatabe, Hyakurihara, Tsukuba and Matsushima bases were nearly complete, but Jimmachi, Koriyama, No 3 Koriyama and Ishioka bases were virtually without equipment.

Wire Communications

The wire communications facilities within Tenth Air Fleet headquarters, between Tenth Air Fleet headquarters and Tokyo, the Navy General Command and Yokosuka Naval District and between Third Air Fleet headquarters and the bases in the Kanto area were completed in late July, but those between Fleet headquarters and the Matsushima Base and between Tenth Air Fleet headquarters and the Jimmachi Base via No 2 Koriyama Base were not started.

As for the wire communications of the bases, 85 percent of the plan was completed at Kasumigaura, Yatabe, Hyakurihara, Tsukuba and Matsushima; approximately 70 percent at Koriyama and Jimmachi; work was not started at Ishioka and No 3 Koriyama.

Installation and Increase of Radars

1. Search radar:

    Yatabe, Hyakurihara, Matsushima, Koriyama -- complete;

> Kasumigaura and Jimmachi -- requisition for equipment was submitted, but work was not started.

2. Radar for firing purpose:

> Kasumigaura completed; other bases without equipment.

3. Guide radar:

> Installation was planned at Yatabe, but work was not started.

Transfer of the Command Post to the Yokosuka Naval District

In mid-July the decision was made to move the 1st Command Post of Tenth Air Fleet to the Yokosuka Naval District and to establish the 2d Command Post at Kasumigaura in accordance with operational necessity, but the war ended while the investigation, preparations and the augmentation of various communications facilities of the Yokosuka Naval District were just underway.

Aircraft Communications Equipment

The equipping of all fighters, carrier attack planes and land attack planes with radio sets was attempted and nearly completed. As for the special attack planes, equipment for one-fourth of all the carrier special attack fighters and carrier special attack bombers, and one-eighth of all the training special attack planes was attempted, but even 50 percent of this goal was unattainable; the training special attack planes in particular were almost entirely lacking in communications equipment. As for radar, the equipping of one-fourth of the land attack planes was attempted, but only 40 percent of the goal was achieved.

Visual Communication Facilities of Bases

Efforts were made to provide these facilities in accordance with the standard established by the Central Agency but at war's end, headquarters and Kasumigaura Base completed 90 percent, and other bases about 50 to 70 percent of their respective plans.

Reinforcement of Personnel

Through repeated strong demands, personnel up to 90 percent of the required number were assigned in early August to Tenth Air Fleet headquarters, the Ou Airfield Unit headquarters, Kasumigaura, Hyakurihara, Yatabe, Jimmachi and Matsushima bases. The No 2 Koriyama and Tsukuba bases received some reinforcements, but the No 3 Koriyama and Ishioka bases received none. As for the air groups, only the Kasumigaura Air Group received any reinforcements.

A survey of the assigned personnel revealed that most of them were special duty warrant officers and reserve officers with a considerable number of the former being poorly qualified.

Flight radiomen (observers) were assigned to one-fourth of all the carrier special attack planes and carrier special attack bombers, and to one-eight of all the training special attack planes.

www.ingramcontent.com/pod-product-compliance
Lightning Source LLC
Chambersburg PA
CBHW082104230426
43671CB00015B/2601